Money in the Late Roman Republic

Columbia Studies in the Classical Tradition

VOLUME 29

Money in the Late Roman Republic

by

David B. Hollander

BRILL

LEIDEN • BOSTON
2012

This paperback was originally published in hardback under ISBN 978 90 04 15649 4.

Cover illustration: Itinerant vendors on the forum. Mural from Pompeii, Italy, 1st CE. Photo credit: Erich Lessing/Art Resource, NY. Museo Archeologico Nazionale, Naples, Italy.

This book is printed on acid-free paper.

The Library of Congress has cataloged the hardcover edition as follows:

Library of Congress Cataloging-in-Publication Data

Hollander, David B. (David Bruce)
Money in the late Roman Republic / by David B. Hollander.
p. cm. — (Columbia studies in the classical tradition ; 29)
Based on the author's Ph.D. thesis, Roman money in the late Republic, presented to Columbia University in 2002.
Includes bibliographical references and index.
ISBN-13: 978-90-04-15649-4
ISBN-10: 90-04-15649-6 (hardback : alk. paper)
1. Money—Rome—History. 2. Coinage—Rome—History. 3. Monetary policy—Rome—History. 4. Rome—Economic conditions. I. Title.

HG237.H636 2007
332.4'93709014—dc22

2006051844

ISSN 0166-1302
ISBN 978 90 04 22549 7 (paperback)
ISBN 978 90 04 41912 9 (e-book)

Published by Brill. Koninklijke Brill NV incorporates the imprints Brill, Global Oriental, Hotei Publishing, IDC Publishers and Martinus Nijhoff Publishers.

For Sylvia and Lucinda

CONTENTS

PREFACE

This book is a much revised version of my dissertation, *Roman Money in the Late Republic*, Columbia University, 2002. I would like to thank first and foremost my advisor, William V. Harris, for his help and support over the years. I am also extremely grateful to the other members of my committee: Richard A. Billows, Ronald Findlay, Adam Kosto and William E. Metcalf. Many other people provided me with advice, criticism, support and/or hospitality as I worked on this project. They include Roger S. Bagnall, Andrew Burnett, John D'Arms, Brian Deimling, Fungya Gong, Joshua Booth Green, Jeffrey Hayes, Farid Heydarpour, Keith Hopkins, Paul Oskar Kristeller, Jinyu Liu, Aliocha Maldavsky, Ralph and Nancy Martin, Allen McCune, Aurelio Muscarà, Livia Puoti, James Rives, Gaius Stern, Peter Temin, Paola Tenti, Emiddio Trotta, Zsuzsana Varhelyi, and Yan Zelener. At Iowa State University I have been fortunate to have a number of generous colleagues. In particular I would like to thank James T. Andrews, Michael Bailey, Patrick Barr-Melej, Charlie Dobbs, Sara M. Gregg, Paul Griffiths, James McGlew, Margaret Mook, Andrejs Plakans and Leonard Sadosky. I must also thank the editorial board of Columbia Studies in the Classical Tradition as well as the editors at Brill. I am, of course, responsible for any errors. Finally, for their support, encouragement and patience thanks are also due to my wife, Lucinda Martin, and daughter, Sylvia, as well as my parents, Neil and Margaret, and sister, Jocelyn.

I must also acknowledge the generous support of Columbia University which provided me with a President's Fellowship (1993–1997). A Thompson Memorial Fellowship (1997–1998) as well as a fellowship from the Lemmermann Foundation (1999) allowed me to study in Rome. A grant from Iowa State's Center for Excellence in the Arts and Humanities helped me complete some revisions in the summer of 2003.

Parts of chapters 2, 5 and 6 appear in slightly different form in "The Demand for Money in the Late Roman Republic," in William V. Harris (ed.), *The Nature of Ancient Money* (forthcoming). Translations of Greek and Latin, unless otherwise noted, come from the Loeb Classical Library. In the notes I have cited secondary literature by author and date; full references appear in the bibliography.

LIST OF TABLES

CHAPTER ONE

INTRODUCTION

Marcus Tullius Cicero provides a tantalizing glimpse at a forgotten sphere of Roman knowledge when, in the middle of the *De officiis*, he notes in passing that it is better to discuss the earning and investment of money (*pecunia*) with "those excellent men who sit at the central gate of Janus" than with any philosopher.[1] Unfortunately, while a few philosophical works on household management survive from antiquity, Cicero's *viri optimi*, the bankers who worked in the Roman forum, have left for posterity no treatises or dialogues on money management. Nevertheless, though the information is widely scattered, the Romans still have a considerable amount to tell us about their use of money. Archaeological, numismatic, and textual evidence reveal many details concerning transactions, banking, and the circulation of money. Using such material, this study examines the nature and use of money in the late Roman Republic (from the creation of the *denarius* system during the Second Punic War down to the battle of Actium in 31 BCE) in order to understand better the development of the Roman economy in this period of rapid imperial expansion and increased wealth.

1.1 Roman Money and Roman Coinage

Roman monetary history, unfortunately, has been largely devoted to the study of Roman coins. In spite of the efforts of such scholars as Max Weber, Karl Polanyi and Philip Grierson to point out that objects other than coinage could and did function as, or in place of, money,[2] most classicists have adopted, explicitly or otherwise, the position expressed by M. I. Finley that, in ancient Greece and Rome, "money was essentially coined metal and nothing else."[3] To a certain degree the prominence of

[1] Cic. *Off.* 2.87: *Sed toto hoc de genere, de quaerenda, de collocanda pecunia (vellem etiam de utenda), commodius a quibusdam optimis viris ad Ianum medium sedentibus quam ab ullis philosophis ulla in schola disputatur.*

[2] Weber (1927) 236–41; Polanyi (1968) 175–6; Grierson (1978) 8.

[3] Finley (1985) 196. Most Roman economic historians adopt a similar position

numismatists in the field of ancient economic history may explain this state of affairs—their work has been important but perhaps too successful, improving yet distorting our view of economic life in antiquity.

While the colloquial meaning of 'money' may be safely regarded as a settled matter, its academic significance remains somewhat controversial. A precise definition for the term 'money' has long eluded the consensus of economists, historians and anthropologists. Indeed such is the confusion surrounding this topic that a scholar can be praised for not even attempting to define the word.[4] In his recent study of Greek coinage and monetization, David Schaps argues that "the question of a proper definition" of money is "not only nonessential but misleading" for historians.[5] As many historians and anthropologists have shown, money can assume a bewildering variety of forms, from cowrie shells to cigarettes,[6] and perform several different functions: medium of exchange, measure of value, unit of account, store of wealth and means of payment. Often different forms of money, each with distinct functions, have coexisted within the same monetary system. For example Karl Polanyi described the monetary system of the kingdom of Dahomey as consisting of cowries "as domestic currency," slaves "as money of account for larger amounts" and gold dust "which was employed in ports of trade and other foreign contacts."[7] As Max Weber noted, during the earlier stages in its development "money in the unitary sense of

---

though it is rarely explicit. Frank (1920) does not define money but treats coinage and money synonymously in his chapter on Roman coinage. Jones (1974) 198 describes cash (as distinct from in kind) payments to soldiers as "money pay." M. H. Crawford's *Coinage and Money under the Roman Republic* (1985), despite its title, deals almost exclusively with coinage. Lo Cascio (1981) 76 writes of "a system in which money was coinage." Duncan-Jones (1994) 20 equates coinage with money while Harl (1996) refers to coinage as "the money of the Roman economy." Even C. Howgego, clearly aware that coinage does not equal money, nevertheless allows coinage to dominate his study of "The Supply and Use of Money in the Roman World 200 BC to AD 300," *JRS* 82 (1992). See also Verboven (2002) 116, who asserts that "pre-industrial economies...were confronted with a very inelastic money supply, consisting almost exclusively of state minted coins." Harris (1993) 21 makes progress, arguing that "although the common assertion that only coins were money in the Roman Empire is in a sense true, the money supply was, to an unquantifiable extent, larger than the supply of coinage, for the Romans knew other instruments that amounted to money or near-money."

[4] Stuard (1989) 207: "Spufford wisely avoids beginning his study with any attempt at defining money."

[5] Schaps (2004) 3.

[6] Cribb (1986). As Seaford (2004) 16 notes "almost anything might in principle serve as money."

[7] Polanyi (1968) 189–90.

today is not to be thought of; rather . . . different species of money exist side by side."[8]

The complexity of and variation among different monetary systems in history has led to a variety of definitions of money, some broad, others quite narrow. Debate tends to focus upon which functions are central to the nature of money and which are incidental. Philip Grierson, for example, argued that the function of measure of value was the most important quality of money.[9] However, modern economists, who are primarily concerned with the activity of markets, tend to emphasize the medium of exchange function, defining money as "the stock of assets that can be readily used to make transactions"[10] and asserting that "the distinguishing feature of money among all assets . . . is its role as the medium of exchange."[11] Furthermore they expect money to be a store of wealth, a unit of account *and* a medium of exchange all in one.[12] This modern conception of money seems to be an unstated assumption in the works of many Roman economic historians,[13] despite the fact that the ascendancy of 'all-purpose' money in monetary systems is a fairly recent development.[14] The use of such a definition seems to limit Roman money to coinage since the Romans possessed few other assets having such versatility and widespread acceptability in market situations.

By limiting our definition of Roman money we risk overlooking important aspects of the Roman economy.[15] Just as a study of the

[8] Weber (1927) 237.

[9] Grierson (1978) 9: "I would insist on the test of money being a measure of value."

[10] Mankiw (1994) 141.

[11] Fischer et al. (1988) 141.

[12] Mankiw (1994) 141. Polanyi (1968) 178: "in modern society the money employed as a means of exchange is endowed with the capacity of performing all the other functions as well."

[13] Polanyi (1968) 177 notes that "historians of antiquity have proved hardly less susceptible to modernizing on the matter of money." De Cecco (1985) 813 asserts that "Roman historians have fallen in our century easy prey to the temptation to interpret Roman monetary history in terms of contemporary history and contemporary economic theory." Snell (1995) 1487 notes that the "normal definition of money may depend too much on modern experience."

[14] This is a common mistake according to Dalton (1965) 45: "[anthropologists often] use the bundle of attributes money has in Western market economy to comprise a model of *true* money. They then judge whether or not money-like stuff in primitive economies is really money by how closely the uses of the primitive stuff resemble our own—a strange procedure for anthropologists who never use the bundle of attributes of the Western family, religion, or political organization in such a way."

[15] Dalton (1965) 61: "[when] any primitive money which does not have all the traits of the Western model is simply ruled out by definition . . . This does not get us very far towards understanding primitive and peasant economies."

economy of New York City that failed to take account of the role of food stamps and vouchers would obviously be incomplete and inaccurate, a study of the Roman economy which failed to take account of the role of bullion, financial instruments, grain and other assets alongside coinage would neglect important aspects of Roman economic behavior.

It must be emphasized, furthermore, that an ideal definition of the word 'money' eludes even modern economists. One well-respected macroeconomics textbook concedes that "since there is a continuum of assets in the world with varying characteristics, it is not clear how to choose a subset to label 'money.'"[16] Karl Polanyi argued that money is an "incompletely unified system" and consequently that "attempts at determining the 'nature and essence' of money" are doomed."[17] As George Dalton put it, "money has no definable essence apart from the uses money objects serve."[18]

One popular strategy for defining money has been to develop hierarchies of money-types. Some scholars, for example, classify all money other than coin and paper-money as 'primitive money,' 'money substitutes' or tokens, while others would distinguish between 'general purpose' or 'all-purpose' money (capable of fulfilling all the functions of money) and 'special purpose' money (objects with limited and specific monetary roles).[19] The use of such terminology often conveys the tacit assumption that these forms of money are inferior to and therefore less important than coinage and paper money. Furthermore, it is sometimes assumed that once general purpose money appears it will wholly replace pre-existing forms of 'primitive' or 'special purpose' money. Philip Grierson, for example, apparently regarded this as an invariable rule, stating that:

> each of the coinage systems...replaced at its creation some earlier form of 'primitive' money, and similar replacements have occurred time and time again as the use of coinage has spread.[20]

---

[16] Mankiw (1994) 473. Notes Flynn (1984) 393: "one of the most complicated current debates in monetary theory involves the question—what exactly should be included in one's definition of 'money'? Are checks money? Are bank notes money? Do savings accounts contain money? Are credit cards money? The debate is endless."

[17] Polanyi (1968) 175.

[18] Dalton (1965) 62.

[19] Einzig (1948); Quiggin (1949); Grierson (1978). Dalton (1965) 44 stresses that primitive money means nothing more than 'different from our own.'

[20] Grierson (1978) 6.

Such replacements, however, are never absolute. Even today many forms of special purpose money, such as stamps, tickets and subway/bus tokens continue to exist alongside general-purpose currency.[21] As Karl Polanyi notes, "to confuse the basic problem of money with that of token money is a source of frequent misunderstandings" because both tokens and 'real money' "function as money objects."[22] Certainly significant differences can exist between various forms of money, and by identifying those differences one can better understand a monetary system as whole, but one must not begin by making arbitrary distinctions. In examining Roman money, it makes sense to begin with the word *pecunia*.

1.2 *Pecunia* and Money

Pecunia and 'money' have much in common and it is hardly surprising that the former is frequently translated into English as the latter. Both terms are polyvalent, possessing a range of potential meanings from 'coinage' or 'cash' to 'wealth' and 'riches.' 'Money,' for example, can mean something quite different in the phrase 'he's got a lot of money' than it does in the phrase 'got any money?' But while 'money' means (colloquially) first and foremost 'cash' and refers only secondarily to other forms of wealth, *pecunia* has as its primary definition 'property' not coinage.[23]

The Roman jurists, whose discussions of the word *pecunia* are practically the only ones to survive, consistently adopted a very expansive definition of it in their writings. Gaius notes in the *Institutes* that:

> the term '*pecunia*' in this Act [a *lex Cornelia*] means everything (*omnes res*); and so if we stipulate for wine or corn or a farm or a slave, this Act must be adhered to.[24]

[21] Dalton (1965) 49 notes that "even where dollars perform all the money uses for all modes of transaction, there are situations in which a limited range of money uses are performed by objects not thought of as money." The ancient Near East provides an excellent example of the failure of coinage to bring about instantaneous economic change. Snell (1995) 1496 notes that "it took hundreds of years of rule by foreign governments that were used to dealing in coins for coinage to seep into the more established economies of the ancient Near East."

[22] Polanyi (1968) 176.

[23] The situation is somewhat analogous to the use of the word χρήματα in Greek. See von Reden (1995) 174.

[24] Gai. *Inst.* 3.124 (Translation: W. M. Gordon and O. F. Robinson): *appellatione autem*

Ulpian, the early third century jurist, declares as a general rule that:

> The designation '*pecunia*' does not only include coinage but absolutely every kind of *pecunia*, that is, every substance (*omnia corpora*); for there is no one who doubts that substances are also included in the designation of *pecunia*.[25]

Hermogenianus later extended the definition ever further. The *Digest* quotes him to the effect that:

> In the designation of '*pecunia*' is included not only coinage but everything (*omnes res*) whether immobile or mobile and whether it is an object or a claim.[26]

The jurists believed that the term *pecunia* embraced not just coins or cash but *omnes res*. Few today would feel comfortable asserting that wine, grain and land or indeed everything is money.

The fact that jurists frequently felt it necessary to provide a definition for *pecunia* suggests the existence of another, more conventional and restrictive, definition in which the word's meaning was, as Ulpian and Hermogenianus imply, limited to coinage. If the jurists were reacting against a popular definition of *pecunia*, their wider definition of the term no doubt arose in response to the real legal situations they confronted. In other words, the fact that objects other than coinage were used in a pecuniary fashion forced the jurists to emphasize their broader conception of *pecunia*. Thus their definition probably reflects Roman economic conditions.

No late Republican source provides an explicit definition of *pecunia*, but we can still learn much from the ways in which Cicero and others used the word. One indication that Romans of this period viewed *pecunia* in much the same way as the jurists can be found in their understanding of the word's origins. Late Republican authors believed that livestock (*pecus*) had been one of the earliest and most important forms of *pecunia*. Varro asserts in both his *De Re Rustica* and *De Lingua Latina* that *pecunia*

---

pecuniae omnes res in ea lege significantur; itaque et si vinum vel frumentum aut si fundum vel hominem stipulemur, haec lex observanda est.

[25] *Dig.* 50.16.178 (A. Watson, trans.): *'pecuniae' verbum non solum numeratam pecuniam complectitur, verum omnem omnino pecuniam, hoc est omnia corpora: nam corpora quoque pecuniae appellatione contineri nemo est qui ambiget.*

[26] *Dig.* 50.16.222 (A. Watson, trans.): *Hermogenianus libro secundo iuris epitomarum. 'Pecuniae' nomine non solum numerata pecunia, sed omnes res tam soli quam mobiles et tam corpora quam iura continentur.*

derived from *pecus*.[27] Cicero makes a similar claim in the *De Re Publica*[28] which Ovid echoes in the *Fasti*.[29] Most strikingly, Varro calls *pecus* the foundation of all *pecunia*.[30] Whether or not the etymology is correct, the fact that Romans believed it is, in itself, highly suggestive. Cattle was or at least was thought to have been *pecunia*.

The modifiers associated with *pecunia* in late Republican texts offer further indication of the word's broad meaning. Cicero frequently uses the expressions *praesens pecunia* and *pecunia numerata* ('ready money') to refer to coins or cash.[31] Since *nummi* (coins) was sometimes used synonymously with *pecunia*, one occasionally even finds the expression *nummi numerati* having the same sense as *praesens pecunia*.[32] These expressions suggest that Cicero and other Republican writers felt the definition of *pecunia* extended beyond coinage to other assets or means of payment just as the English phrase 'ready money' may be taken to imply the existence of checks and credit. While such expressions may be mere figures of speech, we are entitled to wonder whether the Romans had any non-*praesens pecunia* or *pecunia* non-*numerata*.

The differences between the words *pecunia* and 'money' suggest differences between the Roman economy and our own. The fact that *pecunia* can refer to both coinage and other assets indicates an economy in which monetary functions are still dispersed among a variety of objects rather than unified in a single form of currency such as the dollar.

---

[27] Varro *Rust.* 2.1.11: *est scientia pecoris parandi ac pascendi, ut fructus quam possint maximi capiantur ex eo, a quibus ipsa pecunia nominata est*; and *Ling.* 5.92: *pecunia a pecu: a pastoribus enim horum vocabulorum origo.*

[28] Cic. *Rep.* 2.9: *quod tum erat res in pecore et locorum possessionibus, ex quo pecuniosi et locupletes vocabantur.*

[29] Ov. *Fast.* 5.280–1: *aut pecus aut latam dives habebat humum; hinc etiam locuples, hinc ipsa pecunia dicta est.*

[30] Varro *Rust.* 2.1.11: *nam omnis pecuniae pecus fundamentum.*

[31] Cic. *Att.* 2.4.1: *pro eo tibi praesentem pecuniam solvi imperavi*; *Verr.* II 5.17: *pecuniam sibi esse in nominibus, numeratam in praesentia non habere*; and *Leg. agr.* 1.2: *nunc praesens pecunia, certa, numerata quaeritur*; *Fam.* 10.32.1: . . . *magna numerata pecunia, magno pondere auri, maiore argenti coacto de publicis exactionibus*. . .; and *Flac.* 80: *census es praeterea numeratae pecuniae cxxx.*

[32] Cic. *Att.* 13.45.3: *audiverat multos nummos domi esse numeratos quos oporteret quam primum dividi*; Plaut. *Persa* 437–8: *nummi sescenti hic erunt, probi, numerati*; and *Poen.* 594: *hic trecentos nummos numeratos habet.* Verboven (1997) 148 notes that "*nummi* should not be understood as necessarily implying 'coin.' It is frequently used by Cicero as an equivalent of *pecunia* in any form."

1.3 Barter and the Nature of the Roman Economy

Economies in which monetary functions have become largely unified in one form of money (such as coinage) often make a distinction between transactions carried out with their 'all-purpose money' and other forms of exchange, i.e. barter. It is important to recognize that the tendency to distinguish between barter and money transactions can obscure the role of non-numismatic money in the Roman economy. This, often arbitrary, distinction[33] is especially dangerous because it allows historians and economists to dismiss vast sectors of the ancient economy from their consideration. It assumes that some transactions occurred less frequently or were less important solely because payment was made by means of grain or slaves rather than with silver and gold. Though Republican Romans were familiar with the idea of barter (thanks to the Greeks), it is striking that they rarely employ such a concept themselves. Barter seems to be foreign to their economic practices.

The idea of barter as a form of exchange distinct from purchase with 'money' goes back at least to Aristotle who wrote:

> the practice of barter (ἡ ἀλλαγή) was necessary only so far as to satisfy men's own needs... a group divided into several households participated also in a number of commodities belonging to their neighbors, according to their needs for which they were forced to make their interchanges by way of barter, as also many barbarian tribes do still; for such tribes do not go beyond exchanging actual commodities for actual commodities, for example giving and taking wine for corn...[34]

Thus Aristotle viewed barter in much the same way as most inhabitants of industrialized countries do today, that is, as a primitive form of pre-monetary exchange, whose use is confined to backwards populations.[35]

---

[33] Einzig (1948) 327: "Barter merges into primitive money and primitive money into modern money through barely perceptible shades of distinction. In many instances a transaction may constitute barter from the point of view of one party and purchase or sale from the point of view of the other. In other instances each of the two parties considers that it is he who paid with money for the goods supplied by the other party. Since even those directly concerned are apt to disagree whether a transaction is a purchase or a barter, it must be very difficult for the outside observer to make up his mind about it." See also Snell (1995) 1487–8 and Seaford (2004) 19.

[34] Aristotle *Pol.* I 3.12.

[35] According to Polanyi (1957) 93, this passage does not really deal with barter but with the reciprocal sharing of goods. Notwithstanding Aristotle's undoubtedly acute powers of observation, one must question the accuracy of his remarks concerning barter. Aristotle was a relatively prosperous man, moving among the wealthiest strata of

Republican writers never explicitly make Aristotle's kind of distinction, and only Sallust implies that Romans of his time might have thought along those lines. In a passage describing the origins of the Numidians he states that the Persian followers of Hercules settled in North Africa and:

> used as huts the inverted hulls of their ships for there was no timber in the land and there was no opportunity to obtain it from the Spaniards by purchase or barter (*emundi aut mutandi*), since the wide expanse of sea and ignorance of the language were a bar to intercourse.[36]

The ways in which Cicero, Cato and Varro discuss economic and monetary matters strongly suggest that they did not subscribe to Aristotle's categories and tended to conceive of exchange in terms that preclude the idea of a strict barter/purchase dichotomy.

By the end of the first century CE, the barter/purchase distinction was perhaps becoming more prevalent among Romans. This was to be expected because of the ever-increasing monetization (i.e. the increasing supply of coins) of the Empire and Rome's continuing status as center of a vast economic network. Tacitus' remarks in the *Germania* no doubt reflect the typical attitudes of wealthy Romans of that time. In language reminiscent of Aristotle, Tacitus notes that more distant Germanic tribes "use the simpler and more ancient practice of the barter of commodities."[37] Here, as elsewhere, the word translated as 'barter' is in fact *permutatio* which simply means 'exchange.' The Romans did not have a word precisely analogous to 'barter' as it is commonly used today.

In his *Institutes* the Roman jurist Gaius explicitly considered the merits of the barter/purchase dichotomy:

> The contract of sale is concluded when the parties agree on the price... The price must be in money. There is a considerable dispute whether the

Greek society. How much did Aristotle really know about the practices of the typical Greek farmer, a figure whom he tends to idealize in the *Politics*? A study of agriculture in rural Greece undertaken in the twentieth century—almost certainly a more 'monetized' period in Greek history—found that some farmers still act like Aristotle's 'barbarians:' the inhabitants of Methana, the authors noted [Forbes and Foxhall (1995) 81], continue to use olive oil as a "standard by which to gauge the 'true' worth of money."

[36] Sall. *Iug.* 18: *iique alveos navium inversos pro tuguriis habuere, quia neque materia in agris neque ab Hispanis emendi aut mutandi copia erat; mare magnum et ignara lingua commercio prohibebant.* Polybius also seems to make a distinction between purchase and exchange which privileged money-use (34.8.4–10).

[37] Tac. *Germ.* 5: *interiores simplicius et antiquius permutatione mercium utuntur.*

> price of something can consist in other things, a slave, a toga or a piece of land. Our teachers think that it can. That is their inference from the common belief that an exchange of things is a sale, actually the oldest type... The authorities of the other school take a different position and hold that exchange and sale are different contracts. In particular, they think it impossible in an exchange of goods to settle which thing has been sold and which given as price; they hold it absurd, again, that each thing be regarded as both sold and paid as the price.[38]

The comments of Gaius demonstrate that even in the mid-second century CE Aristotle's view of barter, though championed by one group of legal scholars, had not yet prevailed. Some jurists, at least, dismissed the idea that there were significant legal or economic differences between barter (*permutatio rerum*) and purchase (*emptio*). The debate persisted. In the early third century Paulus sided against Gaius,[39] but the broad definitions of *pecunia* offered by Ulpianus and Hermogenianus (see above) may reflect continued support for his arguments.

Though Gaius' arguments come from a legal context, they should nonetheless convince the economic historian. To ignore barter transactions (or to relegate them to second class status) is to ignore some forms of *economic* activity, particularly rural economic activity, and privilege others.[40] In modern economics the distinction between money-use and barter primarily serves to highlight differences in efficiency.[41] Whereas cash can usually be reused quickly since it is generally accepted currency, it takes time to arrange a barter transaction since a buyer must find someone who not only has what the buyer wants but will also accept the buyer's particular goods in payment (i.e. there must be a double-

[38] Gai. *Inst.* 3.139–41 (translation: Gordon and Robinson): *Emptio et venditio contrahitur cum de pretio convenerit... Item, pretium in numerata pecunia consistere debet. nam in ceteris rebus an pretium esse possit, veluti homo aut toga aut fundus alterius rei <pretium esse possit>, valde quaeritur. nostri praeceptores putant etiam in alia re posse consistere pretium. unde illud est quod vulgo putant, per permutationem rerum emptionem et venditionem contrahi, eamque speciem emptionis venditionisque vetustissimam esse... diversae scholae auctores dissentiunt, aliudque esse existimant permutationem rerum, aliud emptionem et venditionem; alioquin non posse rem expediri permutatis rebus, quae videatur res venisse et quae pretii nomine data esse, sed rursus utramque rem videri et venisse et utramque pretii nomine datam esse absurdum videri.*

[39] *Dig.* 18.1.1.1: *Sed an sine nummis venditio dici hodieque possit, dubitatur, veluti si ego togam dedi, ut tunicam acciperem. Sabinus et Cassius esse emptionem et venditionem putant: Nerva et Proculus permutationem, non emptionem hoc esse... sed verior est Nervae et Proculi sententia: nam ut aliud est vendere, aliud emere, alius emptor, alius venditor, sic aliud est pretium, aliud merx: quod in permutatione discerni non potest, uter emptor, uter venditor sit.*

[40] de Ligt (1991) 75 notes that "everywhere, barter and money transactions existed side by side" in rural areas.

[41] Fischer et al. (1988) 141.

coincidence of wants). The use of the term 'barter' implies that none of the goods being exchanged functioned as a medium of exchange. It follows, then, that the barter/money-use distinction will be useful when and where one can detect significant differences in the velocity of circulation of coinage or cash and other goods. Thus the term 'barter' presupposes a highly restrictive, modern, and colloquial definition of the word 'money.' To describe exchanges within the Roman economy as 'barter transactions' simply begs the question of what actually functioned as money then and how quickly it circulated.

The practice of barter is typically associated with primitive economies and high levels of monetization with modern economies. Once a major controversy in the study of the ancient economy, Roman economic history has largely moved beyond a simple choice between these two models.[42] Since the Roman economy lies, as Harris argued, somewhere "between archaic and modern,"[43] we have no model from which to deduce conclusions about Roman money. Instead, we should expect the Roman monetary system to have both modern and archaic characteristics. The modern aspects of Roman money are readily identifiable. Wealthy Romans employed coinage as though it was 'all-purpose' money, and their use of financial instruments demonstrates a high level of sophistication. The archaic aspects of Roman money are less obvious, though this should not be surprising considering the elite bias of the sources. Weber and Polanyi provide the tools with which one can begin to identify the more archaic aspects of the Roman monetary system. They emphasize the need for a broad understanding of 'money,' the ability of different objects to perform different monetary functions, and the likelihood that different forms of money operated in different economic contexts or zones.[44]

[42] Saller (2002) 256–7 argues that Rostovtzeff and Finley were actually in agreement on many aspects of the ancient economy and describes the ongoing debate between 'primitivists' and 'modernists' as "increasingly sterile." Saller concedes, however, that "Finley himself contributed to the polemic." De Neeve (1985) 94 rightly noted that "the dichotomy modern/primitive is too crude."

[43] Harris (1993) 15.

[44] Weber (1927) 237. Von Reden (1995) 172 notes that "we have to accept that money can change its character and function according to the context in which it is used." See also: Snell (1995) 1487.

1.4 Monetary Terminology

Since the Romans clearly viewed money as embracing more than just coinage, it is tempting to devise some new names or categories to describe the forms that Roman money took. This sort of practice has long been a popular among economic historians and can quickly lead to further confusion, rather than clarity.[45] So, for example, in his *General Economic History*, Weber refers to ten different types of money,[46] while Polanyi mentions many more.[47] Modern economics, despite its streamlined definition of money, has also readily indulged in this habit.[48] The profusion of names and categories can be quite confusing and has, as I have already pointed out, some unfortunate consequences. It seems best, then, to choose from among the existing formulations and attempt to compensate for their shortcomings.

Three main alternatives present themselves. We can adopt the position that everything is money, employ the popular 'all-purpose' and 'special-purpose' categories or adhere to a modern definition of money. The first choice is initially appealing because it brings our definition of money literally in line with the Roman jurists' definition of *pecunia* as *omnes res*. However this choice also has certain drawbacks since it veers exceedingly far from the colloquial meaning of 'money' and glosses over significant differences among assets. Some things are *designed* to be money while others only rarely perform monetary functions. Furthermore, if everything is or can be money, what can 'monetization' mean? We should not take the jurists too literally. That anything *could* be Roman money does not mean that everything was.

What of using the 'all-purpose' versus 'special purpose' distinction? I have already noted one of the main drawbacks to this approach: 'special

---

[45] Two recent books on Greek money perhaps reflect increasing frustration with such practices. Schaps (2004) 3 declines to propose any "proper definition," while Seaford (2004) 16–9, taking a novel approach, lists seven characteristics of money "the possession of which by something (x) inclines us to call x money."

[46] Weber (1927) *passim*. I.e.: utility money, clothing money, token money, external and internal money, standard money, credit money, women's money, chieftain money and head money.

[47] Polanyi (1968) *passim*. E.g.: paper money, barley money, gold money, money substitutes, all-purpose money, special purpose money, primitive money, archaic money and exchange-money.

[48] One finds, for example, commodity money, cool and hot money, fiat money, fiduciary money, IOU money, near money, paper money and high-powered money. See Mankiw (1994) and Fischer et al. (1988).

purpose' money tends to become marginalized in the presence of 'all-purpose' money. One might also question the existence of 'all-purpose' money itself. A whole range of geographical, social and political considerations limits the use of both cash and coinage. There are many stores in the United States, for example, where a hundred-dollar bill is not accepted for payment. The term 'all-purpose money' is itself flawed.[49]

A modern (though not colloquial) definition of money seems best, i.e. money is the stock of assets readily available to make transactions.[50] Such a definition need not exclude all assets other than coinage. Modern economic theory does acknowledge differences in usefulness among assets. This can be seen in the different ways the Federal Reserve calculates the U.S. money stock. C, M1, M2, M3, and L designate successively broader definitions of money. While C includes only currency and M1 includes both currency, demand deposits, and traveler's checks, L comprises a wide array of shares, deposits, securities, bonds and other liquid assets. My study reflects similar divisions within the Roman money stock by dealing in successive chapters with coinage (Chapter 2), bullion and financial instruments (Chapter 3), and other assets (Chapter 4). These divisions might almost be termed Roman C, Roman M1 and Roman M2. I treat as forms of Roman money those assets that could be used as a medium of exchange or means of payment and, as I shall demonstrate, the Romans employed far more than just coinage to make transactions. Surprisingly, not much separates the modern definition of money from the jurists' definition of *pecunia*.

The Roman monetary system cannot be fully understood unless we look beyond the various forms money took to the contexts in which they were used. In certain circumstances some Roman assets were more readily usable than others. Thus, in Chapter 5, I have divided the Roman economy into four sectors which I call the commercial, governmental, urban and rural monetary zones. In each zone the assets readily available, the types of transactions made and the power and expertise of the parties involved differed. Furthermore, in each zone some assets functioned in place of money by performing the monetary functions of means of payment, unit of account or store of value. Such assets, while not money *per se*, do nevertheless reduce the *demand* for money. By looking at the use of and demand for various forms of money in these four

[49] Jongman (1988) 46.
[50] Mankiw (1994) 141.

monetary zones, we can better appreciate the complexity of the Roman monetary system as a whole and better gauge the impact on that system of changes in the money supply. This last question will be addressed in the concluding chapter with the help of money demand theory. There I will argue that the changes in the relative size of these monetary zones and the changing economic conditions within them, make it implausible to suppose that the dramatic growth in the Roman coin supply during the late Republic brought about any economic growth.

CHAPTER TWO

ROMAN COINAGE: USE, VOLUME AND COMPOSITION

2.1 Introduction

Coinage arrived in Italy in the sixth century BCE thanks to Greek colonists, and its use spread gradually.[1] Well after the appearance of coinage many Italians continued to employ bullion (*aes rude*) rather than coins for transactions.[2] The Etruscans, for example, used *ramo secco*, copper bars, from the sixth century down to the third century despite their extensive contacts with the Greek world.[3] Only in Apulia did non-Greek populations adopt coinage on any substantial scale before the period of Roman expansion.[4] In the fourth century, however, the development of *aes signatum* ('marked bronze' bars) and *aes grave* ('heavy bronze' cast coins) signaled the beginning of a trend towards coin-use among native Italian populations.[5] Although sources for the early economic history of the Roman Republic are not particularly trustworthy (Crawford describes them as "relentlessly modernizing"),[6] the Romans probably established an official monetary unit, the *as* or a pound of bronze, in the late sixth century BCE.[7] The Twelve Tables and the tradition concerning Servius Tullius both tend to support this conclusion.[8] The earliest Roman coinage dates to the end of the fourth century BCE when the Romans began to mint silver and bronze coins periodically.[9] Regular emissions appear around the time of the Pyrrhic War.[10] The third century brought about a rapid development in Roman minting. This period also witnessed the

---

[1] There are several good overviews of Roman coinage: Burnett (1987); Crawford (1974, 1985).

[2] Harl (1996) 21; Crawford (1985) 1.

[3] Crawford (1985) 3–6; Harl (1996) 21–2.

[4] Crawford (1985) 14.

[5] Harl (1996) 23–4.

[6] Crawford (1985) 17.

[7] Crawford (1985) 20.

[8] Cornell (1995) 288; *The Twelve Tables* 8.3–4, Plin. *HN* 33.43; Crawford (1974) 35.

[9] Burnett (1978) 141–2; (1977) 118. Crawford (1985) 17 notes that there is no evidence to suggests that the Romans made use of the coinage of other states in the period before they began minting their own.

[10] Crawford (1985) 16–7, 29–30; (1974) 131–7.

development of fiduciary bronze coinage (during the First Punic War),[11] an increase in the quantity of coinage produced (between the First and Second Punic Wars), and the first minting of gold coinage (during the Second Punic War).[12] The Second Punic War strained the Roman monetary system and led the Romans to revise it radically. Around 211 BCE they created a new system, usually referred to as the 'denarius system,' consisting of the silver *denarius*, gold *aureus* (worth 25 *denarii*), the bronze *as* (originally a tenth of a *denarius*) and its various fractions. This system (with some minor modifications) remained in use through the end of the Republic. By the beginning of the second century BCE most coins produced in Italy were Roman.

Coins are undoubtedly the most recognizable form of Roman *pecunia* and it is easy to show that Roman coinage fulfilled all of the functions of money. The Roman *aerarium* and numerous coin hoards attest to the fact that coinage was a store of wealth. Republican texts often refer to both public and private financial documents recording transactions in *asses, sestertii,*[13] and *denarii*, indicating that coinage functioned as a unit of account. Frequent references to purchases show Roman coins acting as a means of exchange or payment. Whereas in the next two chapters it will be necessary to discuss in depth the monetary functions of various commodities and financial instruments, with coinage we can immediately turn to the question of the nature and extent of its use.

Although a central purpose of this book is to emphasize the role of assets other than coinage in the Roman economy of the late Republic, I do not wish to suggest that coinage was unimportant. Coins are without question the most versatile form of money. They are easy to carry, widely accepted, usually of unambiguous and stable value, countable, easily hidden and often made out of a valuable commodity such as gold or silver. In certain circumstances coinage was especially useful: for travel or living abroad, army pay, political campaigns (e.g. for bribery), as well as the day-to-day purchases of the urban poor. But, to place the numismatic economy in its proper monetary context, one must be aware of coinage's limitations. Coins are vulnerable to debasement, retariffing and forgery and have few uses beyond exchange and

[11] Harl (1996) 28.

[12] Harl (1996) 30; Crawford (1974) #28, #29 etc.

[13] The *sestertius* is worth a quarter of a *denarius*. Originally this meant two and a half *asses* but after the *denarius* was retariffed c. 141 BCE, the *sestertius*'s value became four *asses*.

decoration. Although coins do not deteriorate in storage the way grain, olive oil and other commodities can, you cannot eat cash—an important consideration in times of food shortage.

The supply of Roman money grew rapidly over the last two centuries of the Republic and it is likely that more and more people came to use coinage for more of their transactions. This chapter examines the state's production of silver, gold, and bronze coins during this period and what that suggests about Roman demand for coinage.

2.2 Silver Coinage

The silver *denarius*, produced in large numbers down to the end of the Republic and beyond, was the most important coin in the monetary system born during the Second Punic War. It has long been believed that more precise information about the amount of *denarii* minted by Rome would provide greater insight into the Roman economy. This is because Quantity Theory, as developed by economist Irving Fisher in 1911, posits a mathematical relationship between the money supply, prices, number of transactions and the velocity of circulation within an economy.[14] Thus studying coin production could lead to new insights into inflation and economic growth in the late Republic. The hunt for coin production figures began in the early 1970s with the pioneering work of Crawford, who made the first serious attempt to estimate production levels. In his *Roman Republican Coinage* Crawford used figures gathered from a selected group of 24 large hoards to extrapolate production figures from known obverse die counts and other estimates of die numbers. He began by observing the frequency in the hoards of coins for which die studies had already been completed (if a reverse die count had been done, Crawford multiplied that figure by 0.8 or 0.9, depending on the issue's date, to arrive at an approximate number of obverse dies).[15] From these ratios (total known obverse dies divided by number of coins found in the selected hoards) Crawford generated multipliers with which he could calculate obverse die numbers for all the other issues.[16] For example, the number of coins of a particular issue dating from between 84 and 58 BCE found in the selected hoards would be multiplied by 2 to arrive at

[14] Ekelund and Hébert (1990) 537.
[15] Crawford (1974) 640–72.
[16] Crawford (1974) 672–3.

a total number of obverse dies for that issue. Then, having assumed that the average Republican die produced around 30,000 coins, Crawford was able to calculate production figures for the period from 157 to 50 BCE.[17] By adding up these annual figures and factoring in an attrition rate (due to hoarding, destruction and the accidental loss of coins) it was then possible to graph the development of the Roman coin supply over time. Keith Hopkins did just this in his well-known "Taxes-and-Trade" article.[18] Assuming that there was an average annual loss of about 2% of the coinage in circulation he calculated that "the money supply at Rome grew substantially, perhaps tenfold" in the late Republic.[19]

A number of scholars have raised doubts about the coin production calculations described above, but T. V. Buttrey has provided the most comprehensive critique.[20] First, he argued that Crawford's method for calculating the number of dies per issue was faulty since he used a "series of elaborate extrapolations from a very small base."[21] Secondly he maintained that it was impossible to know how many coins were produced per die, calling Crawford's estimate only a "guess"[22] and pointing out that several factors beyond simple wear and tear govern the use of dies.[23] Thirdly he asserted that there was no way to know the attrition rate or the coins-per-die ratio because they were "fundamental variables" not constants.[24] Buttrey concluded that "we do not know, and cannot know, the quantity of coin produced at any time under the Roman Republic."[25]

While absolute figures may be beyond reach, relative figures are not. Neither Crawford nor Hopkins claimed to have calculated exact numbers. Crawford claimed only to have "the right order of magnitude" for obverse dies[26] and Hopkins was concerned above all with the shape of his money supply graph. He pointed out that there is no reason to believe that the coins per die average changed significantly from the

---

17 Crawford (1974) 694–707.
18 Hopkins (1980) 107.
19 Hopkins (1980) 107 and 109 fig. 2.
20 Buttrey (1993) 335–51; Buttrey and Cooper (1994) 341–52; Buttrey and Buttrey (1997) 113–35. See also: Hersh (1977) 19–36; Frier (1981) 285–95; Lo Cascio (1982b) 75–97; Volk (1987) 141–222.
21 Buttrey (1993) 347.
22 Buttrey (1993) 347.
23 Buttrey and Cooper (1994) 343.
24 Buttrey (1993) 347.
25 Buttrey (1993) 350–1.
26 Hopkins (1980) 107 notes "Alternate rates of loss, 1 per cent or 3 per cent per year, even of 5 per cent per year, do not radically change the shape of the growth curve."

second to the first century BCE and noted that "any reasonable constant loss rate and any reasonable constant average number of coins minted per die" produced a graph with essentially the same shape.[27] It is true that more die counts would improve the accuracy of production estimates and therefore also estimates of the amount of coinage in circulation but, as some have already observed, this will take a considerable amount of time given the huge quantity and variety of surviving Roman coins.[28] In the meantime it should be mentioned that two studies have subsequently reaffirmed Crawford's results with respect to both the extrapolation of obverse die counts and the overall trend in coin production.[29]

Hoards provide us with another way to gauge the supply of Roman coinage. Dirk Backendorf used data generated from Italian hoards to produce a new graph, one not based on guesses about attrition and production rates. He observed that the hoard evidence reflects the product of the Roman mint, the coins, rather than the means of production, i.e. the dies,[30] and that some basic principles allow one to work backward from the hoards to the general coin supply. First of all, through the hoard evidence one can graph a coin-type's life in circulation. This 'life-curve' has a rather distinct shape.[31] In the years immediately following their production the coins spread quickly and begin to appear more often and in larger quantities in the hoards. However as attrition takes its toll over the years the coin-type is found in hoards less frequently and in fewer numbers. Two factors affect the size of the initial peak in the life-curve: the size of the particular issue and the size of the general population of coins into which it is introduced. As Backendorf describes it:

> If a small issue of coins causes a large increase... the money supply, to which this issue is added, must have been small. If a substantially larger issue later causes a considerably smaller increase... the money supply must have become larger in the meantime.[32]

---

[27] Hopkins (1995/96) 53.

[28] Crawford (1974) 641; de Callataÿ (1995) 290.

[29] de Callataÿ (1995) 292–3 uses early cistophoric coinage to show that, while "the data from hoards are not identical to the die counts, ...it seems hard not to recognize a close general similarity." Lockyear (1999) 241–2 argues that, "although Crawford's figures are incorrect in detail, they are correct in their general trends." He suggests that "the increase in the total coinage pool was between five- and ten-fold."

[30] Backendorf (1998) 202.

[31] Backendorf (1998) 538–40.

[32] Backendorf (1998) 202.

The attrition rate of a coin-type, which governs the later portion of its life-curve, need not be calculated since it is already reflected in the hoard evidence. The sequence of hoards along with their internal structure provide the data to construct aggregate life-curves for coin-types by period, and these data reflect production levels and the money supply during each of these periods. Thus Backendorf was able to reconstruct (relatively) these quantities for the period 150 to 25 BCE. He concluded that the money-supply of Italy fluctuated very much as Crawford and Hopkins suggested it did, i.e. that there was a massive increase in the coin supply in the latter half of the second century, that production diminished slightly towards the end of the first quarter of the first century but soon recovered and rose to even higher levels by 50 BCE.[33]

While precise figures remain beyond our grasp, considerable evidence points to a dramatic growth in the supply of Roman silver coinage in the late Republic. In 50 BCE there was at least five times and perhaps as much as ten times the number of *denarii* in circulation as there had been a hundred years earlier. The possible ramifications of this growth will be considered in Chapter 6.

2.3 Gold Coinage

The Romans minted relatively few gold coins during the late Republic judging from the number of issues and obverse dies. The production of these coins usually occurred during a period of crisis. Of the 59 Republican gold issues 8 come from the period of the Second Punic War,[34] 4 date to the period of Sulla's rule in the 80s,[35] and 44 were minted during the civil wars of the 40s and 30s.[36] Some of the other issues appear to be honorary or celebratory. Greeks rather than Romans may have struck

[33] Backendorf (1998) 542. Backendorf's methods and calculations are by no means simple or obvious, so it is worth mentioning that they earned the approval even of Buttrey (1999) 532, who wrote of Backendorf's findings: "I accept that he is correct."

[34] Crawford *RRC* #28.1–2, #29.1–2, #44.2–4, #50.1, #72.2, #88.1, #105.2 and #106.2.

[35] Crawford *RRC* #359.1, #367.2, #375.1 and #381.1a–b.

[36] Crawford *RRC* #452.1, #456.1a–b, #460.1, #466.1, #475.1a–b and 2, #481.1, #490.2, #491.1a–b and 2, #492.1–2, #493.1a–c, #494.1–15, 20, 22, 26, 34, 35 and 44–46, #495.1, #497.1, #498, #499, #500.2, 4 and 6, #502.1, #505.1 and 4, #506.1, #507.1, #508.1, #509.1 and 3, #511.1, #512.1, #513.1, #514.1, #515.1, #516.1 and 4, #517.1, 4 and 7, #519.1, #521.1, #522.1 and 3, #524.1, #525.1, #526.1 and 3, #527, #528.1, #529, #533.1 and 3, #524.1, #540.1, #541, #544.1–7 and #546.5.

the issue from 196 BCE (*RRC* #548) in honor of T. Quinctius Flamininus.[37] The Cn. Lentulus issue (#549) was also likely honorary,[38] while the gold coins of 71 BCE (#402) were probably struck on the occasion of Pompey's triumph.[39] If Crawford's obverse die estimates are reliable and bear some relation to the number of coins minted, it would seem that the Romans did not produce substantial quantities of gold coinage until Caesar and A. Hirtius produced their issue in 46 BCE (#466). This does not mean that gold coinage was previously unimportant—its appearance in crisis situations suggests otherwise—but that the Romans tended to prefer silver and bronze coinage.

Why did the Romans mint gold so infrequently? A lack of gold, certainly, does not seem to have been a problem, since, as Pliny tells us, there were large quantities of gold bullion in the Roman *aerarium* in the mid-second century BCE[40]—a period when the Romans were not minting any gold coins at all.[41]

Some have suggested that widespread use of foreign gold limited the need for the Romans to mint their own gold coins. J. G. Milne speculated that the Romans in the second and first centuries used eastern gold coins, particularly those of Philip, Alexander and Lysimachus.[42] He thought that these gold coins, sometimes referred to as 'philippics,' were not used as currency but "simply traded as bullion by weight,"[43] a view later echoed by Kenneth Harl who claimed that the Romans "probably adopted a common practice of employing philippics in sealed bags of fixed value whenever gold payments were required."[44] Appealing though this hypothesis may be, the numismatic evidence does not support it. Greek coins rarely appear in late Republican hoards in Italy.[45] Furthermore, if the Romans were so accustomed to using Macedonian

---

[37] Crawford (1974) 544.

[38] Crawford (1974) 545.

[39] Crawford (1974) 83 and 413.

[40] Plin. *HN* 33.55.

[41] Howgego (1990) 13 notes "Rome struck no gold coinage between the Second Punic War and the time of Sulla, and no substantial issues until 46 BC. Yet gold in the form of booty poured in."

[42] Milne (1940) 13.

[43] Milne (1940) 13. Plin. *HN* 33.46 notes that a type of Illyrian coin acted '*mercis loco*' in the late Republic: *is, qui nunc victoriatus appellatur, lege Clodia percussus est; antea enim hic nummus ex Illyrico advectus mercis loco habebatur. est autem signatus Victoria, et inde nomen.*

[44] Harl (1996) 49–50.

[45] Crawford (1977b) 52. The picture has not changed since the seventies. Out of 205 hoards of Republican coins discovered in Italy with closing dates between 208 and 30 BCE, only 10 contained some Greek coins and none contained Greek gold coins.

gold coinage why, when they needed to produce their own gold coins, did they not employ the same weight standard of 8.5 grams?[46] Other than the occasional use of *philippus* to describe a gold coin, Republican literary texts provide scant evidence for Romans using foreign gold coinage. A passage from one of Cicero's letters to Atticus is, however, suggestive.[47] In discussing a transaction with a certain Caelius that involved gold, Cicero uses the word *collubus*, a term that can refer to the exchange of foreign coins. Though *collubus* could denote the exchange rate by which a payment in gold bullion was calculated in terms of coinage, a passage from one of his speeches suggests that Cicero believes a *collybus* must involve foreign coins. Referring to dubious exchange charges exacted from Sicilian farmers by Verres, Cicero asks "How can there be any exchange (*collybus*), where a single coinage is in universal use?"[48]

What of bullion? Perhaps the Romans minted little gold because they preferred to use bullion instead.[49] Gold bars (*lateres*) were kept in the Roman treasury,[50] but we know virtually nothing about their use. So far, gold bars have turned up in just one Republican hoard in Italy (*RRCH* #357) and the only reference to the state making a payment in gold bullion involves the bounty paid for the head of Gaius Gracchus.[51] Harl's claim that "often the Republic settled large purchases in ingots of gold or silver cast in convenient multiples of the pound and certified by official stamps"[52] is appealing but unproven.

A different hypothesis suggests that the Romans associated gold with kingship and so were reluctant to mint coins carrying such dangerous political connotations. Harl argues that the Romans "viewed gold as a regal metal better dedicated to the gods."[53] He notes in particular the coins of T. Quinctius Flamininus that, because of their similarity to Macedonian *staters*, other Roman aristocrats might have found threatening. Harl envisions a Roman policy of "denying aristocrats the chance

---

[46] Harl (1996) 482. Of the Roman issues whose weight standards can be determined only that of T. Quinctius Flamininus corresponds to the Greek system. See Crawford (1974) 593; Botrè and Fabrizi (1994/95) 38.

[47] Cic. *Att.* 12.6.1: *De Caelio vide, quaeso, ne quae lacuna sit in auro. Ego ista non novi, sed certe in collubo est detrimenti satis.*

[48] Cic. *Verr.* II, 3.181: *Nam collybus esse qui poteset, cum utuntur omnes uno genere nummorum?*

[49] Harl (1996) 50.

[50] Plin. *HN* 19.15 and 33.56: *C. Caesar primo introitu urbis civili bello suo ex aerario protulit laterum aureorum,* $\overline{\text{XV}}$ *argenteorum* $\overline{\text{XXX}}$.

[51] Plut. *C. Gracch.* 17.3–5.

[52] Harl (1996) 50.

[53] Harl (1996) 52.

for regal fame by minting staters."[54] He associates the gold coinage of the eighties with Sulla and his king-like position in the Roman state and observes that, once Sulla had resigned from office, the senate stopped minting gold coins.[55] While it is certainly possible that the Romans associated gold with kingship and the gods,[56] it is difficult to prove that such considerations affected the policy of the Roman mint.[57] Sulla's earlier gold issues (Crawford #359.1 and #367.2 and 4) from 84 to 82 BCE are more likely to be related to the financial demands of the civil war. The later *aurei* (Crawford #375.1 and #381.1a–b)—much smaller issues judging from their obverse die counts—could reflect the lessening of the crisis as Sulla consolidated power in 81 and 80 BCE but are probably celebratory issues like the gold coins minted in 71 BCE (Crawford #402.1a and b).[58] Finally, if gold coins did have regal connotations, it is rather ironic that Caesar's assassins would choose to mint them too.[59]

Some scholars would link the minting of gold at Rome to the cessation of minting by other states in the Mediterranean. As Christopher Howgego observed "Rome began to produce a plentiful coinage in gold... only after other principal gold coinages from Macedon, Carthage, Ptolemaic Egypt and Gaul had ceased to circulate."[60] But how should this relationship be understood? Did the Romans ban their new subjects from minting gold and withdraw foreign gold coins from circulation, replacing them with their own issues? Since the Romans betray no sign of having had a consistent monetary policy with respect to the provinces (many cities continued to produce silver and bronze coins)[61] and could hardly embark upon such a program in the midst of the civil wars, this explanation is implausible. Most likely the Romans had simply come to monopolize the gold supply through plunder, indemni-

[54] Harl (1996) 49.

[55] Harl (1996) 52.

[56] As the Greeks did. Kurke (1999) 304 argues that: "gold in the traditional elite systems is strongly associated with the gods (from the time of Homer on), with kingship or sovereignty, with the east and with eastern despots" and "at least part of the reason silver became the metal for Greek civic coinage was symbolic opposition to the elitist identification with gold."

[57] For a critique of this argument see: Johnson (1998) 141.

[58] Crawford (1974) 413.

[59] RRC #506.1, for example, features the head of L. Iunius Brutus on the obverse and the head of M. Iunius Brutus on the reverse.

[60] Howgego (1992) 5. See also: Nash (1978) 22.

[61] Burnett and Crawford (1987) *passim*.

ties, taxation and control of the mines.[62] Access to gold was now too restricted.

The concept of monetary zones may provide the most reasonable explanation for the pattern of gold issues under the Republic. If the Roman state did use gold bullion, it was probably for the purpose of making large payments to companies and merchants involved in building and supply contracts (i.e. the commercial monetary zone). Gold's high value relative to equal weights of silver or bronze made it the most convenient means of transferring large sums. In contrast silver and bronze coins must have played a substantial role in financing the army where many small payments were required. In times of military crisis prices tend to rise and consequently the demand for cash also increases. It becomes more and more difficult to obtain coinage. This situation could impede the government's ability to meet its financial obligations with respect to the army. By minting gold coins, the Romans could restore liquidity to a sector of the economy that relied on the use of coinage.

In the second century and early first century BCE the Romans had plenty of gold bullion, probably did not use very many Greek gold coins and did not hesitate to mint their own *aurei* when occasion dictated. If they struck gold coins rarely, it was because they rarely needed them. In the last decades of the Republic the Romans began to produce gold coins in quantity not to make up for dwindling Hellenistic supplies but because civil war and a growing empire drastically increased their demand for cash.

2.4 Bronze Coinage

Roman bronze coinage, like gold, exhibits a rather odd production pattern in the late Republic. Table 2.1 shows the issues of Roman bronze coins from 211 to 31 BCE. There are two curious gaps in production:

[62] See Strabo 4.6.7 for *publicani* working gold mines in Cisalpine Gaul in the territory of the Salassi. Pliny (*HN* 33.78) refers to an old censorial edict limiting the *publicani* "from having more than 5,000 men" working in the gold mines at Victumulae. The Romans closed the gold and silver mines in Macedonia for a time in the second century BCE (Livy 45.39.11). Furthermore, Strabo (3.2.10) indicates that the state had at one time owned the silver and gold mines in Spain, stating that the "silver-mines are still being worked at the present time; they are not state-property, however, either at new Carthage or anywhere else, but have passed over to private ownership. But the majority of the gold-mines are state-property."

the period from 146 to 114 when the Romans stopped minting the *as* (though its fractions continued to appear regularly) and the period from 82 to 46 when the Roman state virtually ceased production of bronze coins altogether. No source explains the reason for these gaps, but the pattern must reflect the demand for such coins on the part of the Roman government and by extension the supply of bronze coins in circulation. Several factors must have affected the supply and demand for the *as* and its fractions including changes in the nature of government expenditure, the presences of municipal, foreign and counterfeit coinage in circulation, lack of confidence in bronze coinage (and hence depressed demand for them), and a low attrition rate for the bronze coinage produced prior to the gaps.

Table 2.1 Roman Republican Bronze Issues[63]

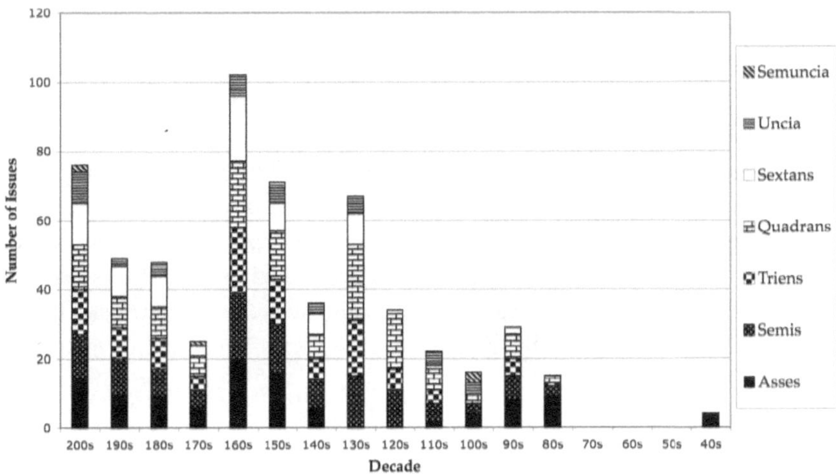

If the Roman government produced coinage primarily to make payments (rather than to facilitate exchange in the general economy),[64] the production of bronze coinage must be related to state demand for them. Crawford suggested that a switch from paying soldiers in bronze to paying them in silver might account for the second century

[63] Crawford (1974) *passim*.
[64] For some discussion of this issue see Crawford (1982) 141; Howgego (1990).

production gap,[65] but this hypothesis faces several difficulties. First, there is no evidence that the Romans ever made such a switch. Secondly, the Romans continued to mint divisors during this period. Thirdly, military salaries, while certainly a major part of the Roman budget, were hardly the only kind of expenditure. A major change in the way soldiers were paid would have some effect on coin production levels but could not be the only factor at work. However, a less extreme change in the way the state paid soldiers, say merely an increased reliance on silver in those payments, if coupled with a steady and considerable state income in bronze, might also explain the cessation of minting.[66] Republican *asses* stayed in circulation for a long time,[67] and it is reasonable to suppose that the Roman state received much bronze coinage as part of its revenue. Why pay taxes in intrinsically valuable silver coins when the government would accept fiduciary bronze?[68]

Municipal bronze coins, foreign coins and forgeries also help explain why the Roman state minted relatively few bronze coins. Paestum, Velia and Heraclea all minted bronze coins during the late Republic,[69] and Roman hoards in Italy do sometimes contain non-Roman issues.[70] It is not clear exactly when, for what purpose, or in what quantities these coins were produced,[71] but they may have supplemented the supply of Roman bronze or replaced it in areas where Roman bronze tended not to circulate. 'Imitations' or forgeries of Roman bronze coins would have helped to accomplish the same end. Crawford identified 117 different groups of Republican imitations,[72] and suggested that they mostly come from the period 100–25 BCE. However, as with municipal coins, it is

---

65 Crawford (1970) 47; (1985) 145–6.

66 Roth (1999) 232 suggests linking the increased demand for silver coins in the latter half of the second century BCE to "a shift in Roman logistics...perhaps the Roman state is relying more on buying grain."

67 Buttrey (1973) 47; Burnett (1982) 131; Crawford (1982) 140; (1985) 185.

68 If the *as* was valued in the market at less than its official rate (one possible reason for the revaluation of the *denarius* c. 141), this explanation becomes even more appealing. See Butttrey (1957) 62 and Plin. *HN* 35.45.

69 Burnett (1982) 127; Crawford (1985) 71–2.

70 E.g. *RRCH* #111, 141, 148, 245, 260.

71 Crawford (1973) 54 suggests that the earlier coins from Paestum were produced to pay local army contingents in the first two Punic Wars and that the later ones were used "to finance distributions of [sic] the citizens" and "not to serve any real fiscal need" [(1985) 72]. Burnett (1982) 128 agrees, stating that "the issues are far too small: they are all rare today and did not circulate in any quantity away from their place of issue." He suggests that such coins amounted to only about 1% of the coins in circulation.

72 Crawford (1982) 139–40. See also: Crawford (1968b) 55–9; (1970) 45.

difficult to date forgeries or imitations precisely, form any estimate of their numbers or even to be sure that they are not merely poor quality official coins. As Crawford notes "Republican bronze coinage itself... is not on the whole remarkable for its high quality."[73] The distribution of finds of imitations tends to support the idea that they provided small change to areas that did not receive a sufficient supply from Rome.[74] Few imitations come from finds in the Tiber, suggesting that "the proximity of the mint meant for the city of Rome the accidental consequence of an abundant supply of small change."[75] Finds from Spain reveal a similar situation: Roman bronze coins were not being produced in sufficient quantities for Spain to get by solely with what arrived from Italy. Burnett believes "local bronze accounted for over half the bronze in circulation, or even more in civilian settlements."[76] The quantity of imitations and municipal coins (as far as that can be ascertained) suggests that they too played an important role in the money supply of the late Republic. That such coins did not circulate in great numbers at Rome but were prominent in other areas (particularly where only Roman silver coins, which were being produced in much greater quantities, penetrated) suggests that they may have been produced in response to a need for the small change which Rome did not supply. Crawford derides the idea that the Roman state paid any attention to the need to supply small change to its subjects,[77] but the existence of municipal coins and forgeries points to other possible explanations. Perhaps Rome, used to *ad hoc* and reactive policy making, was simply content to let others help meet the demand for bronze coins. Alternatively, an abundance of small change around Rome could have concealed the problem from Roman officials. Meanwhile opportunistic forgers and municipalities filled the wider need for small change and thus prevented any widespread liquidity problems from coming to the attention of the central authorities.

The possibility that municipal coins and forgeries were deliberately produced to supplement the inadequate production of Roman bronze coins rests on the assumption that there was a high demand for bronze coins and people were willing to look elsewhere if the Romans did not supply enough. It is equally possible, however, that the Romans ceased

[73] Crawford (1982) 140.
[74] Stannard (1998) 227.
[75] Crawford (1982) 141.
[76] Burnett (1987b) 51. See also: Knapp (1982) 188.
[77] Crawford (1982) 141.

or lowered production of bronze coins simply because there was limited demand for them. Municipal coinage may have been produced for social or political motives, while forgers may have acted out of a desire for illicit gain rather than to ease the transaction of business. There is good reason to believe that some people viewed bronze coins with suspicion or confusion during certain periods of the late Republic. Such attitudes would lower demand for bronze coins and could have prompted the state's decision to mint fewer *asses*.

The fluctuating quality and weight standard of Roman bronze coins no doubt led some to take an unfavorable view of them. As Crawford vividly states, "the weight standard of the bronze coinage of the last two centuries of the Republic goes up and down like a yo-yo."[78] At the end of the Second Punic War the *as* weighed two ounces, considerably less than its pre-war weight.[79] By the 140s the *as* had been reduced to less than an ounce,[80] and at the time of the Social War a semuncial standard was adopted.[81] Occasionally there seem to have been attempts to reverse the decline (e.g. c. 170 and c. 115 BCE) but these were unsuccessful.[82] Consequently a variety of *asses* and fractions were circulating and indeed being hoarded together despite their differing weight standards.[83] Despite T. V. Buttrey's suggestion, based on the contents of hoards, that "the Roman seems not to have been disturbed by the great disparity of weights,"[84] such fluctuations cannot have inspired confidence.

The fiduciary nature of bronze coins, the fact that they were supposed to be worth more than their value in metal, probably discouraged some Romans from using them or at least limited their acceptability. The revaluation of the *denarius* from 10 *asses* to 16 around 141 BCE[85] would have dampened appeal for Roman bronze since this act made bronze coinage less valuable with respect to silver.[86] The descriptions

[78] Crawford (1973) 50.
[79] Crawford (1974) 596; Thomsen (1978) 21.
[80] Crawford (1978a) 149: "It is impossible to identify a point at which the uncial standard was introduced, but it is clear that the average weight of the asses circulating in the middle of the second century BC was roughly uncial."
[81] Crawford (1968a) 3; (1974) 596; (1978) 150.
[82] Crawford (1974) 596.
[83] Buttrey (1973) 47.
[84] Buttrey (1973) 47.
[85] Crawford (1978a) 149.
[86] There are, however, several possible reasons for the revaluation. If the government's revaluation merely brought its exchange rates in line with private usage or if

of the events surrounding the monetary measures of Gratidianus in 85 BCE demonstrate that public confidence in Roman coinage was rather low then and this may also relate to bronze issues. Cicero describes coinage as being "tossed about at that time so that no one knew what he had."[87] He reports that Gratidianus issued a decree to regulate monetary matters and consequently became quite popular with the people.[88] One interpretation of this account is that Gratidianus fixed the exchange rate between silver and bronze, thus allowing everyone to know the value of the coins in their possession.[89] Under this scenario, the praetor's popularity with the *multitudo* is a telling detail since the lower classes would presumably rely the most heavily upon coins of low value. Pliny, however, credits Gratidianus with a law concerning the detection of counterfeit coins and specifically mentions the testing of *denarii* (though this too is described as pleasing to the masses).[90] The brevity and ambiguity of the sources make it unlikely that any interpretation of Gratidianus' actions will ever be considered definitive.[91]

Finally, it is important to note that the persistence in circulation of Republican *asses* even into the Imperial period suggests a low attrition rate and the possibility that the stock of Roman bronze coinage remained strong even in periods when few were minted. That the Roman government did not mint bronze coinage in a particular period does not mean that it did not use such coins. It may be impossible to identify precisely the causes of the gaps in bronze production but these gaps do indicate, at least roughly, levels of state demand. Clearly demand for bronze coinage lagged behind that for silver.

---

it was responding to changes in the price of metals, then the change would not have reduced public confidence in bronze coinage.

[87] Cic. *Off.* 3.80: *iactabatur enim temporibus illis nummus sic, ut nemo posset scire, quid haberet.*

[88] Cic. *Off.* 3.80: *nemo umquam multitudini fuit carior.*

[89] So suggests Crawford (1968a) 3: "the edict of Gratidianus should be regarded as an attempt to prescribe a given relationship between the denarius and the *as*... It also marks the final success of the state in persuading people to accept a token bronze coinage."

[90] Plin. *HN* 33.132: *igitur ars facta denarios probare, tam iucunda plebei lege, ut Mario Gratidiano vicatim tota statuas dicaverit.*

[91] On Gratidianus see also: Lo Cascio (1979); Verboven (1994). For further discussion of the period see: Crawford (1968a) 3; (1970) 42; Yavetz (1970); Barlow (1980) 202–19; Walker (1980) 64; Santalucia (1982) 51–4; Williams (1998) 173–83.

2.5 Conclusion

The supply of Roman silver coinage increased to between five and ten times its initial size in the late Republic and, from the 40s, was supplemented by frequent new issues of gold coinage. The gaps in the production of small change, particularly the *as*, suggest that the government's demand for bronze coinage did not rise at the same pace as that for larger denomination coins. The continued production and circulation of local bronze coinage in certain places probably stems from the failure of Rome to provide sufficient supplies of Roman bronze coinage for the growing Empire. The changing size and composition of Roman money stocks undoubtedly reflects, at least in part, the replacement of local coinage with Roman issues in some new areas of the Empire such as Sicily and North Africa.[92] However, in many places Roman coinage did not begin to circulate until the reign of Augustus or later,[93] so replacement alone cannot account for the increased volume of Roman coinage. The dramatic increase in the Roman money supply must have either brought about significant economic changes (e.g. inflation or growth) or corresponded to major changes in the demand for money. Probably some combination of these phenomena occurred but, before we can evaluate these possibilities, it is necessary to examine the other forms of money available to the Romans and those assets whose use and availability shaped the demand for coinage.

---

92 Burnett (1987) 175–9; Crawford (1987) 43–52.

93 E.g. Syria, Crete and Cyrenaica. See Baldus (1987); Buttrey (1987).

CHAPTER THREE

FINANCIAL INSTRUMENTS

3.1 Introduction

Coinage never circulated alone or unaided in the late Republican economy. Uncoined gold and silver as well as financial instruments (*syngraphae, partes, nomina* and *permutationes*) performed some monetary roles while banks provided ways to make transactions without the physical movement of coins. This chapter examines how and to what extent the Romans used such instruments and institutions. These other forms of *pecunia* and ways of using money, by providing alternatives to coinage, limited Roman demand for coinage.

3.2 Bullion

Bullion clearly played a role in the Republican economy, fulfilling all of the functions of money and, like coinage, considered by the Romans to be *pecunia*. But on what scale was it used? Unfortunately the evidence for bullion use is sparse and frequently ambiguous. It is sometimes unclear whether a text is referring to bullion or coins of precious metal.[1] It can also be difficult to distinguish between bullion and plate. However, the fact that ancient writers usually mention the weight of silver vessels when discussing them suggests that the potential role of plate as bullion was seldom forgotten. Thus I will consider plate together with other forms of uncoined silver and gold.

3.2.1 *Bullion as a Means of Payment*

A number of passages indicate that bullion could function as a means of payment in both private and public transactions. Cicero speaks hypothetically of payments in gold bullion in order to illustrate a moral

[1] When, for example, at *Pro Caelio* 51 Cicero mentions payments of gold made by Clodia to Caelius and by Caelius to the slaves of Lucius Lucceius, does the word *aurum* indicate coins or bullion?

point,[2] and it seems unlikely that he would have chosen a completely unusual activity to serve as an example. Silver bullion could also be used in private transactions. Plutarch records an anecdote concerning Antony's father in which silver plate performed a monetary function. Once, when asked for cash, M. Antonius Creticus, short of funds himself, provided his friend with a silver bowl instead.[3] In this instance silver plate acted as a sort of 'emergency money' replacing coinage. While there is no extant reference to someone buying something from another private individual with bullion in the late Republic, a passage from Cicero's *In Vatinium* offers compelling evidence that bullion was regularly used in long-distance commerce. In the speech Cicero describes the behavior of the quaestor Publius Vatinius at Puteoli where he had been sent during the crisis of 63 BCE to prevent the export of gold and silver.[4] Cicero claims that Vatinius ruthlessly sought out whatever gold and silver he could find, searching homes, warehouses and ships, as well as harassing merchants.[5] Those engaged in long-distance trade were obviously expected to possess and transport gold and silver bullion.

Other surviving references, however, relate to public or at least quasi-public finances. Plutarch states that Cato the Elder gave each of his soldiers a pound of silver in 195 BCE at the end of the campaign,[6] and Opimius in 121 BCE rewarded those who brought him the head of Gaius Gracchus with its weight in gold.[7] Livy, furthermore, records the use of gold bullion to pay contractors who supplied clothing to an army fighting in Spain during the Second Punic War.[8] The Roman state also

---

[2] Cic. *Paradoxa Stoicorum* 21: *An virum bonum dices qui depositum nullo teste cum lucrari impune posset auri pondo decem reddiderit, si idem in decem milibus non fecerit?*

[3] Plut. *Ant.* 1.2–3: κεκτημένος γὰρ οὐ πολλὰ καὶ διὰ τοῦτο τῇ φιλανθρωπίᾳ χρῆσθαι κωλυόμενος ὑπὸ τῆς γυναικός, ἐπεί τις ἀφίκετο τῶν συνήθων πρὸς αὐτὸν ἀργυρίου δεόμενος, ἀργύριον μὲν οὐκ εἶχε, παιδαρίῳ δὲ προσέταξεν εἰς ἀργυροῦν σκύφον ὕδωρ ἐμβαλόντι κομίσαι: καὶ κομίσαντος, ὡς ξύρεσθαι μέλλων κατέβρεχε τὰ γένεια. τοῦ δὲ παιδαρίου καθ' ἑτέραν πρόφασιν ἐκποδὼν γενομένου, τὸν μὲν σκύφον ἔδωκε τῷ φίλῳ χρῆσθαι κελεύσας.

[4] Cic. *In Vat.* 12: *missusne sis a me consule Puteolos, ut inde aurum exportari argentumque prohiberes.*

[5] Cic. *In Vat.* 12: *in eo negotio cum te non custodem ad continendas, sed portitorem ad partiendas merces missum putares cumque omnium domos, apothecas, navis furacissime scrutarere hominesque negotii gerentis iudiciis iniquissimis inretires, mercatores e navi egredientis terreres, conscendentis morarere.*

[6] Plut. *Cat. Mai.* 10.4.

[7] Plut. *C. Gracch.* 17.3. Since at that point Rome had not minted *aurei* in about a century, presumably the sum was paid in bullion.

[8] Livy 27.10.13: *cetero auro usi sunt ad vestimenta praesenti pecunia locanda exercitui qui in Hispania bellum secunda sua fama ducisque gerebat.* The use of the phrase *praesens pecunia* as well

accepted or demanded some payments in bullion. In a letter to Cicero, C. Asinius Pollio describes the tax revenue from Spain as including large amounts of gold and silver in addition to coinage.[9] Caesar reports that Varro required Roman citizens in Spain to pay him not only 18 million *sestertii* and a large quantity of wheat but also 20,000 pounds of silver in order to govern the province.[10] In addition, Roman magistrates often requested or extorted *aurum coronarium* from cities and kings.[11] Ultimately a law was passed limiting such collections to those who had earned triumphs.[12] The Romans may have also collected the *aurum vicensimarium*, a 5% tax on manumissions, in gold bullion since the supply of *aurei* was so limited.

3.2.2 *Bullion as a Unit of Account*

Bullion by weight also functioned as a unit of account. In what few references to the contents of treasuries we have (which presumably derive from their *rationes*), gold and silver were not valued in terms of *asses*, *sestertii*, *denarii* or *aurei* but in pounds. For example, Livy records that in 209 BCE "about 4,000 pounds of gold were brought out" of the *aerarium sanctius*[13] and for the years 156 and 91 BCE Pliny reports the amount of uncoined gold and silver in the Roman treasury by number of pounds alongside figures for coins in *sestertii*.[14] Similarly in the *Pro Cluentio* Cicero reports the theft of both coins and gold from a chest rather than just giving the total value of the stolen wealth in terms of currency.[15] In another speech Cicero accuses someone of hiding the embezzlement of a quantity of gold bullion by changing the *vocabula* and *genera* in his accounts.[16] Although the evidence is meager, it is probable that wealthy

---

as the earlier description of this gold in terms of weight suggest that Livy is referring to the use of bullion.

[9] Cic. *Fam.* 10.32.1: *magna numerata pecunia, magno pondere auri, maiore argenti coacto de publicis exactionibus.*

[10] Caes. *B Civ.* 2.18: *Quibus rebus perterritos cives Romanos eius provinciae sibi ad rem publicam administrandam HS CLXXX et argenti pondo XX milia, tritici modium CXX milia polliceri coëgit.*

[11] See, for example, Cicero *Pis.* 90 and Dio Cass. 42.49.

[12] Cic. *Pis.* 90: *Lex enim generi tui et decerni et te accipere vetabat nisi decreto triumpho.*

[13] Livy 27.10.11: *Cetera expedientibus quae ad bellum opus erant consulibus, aurum vicensimarium, quod in sanctiore ad ultimos casus servabatur, promi placuit. Prompta ad quattuor milia pondo auri.*

[14] Plin. *HN* 33.55–56.

[15] Cic. *Clu.* 179–181: *Cum esset in aedibus armarium, in quo sciret esse nummorum aliquantum et auri...pecunia ablata.*

[16] Cic. *Pis.* 90: *vocabula tantum pecuniarum et genera mutabas.*

individuals as well as the state kept accounts of uncoined gold and silver by weight in addition to coinage.[17]

3.2.3 *Bullion as a Measure of Value*

Gold and silver bullion probably functioned as measures of value only in a few limited circumstances. Aside from tableware (and the head of Gaius Gracchus) it is rare to see objects valued in terms of their weight in gold or silver rather than in some quantity of coinage. In Pliny the Elder's extensive discussion of silver and silver plate, the value of almost every object is given by its weight of silver. Values recorded in *sestertii* are exceptional and seem intended to emphasize the high cost of the workmanship. For example, Pliny notes that Gaius Gracchus purchased some silver dolphins for 5,000 sesterces per pound and that Lucius Crassus had bought *vasa* at 6,000 sesterces per pound of silver.[18] In both cases the object's worth far exceeded its intrinsic bullion value.[19]

3.2.4 *Bullion as a Store of Wealth*

Bullion's most significant monetary role was undoubtedly as a store of wealth both for individuals and the state. Substantial quantities of bullion were brought to Rome[20] and stored in the Roman treasury.[21] The *aerarium sanctius*, in particular, seems to have functioned as a storehouse for gold bullion to be spent only in times of emergency. Caesar removed substantial numbers of gold and silver bars (*lateres*) from the Roman treasury when he took the city in 49 BCE.[22] In the private realm quantities of silver appear in descriptions of general wealth or inheritances,[23] suggesting that silver was a popular means not just of displaying but also of storing wealth. However, gold and silver ingots and ornaments rarely turn up in hoards. Out of 205 published Italian hoards from the late Republic only two contained gold jewelry and just one had gold

[17] Where else could Pliny (*HN* 33.141) get his figures for the amounts of silver owned by the younger Africanus, Allobrogicus and Livius Drusus?

[18] Plin. *HN* 33.53.

[19] In the late Republic a pound of silver yielded only 84 *denarii* or 336 *sestertii*.

[20] See, for example, Plut. *Luc.* 37 and *Mar.* 12.4.

[21] Plin. *HN* 33.55–56.

[22] Plin. *HN* 33.56.

[23] Cicero *Att.* 13.45.3 refers to an inheritance consisting of both coin and silver (though whether it is bullion or plate is unclear). Cicero also deals with a hypothetical inheritance involving both silver and silver coins (*Top.* 3.13 and 13.53). Festus 322 L indicates that bullion formed part of an individual's census declaration.

bars.[24] Similarly only one contained silver ornaments and only one had a silver bar.[25] These findings suggest that bullion was not a major store of private wealth in Italy. Elsewhere, however, particularly in Spain and Romania, silver ornaments appear much more frequently in hoards containing Roman coins.[26] This may reflect the higher level of monetization in Italy relative to these other regions.

3.2.5 *The Use and Circulation of Bullion*

It is clear that bullion had monetary functions, but what was its precise significance in the Roman economy? Bullion was essentially the 'money of last resort' in many cases for both the state and individuals. Gold from the *aerarium sanctius* was spent in emergencies,[27] while, for individuals, gold and silver plate or ornaments served both as useful or ostentatious household instruments and as a reserve fund. If necessary, one could 'spend' plate. So, for example, in July of 47 BCE we find Cicero advising Atticus to prepare for the worst by hiding away some funds "from silver, clothing... [and] furniture,"[28] and in April of 43 Cicero describes Antony as having squandered Sextus Pompeius' silver along with his wine, clothes and furniture, leaving behind only real estate.[29] The people of Ephesus try to get Antony to reduce the amount of money he demanded from them by pointing out that Brutus and Cassius had not only taken all their coinage but also their plate and ornaments as well.[30] Cicero succinctly describes the financial role of

---

[24] *RRCH #345*, a mid-first century hoard from Compito also included a gold bracelet while another hoard, from Policoro and dating to the late 70s BCE had both coins and a gold necklace. For the latter, see Siciliano (1974–75) 103–53. *RRCH* # 357, a hoard from Cadriano dating to 49–45 BCE, contained gold bars.

[25] *RRCH* #470, a mid-first century hoard from Moggio, included silver ornaments while another hoard (*RMISA* Palestrina 1963), closing in 80 BCE, contained a silver bar.

[26] Hoards from Spain containing silver objects other than coin include: *RRCH* #75, 91, 94, 107, 181, 184, 188, 189, 193, 200, and 205. They mostly date to the late third and second century BCE. The following late Republican hoards from Romania with silver bullion or ornaments have come to light: *RRCH* #280, 321, 329, 331 and 456.

[27] Livy 27.10.13.

[28] Cic. *Att.* 11.25.3: *te oro, ut in perditis rebus si quid cogi, confici potest quod sit in tuto, ex argento, [ves]te (quae satis multa est), supellectile, des operam.* In this context *argentum* must refer to silver plate, not coinage.

[29] Cic. *Phil.* 13.11.

[30] App. *B Civ.* 5.6: οἱ δὲ Ἕλληνες ἔτι λέγοντος αὐτου ταῦτα ἐρρίπτουν ἑαυτοὺς ἐς τὸ ἄδαφος, ἀνάγκην καὶ βίαν ἐς αὐτοὺς ἐκ Βρούτου καὶ Κασσίου γενομένας ἐπιλέγοντες οὐκ ἐπιτιμίων ἀξίας εἶναι, ἀλλ' ἐλέου, δόντες δ' ἂν τοῖς εὐεργέταις ἑκόντες ἀπορεῖν διὰ τοὺς πολεμίους, οἷς οὐ τὰ χρήματα μόνον, ἀλλὰ καὶ τὰ σκεύη

silver plate in a speech against Catiline. The consul asks why those who were heavily in debt did not use their silver (among other things) to pay off their creditors.[31] If no coins or credit were available, one turned to bullion or plate. In both the urban and governmental monetary zones, then, bullion functioned as an important form of 'emergency money.'

But how precisely was uncoined gold and silver normally used? Would it be converted into coins or could it be spent as it was? Often plate must have been converted into cash (physically or more likely through sale) before being spent but this need not have always been the case. The Antikythera wreck of c. 80 BCE, thought to have been carrying Greek war reparations to Rome, contained gold bars, jewelry and other valuables as well as coins.[32] Gold had a high prestige value and was frequently offered or 'paid' to gods (both at Rome, Jerusalem and elsewhere), apparently in the form of bullion.[33] Romans generals liked to display gold (*aurum coronarium*) in their triumphs but the state seems to have preferred silver for its regular revenue. Pliny the Elder comments:

> It does indeed surprise me that the Roman nation always imposed a tribute of silver, not of gold, on races that it conquered, for instance on Carthage when conquered together with Hannibal, 800,000 pounds weight of silver in yearly installments of 16,000 pounds spread over 50 years, but no gold. Nor can it be considered that this was due to the world's poverty.[34]

Similarly Polybius reports that the provisions of a treaty between Rome and the Aetolians in 189 BCE specified that:

> the Aetollians shall pay in silver specie, not inferior to Attic money, two hundred Euboic talents at once to the consul then in Greece, paying a third part of the sum if they wish, in gold at the rate of one gold mina for ten silver minae.[35]

καὶ τοὺς κόσμος ἐσενεγκεῖν ἀντὶ τῶν χρημάτων, τοὺς δὲ αὐτα παρὰ σφίσιν ἐς νόμισμα χαλκεῦσαι. Χρήματα here could mean simply coins or both coinage and bullion.

[31] Cic. *Cat.* 2.18: *Tu agris, tu aedificiis, tu argento... ornatus et copiosus sis, et dubites de possessione detrahere, adquirere ad fidem?* Again, the context suggests that *argentum* must mean silver plate here since it appears in a list with land and buildings, other forms of 'emergency money.'

[32] Parker (1992) no. 44.

[33] Cic. *Flac.* 66–9; Livy 43.6.

[34] Plin. *HN* 33.51: *Equidem miror populum Romanum victis gentibus in tributo semper argentum imperasse, non aurum, sicut Carthagini cum Hannibale victae octingenta milia, $\overline{XVI}$ pondo annua in quinquaginta annos, nihil auri. nec potest videri paenuria mundi id evenisse.*

[35] Polyb. 21.32.8: δότωσαν δὲ Αἰτωλοὶ ἀργυρίου μὴ χείρονος Ἀττικοῦ παραχρῆμα μὲν τάλαντα Εὐβοϊκὰ διακόσια τῷ στρατηγῷ τῷ ἐν τῇ Ἑλλάδι, ἀντὶ τρίτου μέρους

Coupled with the relative lack of production of gold coins, these passages indicate that the Roman state did not have a strong demand for gold bullion. However, if the state occasionally made large payments with uncoined gold, it would help explain the apparent disparity in the second and first centuries BCE between the amount of gold Rome took in and the amount it coined.[36] Unfortunately there are only a handful of references to the public use of gold bullion from the late Republic. Livy mentions the use of gold from the *aerarium sanctius* as *praesens pecunia* to pay government contracts during the Second Punic War.[37] The context indicates that it was the use of gold from the *aerarium sanctius* not the use of bullion *per se* that was noteworthy. Appian records that Sulla sold temple treasures and raised 9000 pounds of gold with which to finance his war against Mithridates.[38] A fragment of Lucilius, finally, refers to the use of gold by Roman quaestors and, given that it was composed towards the end of the second century BCE when Roman gold coinage was probably scarce, the poet is almost certainly referring to bullion.[39] These scattered sources suggest that it is likely—if by no means provable—that the Roman government often used gold bullion to make large payments in the late Republic.[40]

It would also be helpful to know more about the private role of bullion, in both finance and long-distance trade (i.e. the commercial monetary zone). A passing reference in Cicero to a barge full of gold is difficult to interpret.[41] It is a vivid image, but how frequently was bullion transported overseas? From Cicero we also know of periodic government restrictions on the export of bullion from Italy and other

τοῦ ἀργυρίου χρυσίον, ἐὰν βούλωνται, διδόντες, τῶν δέκα μνῶν ἀργυρίου χρυσίου μνᾶν διδοντες. See also Livy 38.11.1–9.

[36] See Howgego (1990) 13.

[37] Livy 27.10.11–3.

[38] App. *Mith.* 22: χρήματα δ' οὐκ ἔχοντες αὐτῷ ἐσενεγκεῖν, ἐψηφίσαντο πραθῆναι ὅσα Νουμᾶς Πομπίλιος βασιλεὺς ἐς θυσίας θεῶν διετέτακτο. τοσῆδε μὲν ἦν τότε πάντων ἀπορία καὶ ἐς πάντα φιλοτιμία. καί τινα αὐτῶν ἔφθασε πραθῆναι καὶ συνενεγκεῖν χρυσίου λίτρας ἐνακισχιλίας, ἃς μόνας ἐς τηλικοῦτον πόλεμον ἔδοσαν. Appian's use of the word λίτρα along with the fact that it had been about a century since the Romans last minted gold coinage suggests that he is referring to gold bullion, not coins.

[39] Lucil. 12.456–7: *huic homini quaestore aliquo esse opus atque corago,/ publicitus qui mi atque e fisco praebeat aurum.*

[40] There seems to be a fairly broad consensus on this point. See, e.g., Howgego (1992) 9; Harl (1996) 50; Verboven (2003a) 62.

[41] Cic. *Paradoxa Stoicorum* 20: *Auri navem evertat gubernator an paleae, in re aliquantulum, in gubernatoris inscitia nihil interest.*

provinces.[42] Such measures suggest that the state believed that significant quantities of bullion were circulating around the Mediterranean. Since the shipment of precious metals was subject to *portoria*,[43] it is reasonable to suppose that the senate might be aware (via the *publicani*) of the extent to which bullion circulated within the empire. So far, however, no bullion barges have turned up[44]—perhaps because precautions like those employed by Cato the Younger, who attached cork buoys to the containers of silver in a large shipment, were common practice.[45] Despite the lack of archaeological confirmation, it seems likely that bullion had some role in long-distance trade.

With respect to the private, non-commercial use of bullion it is difficult to move beyond the obvious hypothesis that bullion would be used primarily for large transactions such as purchases of real estate. Cicero seems to refer to bullion use when he wants to emphasize the sheer quantity of money being discussed. In one passage from the *Philippics*, for example, he claims that so many coins were flowing through Antony's house that they were weighed out (i.e. treated like bullion) rather than counted.[46] Bullion use, it seems, is high finance.

3.2.6 *Conclusion*

While Pliny's treasury figures show that bullion formed a substantial part of Rome's reserves and Cicero's writings demonstrate that the private circulation of bullion could be a major concern of the government, it is difficult to judge the overall importance of bullion in the economy of the late Republic. Obviously the use of bullion was mostly limited to the state, the wealthy and traders (i.e. the governmental, commercial and urban monetary zones). Gold bullion and silver plate clearly functioned as 'emergency money' for the government and the wealthy respectively; gold bullion probably played a role in long-distance trade as well.

---

[42] Cic. *Flac.* 67: *exportari aurum non oportere cum saepe antea senatus tum me consule gravissime iudicavit*; and *In Vatinium* 5.12: *missusne sis a me consule Puteolos, ut inde aurum exportari argentumque prohiberes.*

[43] Cic. *Verr.* II 2.176: *Dico te maximum pondus auri, argenti... Syracusis exportasse: his pro rebus quod portorium non esset datum, litteras ad socios misisse L. Canuleium, qui in portu operas daret.*

[44] Howgego (1995) 89 notes that "shipwrecks have not as yet revealed any evidence for the transport of gold and silver ingots from Spain, the principal mining area of the Roman Empire." See also: Parker (1992) 17. It seems likely that bullion shipments went by land whenever possible.

[45] Plut. *Cat. Min.* 38.1.

[46] Cic. *Phil.* 2.97: *Itaque tanti acervi nummorum apud istum construuntur, ut iam expendantur, non numerentur pecuniae.*

Though passages mentioning bullion-based transactions are few, the brevity and offhand nature of such references suggest that Roman authors found the use of uncoined gold and silver in monetary transactions unexceptional. The Romans clearly considered bullion to be a form of *pecunia*. This is demonstrated by the ways in which Roman writers treat bullion in relation to *pecunia* and coinage. For example, in the *Pro Cluentio* Cicero refers to stolen coins and gold collectively as *pecunia ablata* ('carried off money').[47] Caesar, in his description of the monetary habits of the British, states that some of them used iron bars by weight not in place of money (*pro pecunia*) but rather in place of coin (*pro nummo*).[48] He distinguishes between different kinds of money-use rather than between money-use and barter. On occasion one does encounter language that suggests that bullion might be placed outside the category of *pecunia* as when Cicero employs the phrase '*pendebatur aurum, numerabatur pecunia*' ("gold was being weighed out, money counted") to describe the goings-on "amid the wool-baskets" at Antony's house.[49] However, *pecunia* in this phrase is clearly meant to mean coins, not money in general.

3.3 Financial Instruments

In studying the use of financial instruments in ancient Rome one is faced with a number of difficulties. Few sources record such activity and they usually contain only brief and cryptic allusions to it. For the late Republic we must rely almost exclusively on the works of Cicero, who frequently makes reference to *nomina, partes, syngraphae* and *permutationes*, but rarely provides enough information to make the nature of their use entirely clear. In spite of these difficulties, this section will examine the different kinds of financial transactions for which we have evidence and the terminology of such transactions in order to demonstrate that the Romans employed some forms of money or 'near money' which were, strictly speaking, intrinsically valueless (*partes* and *syngraphae*) or indeed purely notional (*permutationes* and *nomina*). The extent to which these financial instruments were used, however, seems likely to remain in the realm of speculation indefinitely.

---

[47] Cic. *Clu.* 179–181.

[48] Caes. *B Gall.* 5.12: *Utuntur aut aere aut nummo aureo aut taleis ferreis ad certum pondus examinatis pro nummo.*

[49] Cic. *Phil.* 3.10.

3.3.1 *Permutationes*

Permutatio and its verbal form, *permutare*, appear a number of times of Cicero's letters. *Permutatio* is usually translated as 'a bill-of-exchange' and *permutare* as 'to negotiate a bill-of-exchange,'[50] but these phrases imply a level of certainty concerning the meaning of these terms that does not exist.[51] The following references to *permutatio* illustrate what is clear and what remains uncertain concerning the use of this financial device:

1. *Ad Quintum Fratrem* 1.3.7 (June 13th, 58 BCE): Cicero, while in exile in Thessalonica, mentions *permutatio* in a discussion of his personal finances: "Why, then, did you write to me about an exchange?"
2. *Ad Atticum* 5.13.2 (July 26th, 51 BCE): Cicero, in Ephesus, states that he has given to Philogenes (probably a freedman of Atticus) an account of a *permutatio* between Atticus and himself.
3. *Ad Familiares* 3.5.4 (July 27th, 51 BCE): Cicero states that he will receive in Laodicea money owed to him "from the public exchange" ('*ex publica permutatione*').
4. *Ad Atticum* 5.15.2 (August 8th, 51 BCE): Cicero, writing from Laodicea, discusses his finances and mentions that he may have to borrow money in order to pay "what I exchanged with you" ('*quod tecum permutavi*').
5. *Ad Familiares* 2.17 (July 18th, 50 BCE): Cicero, writing from Tarsus to Gnaeus Sallustius, complains that Bibulus has unfairly taken credit for an exchange of money ('*pecunia permutaretur*') in a letter to the senate.
6. *Ad Atticum* 11.1.2 (January, 48 BCE): Cicero tells Atticus that he has a large sum of *cistophori* in Asia and that "by the exchange of this money" ('*huius pecuniae permutatione*') his credit can be maintained.
7. *Ad Atticum* 11.24.3 (August 6th, 47 BCE): Cicero, writing from Brundisium, reveals that Atticus had instructed Terentia to *permutare* HS 12,000 but that she only sent ('*misit*') HS 10,000.

---

[50] See Lewis and Short (1879) s.v. *permuto*; Glare (1968) s.v. *permutatio* and *permuto*; Shackleton Bailey (1999) 11.1.2, 12.27.2 and 15.15.

[51] Verboven (2002) 132–40 provides a good overview of the debate about *permutatio*. He argues (132) that it is best "to consider *permutatio* as a procedure *sui generis* to transfer funds without carrying cash." See also: Früchtl (1912) 20–8; Jonkers (1941) 185; Barlow (1978) 168–71; Andreau (1978) 51–5; Maselli (1986) 118–9; Duncan-Jones (1990) 39; Petrucci (1991) 116–20; Nicolet (1994a) 634; Andreau (1999) 132.

8. *Ad Atticum* 12.24.1 (March 20th, 45 BCE): Cicero, in Astura, asks Atticus whether Cicero's son, Marcus, can receive what he will need in Athens ('*quod illi opus erit Athenis*') by exchange ('*permutari*') or if he needs to bring it with him ('*ipsi ferendum sit*').
9. *Ad Atticum* 12.27.2 (March 23th, 45 BCE): Cicero, discussing the same topic mentioned in *Ad Atticum* 12.24, asks Atticus to arrange an exchange of money for Cicero's son ('*nummorum quantum opus erit ut permutetur*'). Atticus accomplished this through his Athenian friend Xeno, who owed him money.[52]
10. *Ad Atticum* 15.15.4 (June 13th, 44 BCE): Having learnt a few days earlier that Xeno has not been providing Marcus with enough money in Athens,[53] Cicero asks Atticus to exchange at Athens ('*permutetur Athenas*') a year's expenses for his son.'

These passages reveal several important aspects of *permutatio*. Obviously it was first and foremost a means of transferring money over long distances, a *procedure* rather than a particular type of financial document. Cicero makes this clear when he asks Atticus whether his son could receive money in Athens or would have to bring it with him. He did not ask if his son should *bring* a *permutatio*. Certainly *permutationes*, like traveler's checks, allowed one to travel without carrying large amounts of cash, but it does not seem as though one could use a *permutatio* for a direct purchase. It is, however, certain that this financial device could be used for both public and private transactions. Cicero uses *permutatio* to get money while governing Cilicia and in order to support his son at Athens. It would be risky and burdensome to carry large amounts of coin when traveling abroad and, if one went from Italy to the east, it would be necessary to exchange all those coins for local currency upon arrival anyway. Under such circumstances *permutatio* provided an ideal solution. It may be that *permutatio* originally signified merely an exchange of currency.[54] Certainly, many of the transactions referred to in the passages listed above involved the conversion of sums of money from one currency system to another. This must be the meaning of Cicero's remark that he had exchanged money "to the advantage of the people" ('*cum quaestu populi*'), which suggests that a favorable exchange

---

52 Cic. *Att.* 13.37, 14.17 and 15.21.
53 Cic. *Att.* 16.1.5: *Xenonem perexigue... praebere.*
54 Andreau (1999) 132: "so its name would suggest."

rate had been obtained.[55] Such a conversion would also have been necessary for Atticus to use Cicero's *cistophori* to satisfy his debtors who were, presumably, Roman.

Two passages indicate that *permutatio* meant more than just the transfer/exchange of money. First, in *Ad Atticum* 11.24, Cicero states that Terentia has sent him HS 10,000. In this passage *permutare* seems to be used interchangeably with *mittere* to mean sending money without there necessarily being an exchange of currency. Indeed, as both Cicero and his wife were probably in Italy at the time of the transaction, it seems unlikely that any currency exchange would have been necessary. In this context *permutatio* would seem to indicate merely a long-distance payment.

Secondly, *Ad Atticum* 5.15 gives a similar impression, although here Cicero seems to have received a loan rather than a payment. This passage is difficult to understand. Cicero writes that he is spending so much money that he may have to resort to *versura* to pay Atticus '*quod tecum permutavi*.' Here, clearly, we are not dealing with a simple transfer of money since in that situation the *permutatio* and Cicero's expenses would be unrelated. However, in this case the more Cicero spends, the more he owes Atticus through their *permutatio*. Cicero seems to have reached an agreement with Atticus so that he could draw on funds which Atticus had on deposit in Laodicea or elsewhere in the east. At some point, then or later, Cicero would pay back in Italy the money withdrawn in the east. Their *permutatio* must have included an agreement on the exchange rate between *denarii* and *cistophori* and might also have specified the terms of repayment. In this particular case, since Cicero was using money he did not actually have, the *permutatio* amounted to a loan (though it is not clear that they would have viewed it that way especially as we are ignorant of the terms of repayment). Such a financial device would be of considerable utility to travelers and traders who could withdraw only as much money as they needed. It would reduce or eliminate the possibility of prematurely running out of money or exchanging too much currency at the beginning of a trip and having to re-exchange it for a loss at the end. For someone like Atticus this system would allow for the reciprocal transfer to Rome of money earned/deposited in the provinces with very little risk. It is likely that the *publicani* used *permutationes* in this fashion extensively in order to avoid the dangerous transportation of coinage between Rome and the provinces.[56]

---

[55] Cic. *Fam.* 2.17.

[56] Nicolet (1996) 22: "The local accounts of the companies in the provinces also

Unfortunately Cicero's writings do not explain the physical nature of *permutatio*. We know virtually nothing about the institutions, processes and special documents (if any) necessary for such transactions to take place. In the public sphere, as Nicolet has observed, there must have been an "efficient annual accounting and annual balancing of totals" in order for the system to function properly.[57] To what extent could those who were not tax farmers or government officials make use of the *publicani*'s *permutatio* system? Cicero, certainly, was able to deposit private funds with the *publicani* in Asia and transfer them later,[58] so clearly the *publicani* did not strictly exclude private transactions. Given the way Romans tended to exploit their social networks, no doubt many were able to employ the publicans' system.[59] Even so, there were other ways to effect a *permutatio*, as Atticus's efforts to provide Cicero's son with money in Athens reveals. Atticus provided Marcus with money by directing his Athenian friend, Xeno,[60] who owed Atticus money, to pay it to Marcus instead. Cicero then compensated Atticus by having the income from some rental properties at Rome paid directly to Atticus. The entire matter was apparently handled by means of letters and does not seem to have required any special documents. This *permutatio* was simply an exchange of financial obligations similar to the transfer of *nomina* used to assign debts to third parties. However, in this case it does not appear that Xeno became Cicero's debtor and Cicero, of course, assigned rents rather than debts to Atticus. Their *permutatio*, while seemingly more complicated than those involving the government and the *publicani*, accomplished the same end: the long-distance transfer of funds without the physical transport of coinage.

Beyond the fact that it was a means of transferring money, much remains unclear concerning the nature of *permutatio*. It is important to note that there are no examples of *permutatio* being used either for

served as the accounts for the money made available by the state to governors, the *ornatio*... this money never moved from Rome to the province; what happened was that the state designated a certain amount in the account of a particular company; the only transaction was a paper transaction, known as *permutatio*."

[57] Nicolet (1996) 22.

[58] Cic. *Att.* 11.1.2; *Fam.* 5.20.9.

[59] However, Andreau (1999) 20 argues that "When sums being transferred were nothing to do with the State or with magistrates carrying out their official duties, no tax-collectors would be involved."

[60] There is considerable doubt as to the nature of Xeno's relationship with Atticus: Rauh (1986) 8; Andreau (1999) 20–1. Rauh considers him to be one of Atticus' 'financial agents' while Andreau notes that "there is nothing to suggest that he was a professional banker or even a financier."

purchase or in short-distance transactions. Most of the extant examples of *permutatio* involve the transfer rather than the use of money. For the most part, *permutatio* seems to have been a means of moving money safely and efficiently rather than a form of 'near money' *per se*. Only in Cicero's transaction with Terentia and one other with Atticus (*Ad Atticum* 5.15.2) is it possible that *permutatio* functioned as a means of payment. It is also difficult to estimate the extent to which Romans employed *permutatio*.[61] Those who might have the means, connections or incentives to participate in *permutatio* transactions would likely have included temple and treasury officials, bankers, merchants, moneylenders, representatives of tax-farming corporations, as well as the rich and influential along with their clients, freedmen, slaves and friends.[62] Cicero's letters do not suggest that such transactions were particularly difficult or unusual.[63] Nevertheless, there simply is not enough evidence to determine the extent to which *permutatio* was used and its economic impact.[64]

3.3.2 *Syngraphae*

Syngraphae were financial contracts of some sort but have no obvious modern equivalent. Because its exact Latin significance is by no means self-evident, the word *syngrapha* has been interpreted in a variety of ways. Many translators opt for facile 'bond' which sounds specific but can, in fact, have an array of meanings. Others have used 'promissory note,' 'note of hand,' 'bill of exchange' or 'contract.' For a Latin equivalent some have proposed *cautio*, suggesting that a *syngrapha* was security for a loan made by a Roman to a provincial.[65] An analysis of the use of the word, appearing primarily in the writings of Cicero, indicates that, even if a precise definition remains elusive, *syngraphae*, at least in some circumstances, had distinct monetary functions.

---

[61] Jonkers (1941) 185 questions whether *permutatio* was used frequently or for commercial purposes. Maselli (1986) 119 also suggests that *permutatio* was not particularly common. However, Barlow (1978) 169 argues that "Such transfers must have been fairly common: they provoke no comment from Cicero when he mentions them."

[62] Andreau (1978) 54–5.

[63] The effort to finance Marcus' stay in Athens is an excellent example of this.

[64] The fact that the term *permutatio* does not appear in the archive of the Sulpicii, a group of businessmen active in early to mid-first century CE Puteoli, could indicate that this sort of financial transaction was not common in Roman commerce. However, since the exact profession(s) of the Sulpicii remain unclear, it would be dangerous to draw any firm conclusions based on this fact. See Camodeca (1999) 24–6; Andreau (1999) 76–9; Verboven (2003b).

[65] Früchtl (1912) 94–9; Maselli (1986) 174–5. See also Torrent (1973).

Syngrapha is a transliteration of the Greek word συγγραφή (which itself has a range of meanings) and would seem to suggest, at the very least, a written agreement between two individuals or parties. In many instances, when Cicero uses the word, he provides little information beyond the names of the two parties involved.[66] *Syngraphae* probably required not only the signatures of those entering into the agreement but also those of witnesses.[67] To this extent a *syngrapha* seems to be merely a type of contract, but Cicero's use of the word often implies that it was much more. Several passages suggest that *syngraphae* were (or could be) monetary instruments created for making payments or for the lending and borrowing of money. Cicero explicitly links *syngraphae* to exchange in a passage of the *Philippics* where he speaks of a *syngrapha* for 10 million *sesterces* which was arranged "in the women's apartment where many things have been bought and sold."[68] Here a *syngrapha* seems to function almost like a check or a promissory note. By means of this *syngrapha* Deiotarus had paid Antonius for Roman recognition of his claim to kingship.[69] Interestingly Cicero indicates that the *syngrapha* had not yet been cashed and suggests that Deiotarus was not legally bound to honor it since he had subsequently reestablished himself as king of Galatia without Roman help.[70]

A tantalizing Ciceronian fragment recorded by Nonius links *syngraphae* to long-distance trade. Cicero writes "we willingly wrote *syngraphae* for Achaean merchants."[71] Little can be made of this brief passage beyond the conclusion that *negotiatores* employed *syngraphae* (which should not be surprising given their obvious utility). Did Cicero use *syngraphae* to invest in business ventures? As Brutus's involvement with the *negotiator* M. Scaptius also suggests (see below), *syngraphae* may have played an

[66] In one speech, for example, Cicero speaks of *syngraphae* made by Byzantine exiles with Clodius' secretary (*Dom.* 129: *si tuus scriptor in illo incendio civitatis non syngraphas cum Byzantiis exsulibus...faceret*). Other than to imply that the making of such *syngraphae* was somehow wrong, the context supplies no further information concerning them.

[67] The phrases *inanibus syngraphis* (Cic. *Verr.* II 4.30) and *syngraphae obsignabantur* (Cic. *Phil.* 5.12) imply that *syngraphae* typically required signatures and witnesses.

[68] Cic. *Phil.* 2.95: *syngrapha sestertii centiens per legatos, viros bonos, sed timidos et imperitos, sine nostra, sine reliquorum hospitum regis sententia facta in gynaecio est, quo in loco plurimae res venierunt et veneunt.*

[69] Antonius apparently inserted statements favoring Deiotarus' recognition into Caesar's notoriously mutable memoranda.

[70] Cic. *Phil.* 2.95–6.

[71] Nonius 334.IL: *Pro negotiatoribus Achaeis syngraphas qua nostra voluntate conscripsimus.* See discussion in Crawford (1994) 312–4.

important part in the process by which *negotiatores* funneled senatorial wealth into provincial investments.[72]

Syngraphae appear most frequently in Cicero's writings in the context of credit. In the *De Haruspicum Responso* Cicero states that Brogitarus had become a king thanks to money lent him by Clodius. He writes "I shall consider [him] to be a king when he has paid you back what you lent him by means of a *syngrapha* (*per syngrapham*)."[73] This passage demonstrates that *syngraphae* were a means of making loans. Two *syngraphae* recording loans appear in a decree from Tenos in honor of L. Aufidius Bassus.[74] The inscription, dating to the mid-70s BCE, states that Bassus' father had left his son two *syngraphae*, for 11,000 and 19,500 Attic drachmas respectively, both with an interest rate of 16.67%.[75] Aufidius was thanked by the city for easing the terms of repayment. A more notorious example involves the loan at 48% interest that Brutus made by means of a *syngrapha* to the community of Salamis on Cyprus.[76] The efforts of M. Scaptius, Brutus' agent, to secure repayment of the loan provide us with the most expansive discussion of *syngraphae* in all of Cicero's works. However, since this discussion is mostly concerned with the legal standing of *syngraphae*, it sheds little light on their use.

In a letter to Atticus from around the same time, Cicero mentions *syngraphae* in a discussion of his provincial edict. One of the edict's two main sections, he reports, contains his provisions concerning state accounts, debt, usury, *syngraphae*, and matters relating to the *publicani*.[77] This passage is important because it implies that issues related to *syngraphae* were distinct from those concerning interest (*usura*) and debt (*aes alienum*) although, as we have seen, a *syngrapha* might involve both debt and interest. Clearly *syngrapha* was not merely a formal term for a debt.

One explanation could be that *syngraphae* were more complex than simple loans, specifying terms beyond or instead of interest rates and repayment dates. Perhaps, to use the example of Clodius and Brogitarus, their *syngrapha* provided for repayment only in the event that Brogitarus became king. Such an explanation might shed light on a passage

[72] Andreau (1999) 137.
[73] Cic. *Har. resp.* 29 (my translation): ... *alterum putabo regem, si habuerit unde tibi solvat quod ei per syngrapham credidisti.*
[74] *IG* XII 5, 860 lines 19–27.
[75] Étienne (1979) 145–7.
[76] Cic. *Att.* 5.21.10–2 and 6.2.7.
[77] Cic. *Att.* 6.1.15.

from Suetonius' *Divus Iulius* where the author describes Caesar's efforts, while serving as proconsul in Gaul, to enlist political support at Rome:

> Then to secure himself for the future, he took great pains always to put the magistrates for the year under personal obligation, and not to aid any candidates or suffer any to be elected, save such as guaranteed to defend him in his absence. And he did not hesitate in some cases to exact an oath to keep this pledge or even a written contract (*syngrapha*).[78]

Suetonius perhaps intended the word *syngrapha* to convey the idea of a monetary contract. The magistrate in question presumably gave a *syngrapha* to Caesar guaranteeing the payment of a sum of money if he failed to act in accordance with Caesar's interests. Admittedly it is difficult to see how such a contract could ever have been legally enforced.

One difference between *syngraphae* and *aes alienum* may have stemmed from the fact that some *syngraphae* could function as money in at least a limited capacity. A passage from a letter Cicero wrote to Gaius Trebatius Testa, criticizing his haste to 'cash in' on financial opportunities abroad, suggests that Romans typically viewed *syngraphae* as a form of 'near money:'

> For you were in a hurry to snatch the money and return home, just as if what you had brought the commander-in-chief was not a letter of recommendation, but a *syngrapha*; and it never occurred to you that even those who went to Alexandria with *syngraphae* have never yet been able to bring away a single penny.[79]

The implication of the first half of this passage is that *syngraphae* are as good as money since, if Trebatius had brought one to Caesar, he would have been justified in expecting to return home with money. But Cicero goes on to undermine this connection somewhat by pointing out the notable example of Ptolemy Auletes who apparently did not honor his *syngraphae*.[80] Several other passages from Cicero's letters indicate that

---

[78] Suet. *Iul.* 23.2: *Ad securitatem ergo posteri temporis in magno negotio habuit obligare semper annuos magistratus et e petitoribus non alios adiuvare aut ad honorem pati pervenire, quam qui sibi recepissent propugnaturos absentiam suam; cuius pacti non dubitavit a quibusdam ius iurandum atque etiam syngrapham exigere.*

[79] Cic. *Fam.* 7.17.1 (adapted from the Loeb translation): *Tamquam enim syngrapham ad imperatorem, non epistolam attulisses, sic, pecunia ablata, domum redire properabas; nec tibi in mentem veniebat, eos ipsos, qui cum syngraphis venissent Alexandream, nummum adhuc nullum auferre potuisse.*

[80] No doubt Ptolemy gave these *syngraphae* to various Roman senators to generate support for his restoration to power following his expulsion in 58 BCE.

syngraphae could require a degree of effort to be turned into cash. Caelius's repeated requests for help from Cicero concerning a '*syngrapha Sittiana*' suggest that he anticipated difficulties,[81] and the *syngrapha Salaminiana* certainly caused quite a lot of trouble for all parties involved. It is not surprising, then, that Seneca would refer to *syngraphae* as the "empty shades of possession."[82]

It is likely that, as with the word 'bond,' *syngrapha* had both general and technical meanings. However it is clear that some *syngraphae* could function as money. They were certainly stores of wealth, if not always the most liquid asset since their use might involve high transaction costs. A *syngrapha* was a form of money to the same extent that a promissory note is. Modern paper currencies are also promissory notes issued by banks or governments. Although there is some reason to suppose that *syngraphae* could be used as a means of payment or exchange, there is no evidence concerning their use by third parties (though the *syngrapha Sittiana* may represent such an instance).[83] Some *syngraphae* may have been merely records of payment rather than the payments themselves and so would constitute 'a means of payment' only in the loosest sense. *Syngraphae*, then, were a limited form of 'near money' sometimes used for large transactions. Though we have evidence for their use by several foreign rulers, there is no indication that the Roman state employed *syngraphae*.

3.3.3 *Partes*

Three brief passages from the works of Cicero and Plutarch demonstrate that the Romans possessed and traded shares (*partes*) in tax-farming and commercial companies.[84] In the *Pro Rabirio Postumo* Cicero provides a rather ambiguous reference to such practices. In a discussion of Rabirius' financial activities, Cicero notes that he "held many shares in state enterprises."[85] It is not entirely clear how this passage

[81] Cic. *Fam.* 8.2.2, 8.4.5, 8.8.10 and 8.9.3.

[82] Sen. *Ben.* 7.10.3.

[83] If Caelius was trying to make use of the *syngrapha Sittiana* himself, it must have been signed over to him by Sittius. It is also possible that Caelius wrote on behalf of a friend—presumably a very good friend since he raises the subject in four separate letters—but in that case the owner of the *syngrapha* could hardly have been *the* P. Sittius, as Rauh (1986) 23 would have it, since he was a friend of Cicero's in his own right and would hardly need someone else to intercede on his behalf.

[84] See Malmendier (2005) 31–42 on Roman shares.

[85] Cic. *Rab. Post.* 4: *magnas partis habuit publicorum.*

should be interpreted. The context is Rabirius' activities as a lender and as a friend/patron. Cicero states that he lent money even to nations and kings, having financial dealings throughout the provinces.[86] It seems reasonable to conclude therefore that Rabirius had invested in some corporations involved in state contracts and that such corporations raised capital not through traditional borrowing but through the sale of *partes* (shares). These corporations were most likely involved in tax-farming since such enterprises were the most capital intensive, requiring the maintenance of large provincial staffs and periodic payments to the government in Rome.[87] The passage also indicates that these shares could be alienated since Rabirius gave them to his friends.

Cicero's other remark concerning *partes* occurs in the *In Vatinium* of 56 BCE and tends to reinforce the conclusions drawn from his cryptic remarks in the *Pro Rabirio Postumo*. Cicero accuses Vatinius of *repetundae* (extortion) while a tribune of the plebs and asks him: "did you not at the same time filch shares (*partes*) when they were at their most expensive, in part from Caesar, in part from the tax-farmers."[88] Though brief and ambiguous, this passage does associate *partes* more explicitly with the publicans. Furthermore, Cicero's reference to the *partes* as most expensive at a particular time ('*illo tempore carissimas*') shows that these shares not only could be exchanged but also fluctuated in value. Presumably, therefore, they were regularly traded. This may also be inferred from one of Cicero's letters which, while not explicitly mentioning *partes*, refers to someone who had invested in the tax farming companies and suffered great losses.[89]

The brevity of Cicero's references to *partes* is in itself notable. This suggests that *partes* were a relatively well-known phenomenon, requiring no special explanation or description for the orator's audience. It is reasonable to suppose that such shares in public companies were, as Ernst Badian asserted, "as old as the companies themselves" and "widely

[86] Cic. *Rab. Post.* 4: *credidit populis; in pluribus provinciis eius versata res est; dedit se etiam regibus.*

[87] Lintott (1993) 89 makes a strong case for the *publicani*'s payments coming at the end of the *lustrum* but the *Monumentum Ephesenum* lines 99–101 suggests annual payments. See Malmendier (2005) 34.

[88] Cic. In *Vat.* 29 (adapted from the Loeb translation): *eripuerisne partes illo tempore carissimas partim a Caesare, partim a publicanis?*

[89] Cic. *Fam.* 13.10.2: ... *deinde, quod mature se contulit in societates publicanorum, quod quidem nollem; maximis enim damnis affectus est.*

held by senators" and other wealthy Romans in the late Republic,[90] but unfortunately, there are very few references to shareholders.[91]

The third reference to shares comes from Plutarch's biography of Cato the Elder. Although this passage concerns a private venture rather than a tax-farming company, it supplies us with the most detailed account of the use of shares in the Republican period. Plutarch writes that Cato, in his search for bigger and surer profits, hit upon a way to maximize profits and minimize risk through the formation of trading companies:

> He used to loan money also in the most disreputable of all ways, namely, on ships, and his method was as follows. He required his borrowers to form a large company, and when there were fifty partners and as many ships...he took one share in the company himself, and was represented by Quintio, a freedman of his, who accompanied his clients in all their ventures. In this way his entire security was not imperiled, but only a small part of it, and his profits were large.[92]

Since Cato's company was formed after he had lent money to his clients, presumably the loans themselves were regular (i.e. secured by land) and not bottomry loans (with ship and cargo as security).[93] Thus Cato's scheme combined the high profitability of long-distance trade with the minimal risk of non-maritime loans since his clients would still owe Cato money even if the company's ships sank. The role of Cato's freedman, Quintio, apparently allowed Cato to manage the affairs of the company closely, although it is unclear how he could accompany Cato's clients (debtors/fellow share-holders) on all their ventures unless either very

---

[90] Badian (1972) 102–3. However, as Harris (1975) 436 points out, Badian's conclusions about the scope of ownership of shares goes well beyond what the sources actually say.

[91] Malmendier (2005) 38 notes that Cicero "refers to shareholders as *participes*; other authors denote them as *adfines*" but both words seem to imply a more active role in the running of a company than 'shareholder' implies in a modern context. Livy 43.16 suggests that an *adfinis* might bid at an auction on behalf of the company.

[92] Plut. *Cat. Mai.* 21.6: ἐχρήσατο δὲ καὶ τῷ διαβεβλημένῳ μάλιστα τῶν δανεισμῶν ἐπὶ ναυτικοῖς τὸν τρόπον τοῦτον. ἐκέλευε τοὺς δανειζομένους ἐπὶ κοινωνίᾳ πολλοὺς παρακαλεῖν, γενομένων δὲ πεντήκοντα καὶ πλοίων τοσούτων αὐτὸς εἶχε μίαν μερίδα διὰ Κουϊντίωνος ἀπελευθέρου τοῖς δανειζομένοις συμπραγματευομένου καὶ συμπλέοντος. ἦν δ' οὖν οὐκ εἰς ἅπαν ὁ κίνδυνος, ἀλλ' εἰς μέρος μικρὸν ἐπὶ κέρδεσι μεγάλοις.

[93] Note, however, Rougé (1980) 292–3 who argues, based on Plutarch use of the words τῷ διαβεβλημένῳ μάλιστα, that these were maritime loans. See also: von Lübtow (1975); D'Arms (1981) 39–41; Andreau (1999) 56; Verboven (2002) 282 n. 282.

few voyages were made or all 50 ships traveled together.[94] Neither scenario appears likely or indeed conducive to profit. One must conclude that either Plutarch or his source for this anecdote was somewhat confused.[95] In spite of the numerous difficulties and uncertainties surrounding this passage, it does establish that *partes* were in use as early as the second century BCE and could play a role in private trading ventures.

The evidence concerning *partes*, scanty though it is, demonstrates that they were a store of value and perhaps also occasionally a means of payment. Their use was undoubtedly confined to the commercial and urban monetary zones.

3.3.4 *Nomina*

Romans referred to the money owed them as *nomina* or 'names,' because they entered the sums they were owed into their account books under the name of the debtor. Cicero frequently uses the word *nomen* in this sense, both in his letters and speeches. So, for example, Cicero writes to Atticus that, if necessary, he would be willing to borrow money to pay off a loan made to him by Oppius because he does not wish to wait to receive the cash owed him by his own *nomina*.[96] By the late Republic *nomina* had come to represent more than just debts; they were an abstract store of wealth and, as such, were also used as a means of payment.

A vivid example of *nomina* as a store of wealth comes from the *Verrine Orations* when Cicero describes the plight of a victim of Verres' avarice:

> As they were hurrying him off, the poor wretch kept crying out that he was innocent, that he had done no wrong, that all his money was invested (*pecuniam sibi esse in nominibus*) and that he had no ready cash.[97]

Dio, another Sicilian from whom Verres extorted money, had to borrow, sell land and "call in his debts" ('*nomina sua exegisse*') to pay off the governor.[98]

---

[94] Rougé (1980) 293 argues that the ships traveled in a convoy in order to provide mutual assistance.

[95] A passage from Justinian's *Digest* (22.2.4) considers the possibility of 'a slave traveling in connection with a transmarine loan' which seems to parallel Quintio's position.

[96] Cic. *Att.* 5.1.2: *de Oppio, factum est <ut> volui, et maxime quo<d> HS DCCC aperuisti; quae quidem ego utique vel versura facta solvi volo, ne extrema exactio nostrorum nominum exspectetur.*

[97] Cic. *Verr.* II 5.17.

[98] Cic. *Verr.* II 1.10.28.

Provided all parties agreed, one could transfer a *nomen* to settle a claim rather than pay cash. The consent of all parties was required because one *nomen* was not necessarily as good as another. In 62 BCE Cicero was able to boast to P. Sestius that he was considered a *bonum nomen* ('good name') because he had successfully defended the interests of money-lenders during his consulship. Someone with a 'good name' could borrow money more easily and good *nomina* were more easily delegated (i.e. assigned to third parties by way of payment). A good example of the delegation of *nomina* (and its associated risks) comes from a letter Cicero wrote to Atticus in 45 BCE. A certain Faberius wanted to pay off a debt by assigning to Cicero some of his own *nomina* (i.e. debts owed to Faberius). Cicero tells Atticus, who was arranging the transaction, that he approves of "those debtors" ('*ista nomina*') even though some appear less than ideal (i.e. not entirely reliable).[99]

The use of bullion, *partes*, *syngraphae*, and *permutationes* was undoubtedly limited to the wealthy, the government and those serving their interests. The use of *nomina*, however, required nothing more than an entry in an account book and the sums involved could be large or small. Anyone could be a lender or a borrower and, given the repeated debt crises throughout the Republican era, it is likely that the use of *nomina* extended from the top of the Roman social hierarchy to its bottom. Like *permutatio*, the use of *nomina* allowed funds to be transferred or payments to be made without any physical movement of coinage. Like all forms of credit, *nomina* "helped to expand the money supply"[100] and could prove especially useful when cash was in short supply. So, early in 49 BCE, when the start of civil war had greatly constricted the supply of coinage, we can observe Quintus Cicero trying to pay off a loan to Atticus by assigning to him a debt owed to Quintus by Egnatius.[101]

---

[99] Cic. *Att.* 13.3.1.

[100] Barlow (1978) 237.

[101] Cic. *Att.* 7.18.4: *Quintus frater laborat ut tibi quod debet ab Egnatio solvat; nec Egnatio voluntas deest nec parum locuples*. Shackleton Bailey (1965) 315 suggests that Quintus expected to receive cash from Egnatius rather than delegate his debt directly to Atticus. However, *delegatio* appears more likely since Cicero emphasizes that Egnatius was willing as well as rich (i.e. a good risk) and later notes that he does not actually have any cash at the moment.

3.4 Financial Institutions

Due to the nature of the sources, my discussion of financial instruments has, up to this point, mainly focused on the Roman elite. Little information about the financial practices of other Romans survives but, in light of the papyrological evidence for banking from Ptolemaic and Roman Egypt, it is important to consider the possibility that in the Roman world, as in Hellenistic Egypt, there was "democratized access to banking."[102] Several basic questions need to be addressed: what kind of financial institutions existed in late Republican Rome? What banking services were available? Who used such services? And, finally, what impact did the use of banks have upon the supply of and demand for money? The answers (to the last two questions especially) will, of course, be rather speculative.

Bankers appear at Rome in the late fourth century BCE,[103] the institution having been imported from the Greek world where banks had existed since the fifth century.[104] The Romans occasionally appointed public bankers (i.e. the *quinqueviri mensarii* in 352 BCE and the *triumviri mensarii* in 216 BCE)[105] to deal with emergencies but their responsibilities and capabilities seem to have been quite limited.[106] *Argentarii* (private bankers) assayed and changed money, but also accepted deposits, made payments on behalf of clients and came to have an important role at auctions where they provided credit to buyers.[107] *Nummularii* were active in Italy by the end of the second century,[108] but confined their activities to assaying and money changing until well into the imperial period.[109] Barlow argues that "a tremendous expansion of Roman banking and moneylending" began in the late second century BCE.[110] *Coactores argentarii* ('deposit bankers') appear early in the first century,[111] as did the *tesserae nummulariae* which may have facilitated the long-distance transport

102 Bogaert (2000) 29.
103 Andreau (1999) 30; Bogaert (2000) 45.
104 Bogaert (1968) 343; Andreau (1999) 30.
105 Livy 7.21, 23.21, 24.18.12, 26.36.5.
106 Andreau (1999) 115–6; Bogaert (2000) 48.
107 Barlow (1978) 239; Maselli (1986) 116–7; Bogaert (2000) 50.
108 Andreau (1999) 31. Bogaert (2000) 50 puts this development in the first century.
109 Andreau (1999) 31.
110 Barlow (1978) 233.
111 Bogaert (2000) 47; Andreau (1999) 31.

of coinage.[112] By the late Republic, Italy seems to have a sizable banking sector[113] with the *argentarii* most prominent within it.[114]

Greek and Roman bankers provided their clients with a variety of services. Written orders of payment, giro transfers and checks appear in the Greek world by the third century.[115] By the first century Ptolemaic bankers were transferring money between accounts, maintaining accounts with other bankers and accepting their checks.[116] One of the most important services offered by bankers was to make payments. The written order of payment, a document given to either one's banker or the payee (or both), was one way to accomplish this.[117] In Egypt these orders were used even for quite small payments.[118] At Rome the same practices prevailed and information about payments typically appeared in a banker's *rationes* (accounts).[119] Scipio Aemilianus used his banker to pay his aunts' dowries around 162 BCE.[120] Plautus refers to the practice as well.[121] The *receptum* also allowed bankers to make payments on behalf of (and in the absence of) a client.[122]

Another way to make a payment was to use a check. As Bogaert and others have emphasized such checks were "not modern checks."[123] They were neither protected by law nor endorsable[124] and their use was inevitably limited to people who knew each other well since bankers lacked the technology to verify identities and banks did not have multiple branches or correspondents.[125] Thus most banks, except for the Ptolemaic royal banks, were local banks.[126] Nevertheless the number of

---

[112] Bogaert (2000) 52.
[113] Andreau (1999) 147; Hopkins (1980) 102.
[114] Bogaert (2000) 49.
[115] Bogaert (2000) 27.
[116] Bagnall and Bogaert (1975) 107–8; Bogaert (1983) 216; Andreau (1999) 43; Bogaert (2000) 29. Von Reden (2001) 71 notes that "there is no conclusive evidence that in Ptolemaic Egypt giro transfers between accounts at different banks were possible."
[117] Bagnall and Bogaert (1975) 103.
[118] Bagnall and Bogaert (1975) 93 note that the Florida papyri rarely record payments of more than 12 silver drachmas while Bogaert (1983) 218 observes that the sums in *BGU* XIV 2401–16 (another group of orders for payment) are even smaller.
[119] Bogaert (2000) 53–4.
[120] Polyb. 31.27; Andreau (1999) 142; Bogaert (2000) 54.
[121] Plaut. *Asin.* 440; Bogaert (2000) 47.
[122] Andreau (1999) 43; Bogaert (2000) 58.
[123] Bogaert (2000) 28.
[124] Bagnall and Bogaert (1975) 107–8; Andreau (1999) 42; Bogaert (2000) 29.
[125] Bogaert (2000) 29, 50–1.
[126] Bogaert (2000) 60.

surviving examples of these documents suggests that their use was not at all unusual.[127]

Banks could manage the movement of commodities as well as money. In Egypt, at least, one could use a check to make a payment in kind and such checks could be transferred to a third party.[128] While there is little evidence for such transactions elsewhere in the Mediterranean world,[129] there is no good reason to doubt that they occurred. As Rathbone has argued, Egypt "was not so exceptional a province."[130]

Another major service provided by bankers was the provision of credit to their clients. Plautus refers to bankers providing credit, indicating that this practice dates to the early second century at the latest.[131] *Argentarii* became especially important at auctions where they would provide short-term credit to purchasers.[132] Debts were a standard item in Roman account books.[133]

Who used Roman banks? Though we have very little information about their clientele,[134] everyone seems to have known about them. There were bankers working throughout the city of Rome and elsewhere.[135] The scattered casual references to bankers and banking services in the plays of Plautus and Terence suggest their familiarity to a Roman audience.[136] Moneylending appears common in both urban and rural areas.[137] One view holds, however, that the Roman elite (senators and *equites*) were not among the clients of the professional bankers but instead used aristocratic *feneratores*, financiers who operated with a different set of procedures and lent out their own money and that of their friends.[138] If professional bankers lacked the social connections and economic clout to grow substantially, it might explain why their banks "failed to develop into major financial

[127] Bagnall and Bogaert (1975) 107–8.
[128] Bagnall and Bogaert (1975) 103; Preisigke (1910).
[129] Howgego (1992) 27.
[130] Rathbone (1996) 325.
[131] Plaut. *Aul.* 530; Bogaert (2000) 55.
[132] Maselli (1986) 116; Rauh (1989b) 54–60; Andreau (1999) 133; Bogaert (2000) 57.
[133] *Dig.* 2.6.3; Andreau (1999) 44; Bogaert (2000) 54.
[134] Bogaert (2000) 60.
[135] Bogaert (2000) 47.
[136] Bogaert (1968) 339. See, e.g., Ter. *Phorm.* 923–4 and Plaut. *Curc.* 679–82.
[137] Howgego (1992) 13–4.
[138] Andreau (1978) 48–50; (1995) 310; (1999) 15–7.

institutions."[139] Nevertheless, there are good reasons to be skeptical of a neat division of banking clientele at least in this period. As Nightingale has noted, in the late Republic "both the banker and some of his clients seem to have been socially more exalted."[140] Furthermore, some elite Romans did employ professional bankers at least by means of intermediaries.[141] This suggests that Roman financial networks may have been bigger and more widespread than our sources indicate. Through their connections with merchants, local bankers may well have forged long-distance financial relationships. Certainly, however, the participation of bankers was not essential for the creation of complex financial networks. The elite could turn to their friends and clients while *collegia* and *eranos* loans might serve the needs of businessmen.[142]

The macro-economic impact of Roman banks may well have been considerable. By facilitating payments with checks, orders for payment and transfers, banks lowered transaction costs, making money easier to use. The *nummularii* did the same thing by providing customers with confidence in the coinage they used. *Tesserae nummulariae*, though their use may have been quite limited, also decreased transaction costs since they reduced the need for the counting and checking of coins.[143] Even if most banking operations were local and small-scale,[144] the provision of credit and the ability to make payments without the use of coin effectively increased the quantity of money in circulation.[145] The extent to which banks expanded the Roman money supply remains unknowable and perhaps even beyond reasonable estimates, but it is certainly possible that Republican banking was as widespread and economically significant as the papyrological evidence suggests was the case in contemporary Egypt and the juristic evidence and *Tabulae Pompeianae* suggest was the case in the imperial period.

---

139 Von Reden (2002) 148.
140 Nightingale (1989) 176–7.
141 Andreau (1995) 310.
142 See Rauh (1993) on the business community of Hellenistic Roman Delos, especially chapter 6.
143 Andreau (1999) 88–9, 117; Barlow (1978) 117; Bogaert (2000) 52–3.
144 Greene (1986) 64.
145 Hopkins (1995/6) 63; Cohen (1992) 18.

3.5 Conclusion

The types of 'near money' (*syngraphae, partes* and *nomina*) and monetary processes (*permutatio*) examined in this chapter all constituted crucial financial instruments at the disposal of the Roman government, the wealthy, businessmen and (in the case of *nomina*) even the lower classes. As stores of value and means of payment, they lowered transaction costs (by making the physical transportation of coinage unnecessary) and thereby allowed money to move more quickly and efficiently throughout the Roman economy even though they were essentially abstract substitutes for real assets. When used, such instruments and institutions, though indicative of a highly monetized society, effectively reduced the demand for coinage. A transaction accomplished with *nomina* could be quick and easy but did not require the presence of any cash.

CHAPTER FOUR

PECUNIARY ASSETS

4.1 Introduction

The purpose of this chapter is twofold: first, to explore the possibility that some assets beyond coinage and bullion, since they were readily usable for transactions at least in some monetary zones, did function as money; and secondly, to identify those other assets which, while not rising to the status of money were so important in fulfilling certain monetary functions (e.g. means of payment) that they reduced the demand for coinage. So, for example, if farmers typically paid for seasonal labor with grain, that would not, in and of itself, make grain a form of money but it undoubtedly reduced the farmers' need to hold cash. If grain could be used in a *variety* of transactions, not just to pay laborers, then it would constitute a form of money—at least in those monetary zones where such transactions were possible. I will focus primarily on the role of assets as means of payment and stores of wealth since the bulk of the available evidence addresses these functions. Media of exchange and units of account will also receive some attention though it is clear that coinage had already achieved dominance with respect to these monetary functions by the late Republic.

4.2 Means of Payment

A means of payment is any asset (or the performance of certain actions)[1] used to complete a transaction or discharge a debt or obligation.[2] It is important to note that use of an object as a means of payment does not necessarily imply that it is also used as a medium of exchange.[3] Thus, for example, an amphora of wine used to purchase a slave is a means of payment but would only be a means of exchange if it could also be used

[1] See Dalton (1965) 49. For example: labor, although incorporeal, can be used to discharge a debt or obligation.

[2] Polanyi (1968) 181 and 197.

[3] See Weber (1927) 236; Dalton (1965) 60.

to purchase many other goods and if people tended to acquire wine in order to make such purchases.

The Romans used grain as a means of payment in many different circumstances. We are best informed about its role in taxation. Grain revenues were vital to the Roman state. Cicero describes a transaction by which Verres gave a quantity of grain to the actress Tertia as "taking away from the lifeblood of the *aerarium*."[4] Many provinces, most notably Sicily, paid some taxes to the Romans in the form of grain. Sicily paid a tithe—and occasionally a second tithe was purchased—of its grain production.[5] Several other provinces probably paid an annual percentage of their yield to Rome.[6] In some cases the right to collect such taxes may have been sold to *publicani*, and, as Nicolet has suggested, under these circumstances the state would have received coins even if many individuals and communities had paid with grain.[7]

As Cicero makes clear, all provincial governors had the right to requisition grain from the communities in their provinces for their own maintenance.[8] This constituted a second grain tax for which the provinces were liable. Much of the *Verrines* concerns the extent and nature of this privilege. This tax could also be converted from a payment in grain to one in coin via a process known as *adaeratio*. But Roman governors and generals needed to collect grain for other purposes as well. Fonteius, while praetor in Gaul in the 70s, requisitioned grain that was sent to feed Roman armies in Spain.[9] Varro demanded a large amount of grain in addition to coins and bullion as the price of governing Spain in 49 BCE.[10] A payment of grain might also serve as a means of punishment. Thus, Caesar fined the city of Thysdra a quantity of grain in 46 BCE.[11]

---

[4] Cic. *Verr.* II 3.83: *Hoc nomine videtis tritici modium MMM de capite esse dempta, quae cum de populi Romani victu, de vectigalium nervis, de sanguine detraxisset aerarii, Tertiae mimae condonavit.*

[5] Cic. *Verr.* II 3.227: *Hinc cum unae decumae lege et consuetudine detrahantur, alterae novis institutis propter annonae rationem imperentur*...

[6] For the grain tax in Asia see Appian *B Civ.* 5.4.18–20. Livy refers to tithes of grain from Sardinia several times (36.2.12; 37.2.12; 37.50.9 and 42.31.8) usually also noting the grain's destination. The evidence for Africa is somewhat more problematic. See section 5.2.1.

[7] Nicolet (1994b) 215–30.

[8] Cic. *Verr.* II 3.188: *Nam cum ex senatus consulto et ex legibus frumentum in cellam ei sumere liceret*...

[9] Cic. *Font.* 13: *maximum frumenti numerum ad Hispaniense bellum tolerandum imperavit.*

[10] Caes. *B Civ.* 2.18: *Quibus rebus perterritos cives Romanos eius provinciae sibi ad rem publicam administrandam HS CLXXX et argenti pondo XX milia, tritici modium CXX milia polliceri coëgit.*

[11] Caes. *B Afr.* 97: *Thysdritanos propter humilitatem civitatis certe numero frumenti multat.*

The use of grain as a means of payment extended well beyond the realm of taxation. The state made payments in grain to the citizens of Rome (the grain distributions instituted by Clodius in 58 BCE) and to soldiers. According to Polybius the cost of a soldier's grain would be deducted from his pay, indicating that the grain formed part of his salary.[12] The state even engaged in the lending of grain (to the cities of Sicily c. 101–99 BCE).[13]

Although we have much less evidence for private transactions involving grain, what we do have strongly suggests its regular use to make payments in the rural monetary zone. Cato speaks of the *vilicus* (estate manager) having a grain account and recommends that he limit his lending and borrowing of grain and other commodities to only two or three households.[14] This advice implies that the lending and borrowing of agricultural commodities was a common and necessary part of rural life. Cato also indicates that the *vilicus* paid for part-time agricultural labor with grain (or other commodities) rather than with coinage. He gives specific proportions to be paid to harvesters, millers and others based on the quality of the land under cultivation and the type of produce.[15] Such payments 'in kind' must have been typical throughout the ancient Mediterranean at least for seasonal labor but, outside of Egypt, little evidence for them survives. Certainly in more recent times and in more 'sophisticated' economies this sort of practice has persisted.[16] It is also likely that many tenants paid their rents in grain (or other commodities) as was done elsewhere in the imperial period.[17]

Under the Republic payments in grain could even play a role in long-distance trade. Livy records that in 202 BCE "supplies from Sicily and Sardinia lowered the price of grain so much that the merchant would leave his grain with the mariners to cover the freight."[18] The situation

---

[12] Polyb. 6.39.

[13] Cic. *Leg. agr.* 2.83: *Sicilia civitatibus bello fugitivorum M'. Aquilius etiam mutuum frumentum dedit.*

[14] Cato *Agr.* 5.3–4: *Satui semen, cibaria, far, vinum, oleum mutuum dederit nemini. Duas aut tres familias habeat, unde utenda roget et quibus det, praeterea nemini.*

[15] Cato *Agr.* 136: *Politionem quo pacto partiario dari oporteat. In agro Casinate et Venafro in loco bono parti octava corbi dividat, satis bono septima, tertio loco sexta*...

[16] In South Africa, for example, workers on vineyards are often paid in wine: Braid (1998) 9. For twentieth century French vineyards see: Goujard (1975) 189.

[17] For Egypt see: Rathbone (1991) 183; Rowlandson (1996) 240–52; Bagnall (1997) 29. For Roman Gaul: Whittaker (1985) 60.

[18] Livy 30.38.5: *Per eos dies commeatus ex Sicilia Sardiniaque tantam vilitatem annonae effecerunt ut pro vectura frumentum nautis mercator relinqueret.* It is difficult to understand the precise meaning of Livy's remark. If the sale price of grain was so low that it equaled the cost

seems, however, to have been exceptional; I know of no other instance in which a trader used grain to make payments in the late Republic. Given the nature of the sources, however, it would be dangerous to draw any conclusions from this silence.[19]

Papyrological evidence from Roman Egypt reveals the level of sophistication to which the monetary use of grain might have risen in the late Republic. The *sitologoi* used grain like bankers used money; their documents include orders for payment of grain between private individuals as well as receipts for such payments.[20] Grain was also loaned and used to pay laborers.[21] Rathbone's study of the Heroninos archive, while showing that the Appianus estate was highly monetized, indicates that many laborers received some part of their pay in wheat or other commodities.[22] The tenants of arable land also paid their rent in wheat.[23] Documents recording wheat transactions tend to be very specific about what grain is being used. One document, for example, specified "12 artabas of 5th year wheat."[24] This reflects a considerable drawback to the use of grain to make payments: grain deteriorated in storage and so older grain might not be as valuable as that from more recent harvests.

Wine and olive oil had more limited roles as a means of payment. Cato considered inferior wine to be part of the payment for the extra laborers hired to deal with wine-making. He writes: "gather the inferior grapes for the sharp wine for the hands (*operarii*) to drink."[25] In contracts for the harvest, milling and sale of olives, Cato specifies quantities of both olive oil and olives as part of the price in addition to sums in coin-

of transport, why would a merchant bother to trade it at all? One possible explanation is that grain prices fell after the merchants had acquired the grain and while it was being stored in rented *horrea* (storehouses) in port cities. The merchants would then have a motive for giving their grain to the shippers since they would then cease to incur rental costs and at the same time stay on good terms with the shippers.

[19] Rickman (1980b) 14 says that "shippers were... allowed to retain a small percentage of the actual cargo" so it is possible that in kind payments typically formed part of the cost of transport. However, Rickman, who provides no examples this practice, may be referring only to late Imperial practice.

[20] See, for example, *P. Oxy.* 516 and 517.

[21] For example: *P. Oxy.* 2591.

[22] Rathbone (1991) 160–4.

[23] Rathbone (1991) 183; Bagnall (1997) 29.

[24] Stephens (1978) 150.

[25] Cato *Agr.* 23.2: *uvas miscellas, vinum praeliganeum quod operarii bibant, ubi tempus erit, legito.* Cato is always careful to distinguish between hands (*operarii*) hired for specific tasks (cf. *Agr.* 4.2: *operarios facilius conduces*) and the estate's own slaves (*servi* or the *familia*). Indeed, a later passage provides detailed instructions concerning how much and what kind of wine the slaves are to receive throughout the year (*Agr.* 57).

age.[26] Fifty pounds of oil even form part of the cost, along with 400 *sesterces*, of an oil press purchased at Suessa.[27] Wine and oil both appear in the list of commodities (mentioned above) which Cato recommends the *paterfamilias* forbid (or at least limit) his *vilicus* from lending.[28] While the lending of such goods in itself might seem rather unspectacular and indeed the act of a kind neighbor, the context is critical. Cato writes here of lending with respect to credit in general and the accounts of the estate. Furthermore, there is a substantial difference between lending seed-grain, for example, and lending a cup of flour. One has the sense that rural commodity exchanges flourished in Cato's day, and that he felt such practices were dangerous to the financial well-being of the farm. However, there are no references to the use of wine or oil as means of payment in agriculture from the last century of the Republic. Such payments likely continued but were perhaps either too traditional or too minor a part of the cost of labor to deserve mention.

There is considerable evidence for the use of livestock as a means of payment though it is difficult to interpret. Varro tells us that fines were still levied in oxen and sheep even during his own times (*etiam nunc*).[29] Cicero, however, seems to imply that such practices had long since come to an end when he remarks in the *De Re Publica* that fines in livestock were instituted by Romulus because "wealth at that time consisted of domestic animals."[30] To further complicate the issue, Crawford has forcefully argued that the Romans never used cattle for payments of any kind:

> I find it incredible that fines were ever levied in Rome in cattle and sheep. Just as in the Homeric world the fact that wealth was thought of as consisting in part of cattle and evaluated in terms of cattle does not mean that cattle were ever used as money for purposes of payment, so for Rome it does not follow from the existence of wealth in the form of cattle that cattle were levied as fines.[31]

Two objections can be made to this argument. First, although Crawford is correct when he draws attention to the disagreement among ancient

[26] Cato *Agr.* 144–6.
[27] Cato *Agr.* 22.3: *Trapetus emptus est in Suessano HS CCCC et olei P.L.*
[28] Cato *Agr.* 5.3.
[29] Varro *Rust.* 2.1.9: *quod multa etiam nunc ex vetere instituto bubus et ovibus dicitur.*
[30] Cic. *Rep.* 2.9: *multaeque dictione ovium et bovum (quod tum erat res in pecore et locorum possessionibus, ex quo pecuniosi et locupletes vocabantur), non vi et supliciis coërcebat.*
[31] Crawford (1985) 20.

writers concerning the exact nature of the *suprema multa* (the largest fine that could be imposed in livestock),[32] the ancient sources do agree that fines were exacted in sheep and cows. At least a half dozen writers mention the existence of such fines and they provide an impressive amount of detail concerning the legal and administrative aspects of livestock fines. Both Cicero and Varro mention this sort of fine repeatedly,[33] while Dionysius of Halicarnassus, Plutarch, Festus and Aulus Gellius also refer to them.[34] It should be noted that, although most of these writers quote earlier sources and write of eras long past, they never express any doubts concerning the practice. Clearly they did not consider such fines implausible. Secondly, there is an overwhelming amount of evidence for the use of cattle as a means of payment for a variety of purposes (including fines) in many other cultures both ancient and modern.[35] Though in some societies cattle may have served merely as a unit of account without being physically exchanged in transactions, it is not clear that their use was so limited in ancient Rome.[36] Nevertheless, it is likely that the use of livestock to make payments (and fulfill other monetary functions) diminished as Rome developed from pastoral to agrarian state. By the late Republic, payment by means of livestock was undoubtedly rare.

Although both the Roman government and private individuals preferred to use the *profits* of land rather than the land itself in their transactions, both groups could and did resort to the use of land as a means of payment when it was convenient or necessary. The Roman state made

[32] Crawford (1985) 19. In some texts the *suprema multa* is said to have been 2 cows and 30 sheep, in others it is given as 2 sheep and 30 cows or just 30 cows.

[33] Cic. *Rep.* 2.9 and 2.60: *annis postea viginti ex eo, quod L. Papirius P. Pinarius censores multis dicendis vim armentorum a privatis in publicum averterant, levis aestumatio pecudum in multa lege C. Iulii P. Papirii consulum constituta est*; and Varro *Rust.* 2.1.9. Aulus Gellius 11.1.1–5 also cites Varro's *Rerum Humanarum* concerning fines in livestock.

[34] Dion. Hal. 10.50.2; Plut. *Publicola* 11; Festus 268–70 L and 129 L; Gell. *NA* 11.1.1–5.

[35] The Greeks evidently believed that cattle served as money in Homeric society—and not just as a measure of value. Laertes purchased Eurycleia for twenty oxen (*Od.* 1.429–31). Cattle served as money for a variety of purposes (including fines) among the Masai: Maguire (1928) 12–7 and Shelford (1910) 269. For the monetary use of cattle elsewhere in Africa see: Schapera (1934) 562; Mors (1954) 23; Schneider (1974) 260; Turyahikayo-Rugyema (1976) 288; Hutchinson (1992) 306 and MacKinnon (1999) 107. Cattle were also used as money in medieval Ireland: O'Donovan (1940) 17.

[36] Varro, it should be emphasized, refers both to estate managers keeping *rationes pecuarias* (*Rust.* 2.10.10) and to fines still being levied in cattle. If slaves could be pledged to the treasury as security, the Roman government must have been able and willing to take possession of them. Why would the state balk at cattle?

payments in land to its soldiers on a regular basis. Livy reports that near the end of 201 BCE the Senate directed the urban praetor to create a decemvirate to distribute land to Scipio's African veterans.[37] In the following year it was decided that these soldiers should receive 2 *iugera* of land for every year of their service, as though the land formed part of their salary.[38] In 199 BCE the propraetor C. Sergius supervised the distribution of land to veterans of Sicily and Sardinia as well as Spain.[39] Land remained an important part of a soldier's discharge bonus down to the reign of Augustus,[40] and the state distributed as many as a quarter million land allotments in the period from 82 to 25 BCE.[41]

In both the public and private spheres debt crisis prompted the use of land as a means of payment. Though in many cases individuals would sell their land to get cash with which to pay off debts or make other payments, in some circumstances the land itself served as the means of payment. Short on coinage, the Roman state resorted to such a measure in 200 BCE in order to pay the third and final installment of money it owed to those individuals who had made loans to the State in 210 BCE to finance the war against Hannibal.[42]

In 49 BCE Julius Caesar employed the same solution to deal with a public debt crisis. The *Lex Iulia de bonis cedendis* created a means by which cash-strapped debtors could pay their creditors in land without suffering the indignity of bankruptcy. With the permission and under the supervision of Roman magistrates an individual could use land or other

---

[37] Livy 31.4: *exitu huius anni cum de agris ueterum militum relatum esset qui ductu atque auspicio P. Scipionis in Africa bellum perfecissent, decreuerunt patres ut M. Iunius praetor urbanus, si ei uideretur, decemuiros agro Samniti Apuloque, quod eius publicum populi Romani esset, metiendo diuidendoque crearet.*

[38] Livy 31.49.5: *Et de agris militum eius decretum ut, quot quisque eorum annos in Hispania aut in Africa militasset, in singulos annos bina iugera agri acciperet; eum agrum decemviri adsignarent.*

[39] Livy 32.1: *prorogata imperia praetoribus prioris anni, C. Sergio ut militibus qui in Hispania Sicilia Sardinia stipendia per multos annos fecissent agrum adsignandum curaret.*

[40] Dio Cass. 54.25.5 reports that Augustus ceased distribution of land to discharged veterans in the early first century CE. However Brunt (1962) 83 notes that, according to Tacitus (*Ann.* 1.17), Augustus was still giving land to some soldiers at the end of his reign.

[41] Brunt (1971) 300–44; Skydsgaard (1980) 69.

[42] Livy 31.13: *Cum et privati aequum postularent, nec tamen solvendo aere alieno res publica esset, quod medium inter aequum et utile erat decreverunt, ut, quoniam magna pars eorum agros volgo venales esse diceret et sibimet emptis opus esse, agri publici qui intra quinquagesimum lapidem esset, copia iis fieret: consules agrum aestimaturos et in iugera asses vectigal testandi causa publicum agrum esse imposituros, ut si quis, cum solvere posset populus, pecuniam habere quam agrum mallet, restitueret agrum populo. Laeti eam condicionem privati accepere; trientabulumque is ager, quia pro tertia parte pecuniae datus erat, appellatus.*

property to settle his debts.[43] Such a process might lead creditors into difficulties of their own, as Cicero reveals in a letter to L. Papirius Paetus. Paetus apparently received a good deal of land by means of *cessio bonorum* but was unable to sell any of it to get the *denarii* he required.[44]

Later legal sources clearly conceived of the possibility that someone might use land as a means of payment outside the context of *cessio bonorum*,[45] and references to such activity in the late Republic do survive. In the *Pro Flacco* Cicero accuses an opponent of offering land to a witness in exchange for false testimony.[46] In the *Philippics* Cicero refers to a payment of Leontine land made by Antonius to a Sextus Clodius, allegedly as payment for speaking lessons.[47] Admittedly Cicero may be twisting a gift into wages for rhetorical purposes here. In another letter Cicero refers to those who "have given kingdoms to tetrarchs as though they were farms (*praedia*) and large amounts of money (*immanes pecunias*) to a few men."[48] Here again it is difficult to distinguish gift from payment, but the apposition of *praedia* and *pecunia* in the passage is telling. It is likely that some bequests of land were essentially payments for the services of lawyers whom the *Lex Cincia* barred from charging fees.[49] Valerius Maximus indicates that advocates were among those who could reasonably expect to receive something from a client's will.[50]

Slaves too could serve as a means of payment. Suetonius notes that Caesar would occasionally give a slave to each of his men.[51] It is unclear whether such distributions of booty should be categorized as gift-giving or bonus pay, but Suetonius at least associated it with the doubling of soldiers' salaries. Soldiers expected and received these kinds of bonuses after successful engagements, upon discharge or as inducements to service. In most cases such slaves were probably put to work by the soldiers

---

43 For a full discussion see: Frederiksen (1966) 135.

44 Cic. *Fam.* 9.18.4: *aestimationes tuas vendere non potes neque ollam denariorum implere.*

45 Gai. *Inst.* 3.141.

46 Cic. *Flac.* 51: *pecuniam adulescentulo grandi faenore, fiducia tamen accepta, occupavisti. Hanc fiduciam commissam tibi dicis; tenes hodie ac possides. Eum tu testem spe recuperandi fundi paterni venire ad testimonium dicendum coegisti.*

47 Cic. *Phil.* 2.43: *Duo milia iugerum campi Leontini Sex. Clodio rhetori adsignasti, et quidem immunia, ut populi Romani tanta mercede nihil sapere disceres.*

48 Cic. *Att.* 2.9.1: *qui regna quasi praedia tetrarchis, qui immanes pecunias paucis dederunt.*

49 On this law see: Shatzman (1975) 70–3.

50 Val. Max. 7.8.7. See also Kroll (1933) I.111.

51 Suet. *Iul.* 26: *Legionibus stipendium in perpetuum duplicavit. Frumentum, quotiens copia esset, etiam sine modo mensuraque praebuit ac singula interdum mancipia e praeda viritim dedit.*

themselves or sold to others for cash. Sallust, however, does record one instance in which Roman soldiers in North Africa used the slaves they had acquired to purchase wine and other goods.[52] Roman traders also accepted slaves in payment for Italian wine in Gaul. Diodorus, the first century BCE historian, writes:

> the Gauls are exceedingly addicted to the use of wine and fill themselves with the wine which is brought into their country by merchants, drinking it unmixed... Consequently many of the Italian traders, induced by the love of money which characterizes them, believe that the love of wine of these Gauls is their own godsend. For these transport the wine on the navigable rivers by means of boats and through the level plain on wagons, and receive for it an incredible price; for in exchange for a jar of wine they receive a slave, getting a servant in return for the drink.[53]

Cicero's *Pro Flacco* shows slaves also being used to pay off debts. A certain Heraclides was brought to court by a creditor for failure to repay a debt and ends up in his creditor's custody until he manages to repay it.[54] Cicero records that Heraclides gave some slaves to his creditor Hermippus in order to free himself.[55] Although Cicero twice describes this transaction as a sale, it is clear that Heraclides used the slaves to pay off his debt since Hermippus subsequently released him.

Under the empire, slaves probably continued to function as a means of payment in some circumstances. Gaius refers to the possibility of using a slave to make a payment on two occasions, once, as I have

---

[52] Sallust *Iug.* 44: *pecoris et mancipiorum praedas certantes agere eaque mutare cum mercatoribus vino advecticio et aliis talibus.*

[53] Diod. Sic. 5.26.3: κάτοινοι δ' ὄντες καθ' ὑπερβολὴν τὸν εἰσαγόμενον ὑπὸ τῶν ἐμπόρων οἶνον ἄκρατον ἐμφοροῦνται, καὶ διὰ τὴν ἐπιθυμίαν λάβρῳ χρώμενοι τῷ ποτῷ καὶ μεθυσθέντες εἰς ὕπνον ἢ μανιώδεις διαθέσεις τρέπονται. διὸ καὶ πολλοὶ τῶν Ἰταλικῶν ἐμπόρων διὰ τὴν συνήθη φιλαργυρίαν ἕρμαιον ἡγοῦνται τὴν τῶν Γαλατῶν φιλοινίαν. οὗτοι γὰρ διὰ μὲν τῶν πλωτῶν ποταμῶν πλοίοις, διὰ δὲ τῆς πεδιάδος χώρας ἁμάξαις κομίζοντες τὸν οἶνον, ἀντιλαμβάνουσι τιμῆς πλῆθος ἄπιστον· διδόντες γὰρ οἴνου κεράμιον ἀντιλαμβάνουσι παῖδα, τοῦ πόματος διάκονον ἀμειβόμενοι. Strabo 5.1.8 reports such exchanges also taking place in Illyria among the indigenous peoples.

[54] Cic. *Flac.* 48–50: ... *Cum iudicatum non faceret, addictus Hermippo et ab hoc ductus est... Atque is ab Hermippo missus, cum ei pauca mancipia vendidisset, Romam se contulit, deinde in Asiam rediit, cum iam frater meus Flacco successisset. Ad quem adiit causamque ita detulit, recuperatores vi Flacci coactos et metu falsum invitos iudicavisse. Frater meus pro sua aequitate prudentiaque decrevit ut, si iudicatum negaret, in duplum iret; si metu coactos diceret, haberet eosdem recuperatores. Recusavit et, quasi nihil esset actum, nihil iudicatum, ab Hermippo ibidem mancipia quae ipse ei vendiderat petere coepit... Petit Heraclides a C. Plotio senatore, viro primario, qui legatus in Asia fuerat, mancipia quaedam quae se, cum iudicatus esset, per vim vendidisse dicebat.*

[55] Cic. *Flac.* 48–50.

already noted, in setting out a definition of *pecunia* and later with respect to the purchase of land.[56] However, aside from Sallust's soldiers in North Africa, there is no record from the Republic of a Roman purchasing something by paying with a slave or slaves.

Finally, we must explore the use of labor as a means of payment in the late Republic. Although, it must be conceded, there is little evidence for the practice, it is likely that the use of labor to extinguish debts or other obligations and help pay rents was quite widespread.

Operae, services performed by a manumitted slave for his or her former master, may well have been the most common form of labor payment in the late Republic since considerable numbers of slaves received their freedom in this period[57] and the imposition of *operae* on *liberti* allowed their patrons to continue to receive tangible benefits from them. As *nexum* was essentially the paying off of a debt through the exploitation of the enslaved debtor's labor, so *operae* were payments of the freedman's labor in exchange for the *beneficium* of freedom.[58] Paul defines *operae* as "the work performed in one day."[59] The number of days of work as well as the nature of that work would vary depending on the profession of the slave in question and what sort of agreement he or she had made with his or her patron.[60] Celsus, describing a hypothetical situation, writes of a freedman who swore "to perform a thousand days' services" so, while *operae* were finite, they could nevertheless be substantial.[61] The rights to a freedman's *operae* could be inherited,[62] but might also, in some circumstances, be extinguished without payment.[63] A patron might rent

---

56 Gai. *Inst.* 3.141: *sed ait Caelius Sabinus, si rem tibi venalem habenti, veluti fundum, [acceperim et] pretii nomine hominem forte dederim, fundum quidem videri venisse, hominem autem pretii nomine datum esse, ut fundus acciperetur.*

57 Scheidel (2005) 78 estimates for the first century BCE "the presence of up to 200,000 freedmen in the cities and of another 100,000 or so in the countryside."

58 Treggiari (1969) 16–7. *Dig.* 38.1.1–51 provides a variety of rules and scenarios concerning *operae*.

59 *Dig.* 38.1.1 (A. Watson, trans.): *Operae sunt diurnum officium.*

60 *Dig.* 38.1.7: *Ut iurisiurandui obligatio contrahatur, libertum esse oportet qui iuret et libertatis causa iurare.*

61 *Dig.* 38.1.15 (Watson, trans.): *si communis libertus patronis duobus operas mille daturum se iuraverit.*

62 *Dig.* 38.1.4–6.

63 *Dig.* 38.1.15: *Libertus, qui post indictionem operarum valetudine impeditur, quo minus praestaet operas, non tenetur: nec enim potest videri per eum stare, quo minus operas praestet; Dig.* 38.1.34: *si liberta, quae operas promisit, ad eam dignitatem perveniat, ut inconveniens sit praestare patrono operas, ipso iure hae intercident.*

out the *operae* of a *libertus*,[64] or receive cash from his client in lieu of that work.[65]

While some freedmen provided their patrons with *operae* they did not technically owe, no doubt out of gratitude or loyalty,[66] often the relationship between freedman and former owner was more contentious. Some patrons sought more than they were entitled to, while some clients tried to avoid the *operae* they were legally obliged to perform. In response to the excessive demands of some patrons, the praetor P. Rutilius Rufus limited their legal recourse around 118 BCE.[67] Chrysippus, a freedman of Cicero, provides a good example of the potential consequences of nonperformance of *operae*. In a letter to Atticus written at Brundisium in November of 50 BCE, Cicero complains that Chrysippus and another freedman, who were supposed to accompany Cicero's son, had instead run off.[68] Since Chrysippus apparently either failed to fulfill the *operae* he had sworn to perform or had refused to commit himself upon manumission to the *operae* he had agreed to while still a slave,[69] Cicero contemplated revoking the manumission itself.

Roman and municipal officials could also demand *operae* from the inhabitants (both free and otherwise) under their jurisdiction. These *operae* were essentially a tax paid in labor. Near the beginning of his agricultural manual Cato lists the possible excuses an estate owner might hear from his *vilicus* for inadequate performance. Along with sick slaves, bad weather and runaway slaves, Cato mentions *opus publicum*.[70] No explanation of the *opus* is supplied but maintenance work on nearby roads or other aspects of the communal infrastructure seems likely.[71] Both the late Republican *Lex Coloniae Genetivae Iuliae* and the Flavian *Lex Irnitana*, municipal regulations of Roman communities in Spain,

---

[64] In the imperial period there were limits on this practice (*Dig.* 38.1.25, 27) but Treggiari (1969) 76 notes that in the late Republic "it appears that *locatio* was allowed exactly as it suited the patron."

[65] *Dig.* 40.9.32.1–2.

[66] *Dig.* 38.1.31.

[67] *Dig.* 38.2.1. Broughton (1951) 527 dates Rutilius' praetorship to no later than 118 BCE.

[68] Cic. *Att.* 7.2.8.

[69] As Treggiari (1969) 258 notes, Cicero's remarks are subject to several equally plausible interpretations as to the exact nature of Chrysippus' behavior.

[70] Cato *Agr.* 2.2: *Si ei opus non apparet, dicit vilicus sedulo se fecisse, servos non valuisse, tempestates malas fuisse, servos aufugisse, opus publicum effecisse, ubi eas aliasque causas multas dixit, ad rationem operum operarumque vilicum revoca.*

[71] So suggests Goujard (1975) 126, noting that roadwork is explicitly mentioned shortly thereafter (*Agr.* 2.4) as something the slaves could do on festival days.

suggest how such a *corvée* may have functioned.[72] The *aediles* (or whoever was designated to supervise the work) could demand up to five days of labor per year from each man between the ages of 15 and 60 living in the town's territory. The *Lex Irnitana* suggests that such labor could be used for a variety of public works including the creation or alteration of roads, paths, streams, ditches and sewers.[73] Projects might stem from the needs of the community or be imposed by a regional authority. Cicero indicates that Marcus Fonteius mandated road building throughout Transalpine Gaul during his praetorship.[74] The *Tabula Heracleensis* records a slightly different system to ensure proper maintenance of the roads in and around Rome. It required property owners to maintain the roads adjacent to their lands or buildings (another *corvée*), but let contracts for the maintenance of the streets bordering on public property.[75]

Two other forms of labor payment may have existed in the late Republic: labor as a component of rent and the use of labor to pay off debts. There is no direct attestation of either practice but some circumstantial evidence strongly suggests that they occurred.

The practice of requiring services as a part of rent for tenants was once considered to be a medieval phenomenon,[76] but it is clear that the practice developed earlier.[77] There is, in fact, ample evidence for the use of labor in this fashion from the Empire, though those who have dealt with this material have often resisted referring to such labor as either a payment or rent.[78] Once again Egypt provides the best evidence. Oxy-

---

[72] *Lex Coloniae Genetivae Iuliae* ch. 98; *Lex Irnitana* ch. 83.

[73] *Lex Irnitana* IXa, ll. 30–3: *Quas vias itinera flumina fossas cloacas inmittere commutare eius municipi IIviri ambo alterve volet, dum ea ex decurionum conscriptorumve decreto et intra fines eius municipi et sine iniuria privatorum fiant, IIviris ambobus alterive fa[c]ere ius potestasque esto.*

[74] Cic. *Font.* 17.

[75] *Tabula Heracleensis* ll. 20–55.

[76] Spufford (1988) 16, 21 and 35 argues that labor-rent or rent in service was "a new form of rent" which first appeared in sixth-century Italy but later became common in many parts of Europe.

[77] Percival (1969).

[78] Kuziscin (1984) 235, for example, envisioned "free services" developing alongside, but apparently distinct from, rent in the second century CE. Foxhall (1990) 104 notes that "tenants might... be leaned upon to supply commodities and labour to large landowners" but she is more interested in associating this phenomenon with patronage and dependency rather than with any kind of economic transaction. Those who study Roman tenancy have apparently taken to heart Finley's remark [(1976) 107] that "one cannot even speculate intelligently" concerning tenants' rents. This has resulted in a tendency to label payments or obligations in the form of labor owed by tenants to landlords as anything but 'rent.'

rhynchite papyri include sharecropping agreements in which tenants agree to turn over a proportion of the crop but keep the rest "in return for the work we do and the seed and expenses we provide."[79] The Titianus estate exacted 24 days of labor in addition to 40 drachmas and a piglet per *kella* (room).[80] Three passages from Columella's agricultural manual indicate that labor services could form part of the payments owed by tenants to their landlords in early imperial Italy. In the first passage, Columella notes that it is more important to exact work from tenants than payments.[81] Though he did not apparently consider this work (*opus*) to be part of the rent (*pensiones*), it is nevertheless clear that tenants were obliged to provide it. In the second passage, Columella advises the landlord not to be too strict in exacting all he is owed from his tenants.[82] He indicates that a tenant might owe his landlord other minor things (*ceteris parvis accessionibus*) in addition to money and firewood. The description of these other things as "more annoyance than expense" (*maiorem molestiam quam impensam*) implies that he is referring to labor rather than commodities. The third passage describes how an estate manager should encourage his *coloni* to work hard—something which was always in the owner's interest—but these *coloni* seem to work directly under the supervision of the *vilicus* rather than independently.[83] Three second century inscriptions from North Africa attest to the practice of requiring labor from tenants on imperial estates there.[84] The texts specify the number of days and types of *opera* (plowing, reaping and hoeing) owed.

By the early first century BCE (if not earlier) tenancy had become a common method for exploiting Roman land.[85] In several instances Cicero refers to *coloni* who are clearly tenant farmers. A tenant works a *fundus* for Caesennia and provides Caecina with his accounts.[86] Verres'

[79] Rowlandson (1996) 214–5, quoting *P. Oxy.* XLV 3256.

[80] Rathbone (1991) 178.

[81] Columella *Rust.* 1.7.1: *et avarius opus exigat quam pensiones.*

[82] Columella *Rust.* 1.7.2: *Sed nec dominus in unaquaque re, cui colonum obligaverit, tenax esse iuris sui debet, sicut in diebus pecuniarum vel lignis et ceteris parvis accessionibus exigendis, quarum cura maiorem molestiam quam impensam rusticis adfert.*

[83] Columella *Rust.* 11.1.14: *Plurimum enim refert colonos a primo mane opus aggredi nec lentos per otium pigre procedere.*

[84] *CIL* 8.10570, 14428 and 25902.

[85] de Neeve (1984) 151 argues that the use of tenancy in Roman agriculture greatly expanded beginning in the late second century BCE. See also: Brunt (1975) 629; Finley (1976) 106; Foxhall (1990) 98.

[86] Cic. *Caecin.* 57 and 94.

tax collectors scare off a Sicilian tenant and then sue the owner's husband.[87] In a letter to M. Iunius Brutus of 46 BCE, Cicero mentions that the people of Arpinum had sent some *equites* to investigate their tenants on Gallic properties.[88] Furthermore, the Salvian Interdict, which according to Gaius was "used by a landowner to obtain things pledged by his tenant for rent," seems to date to the early first century BCE.[89] The existence of tenancy in the late Republic does not, of course, prove that labor contributed to rent then. It would be surprising, however, if it did not. The institution of *operae* with respect to freedmen shows that the conceptual framework necessary to permit labor rents already existed. Furthermore, if tenants typically were obliged to provide labor for their landlords, it would account for the occasional appearance of *coloni* in some late Republican armies.

On two occasions *coloni* appear to have taken the field on behalf of their patrons. Caesar twice mentions that Lucius Domitius Ahenobarbus manned several ships at Massilia with his Italian *coloni*.[90] Slaves, freedmen and shepherds also formed part of the crews. Though *coloni* here could simply mean 'farmers,' the description of them as "his *coloni*" implies that there was a special relationship, as does Domitius's specific request for ships for them.[91] If these *coloni* were neither slaves nor freedmen, surely they must have been tenant farmers who worked their patron's land. Sallust may also record the presence of *coloni* in Catiline's makeshift army. In the final battle Catiline deployed these *coloni* near where he himself was stationed and alongside his *liberti*. If *coloni* rather than *calones* (camp servants) is the correct reading,[92] it must be a reference to tenants rather than simply farmers or colonists. Their proximity

[87] Cic. *Verr.* II 3.55: *uxoris fundus erat colono locatus.*

[88] Cic. *Fam.* 13.11.1: *Quia semper animadverti studiose te operam dare, ut ne quid meorum tibi esset ignotum, propterea non dubito, quin scias, non solum cuius municipii sim, sed etiam quam diligenter soleam meos municipes, Arpinates, tueri. Quorum quidem omnia commoda omnesque facultates, quibus et sacra conficere et sarta tecta aedium sacrarum locorumque communium tueri possint, consistunt in iis vectigalibus, quae habent in provincia Gallia. Ad ea visenda pecuniasque, quae a colonis debentur, exigendas totamque rem et cognoscendam et administrandam legatos equites Romanos misimus.*

[89] Gai. *Inst.* 4.147 (Gordon and Robinson, trans.): *Interdictum quoque, quod appellatur Salvianum, apiscendae possessionis causa comparatum est, eoque utitur dominus fundi de rebus coloni, quas is pro mercedibus fundi pignori futures pepigisset.* On the date of the interdict see de Neeve (1984) 47–8.

[90] Caes. *B Civ.* 1.34: *navibus actuariis septem, quas Igilii et in Cosano a privatis coactas servis, libertis, colonis suis compleverat.*

[91] Caes. *B Civ.* 1.56: *Certas sibi deposcit naves Domitius atque has colonis pastoribusque, quos secum adduxerat, complet.*

[92] de Neeve (1984) 177–8 reviews the inconclusive arguments in favor of one reading over the other.

to Catiline in the formation implies a special relationship with him (as the *liberti* certainly had) and surely farmers and colonists were scattered throughout the army.[93] If these passages do refer to tenants fighting on behalf of their landlords, it probably represents the abuse by the landlord of his right to his tenants' services. As the Salvian Interdict suggest, landlords could take possession of their tenants' property if owed rent. The threat of confiscation or other legal action might well have been sufficient motivation to get indebted tenants to follow their landlords even into battle. Debt-bondage, as we shall see, may have offered even less advantageous terms for the paying off of debts. Military service was no doubt an extreme form of labor payment (if, indeed, it was used at all). While no proof exists, it remains likely that, at least in some cases, *agricultural* labor played a role alongside cash and commodities in the economic relationships between landlord and tenant in the late Republic.[94]

Debt-bondage may also have provided a situation in which labor served as a means of payment. The institution of *nexum* allowed for just that sort of transaction in the early Republic. Varro defined the *nexus* as a "free man, who gives his work in servitude for the money which he owes until he has paid up."[95] Here Varro clearly identifies labor (*operae*) as a substitute for money (*pro pecunia*). Although the institution of *nexum* had been abolished by the *lex Poetelia* in 326 BCE, other forms of debt-bondage did exist in the late Republic, if not in Italy.

According to Varro *obaerarii*, free individuals obliged to provide *operae* for others, still (*etiam nunc*) worked the land in Asia, Egypt and Illyricum in his own time.[96] The passage indicates that *obaerarii* are no

---

[93] Cicero (*Cat.* 2.20) lists Sulla's veteran colonists as a major source of Catiline's support. Given Catiline's appeal to the indebted, surely many of his followers were at least *former* farmers who had lost their land.

[94] Aubert (1994) 118 n. 4 argues: "the silence of the sources is perhaps due to the nature of the material, and in any case arguments from silence are weak. One should not discount the possibility of local variations and other forms of pressure on the part of large landowners in order to exact labor services from the local peasantry." Kehoe (1997) 148 argues that "cash is almost universally assumed as the form of the rent payment" in the legal sources, but the jurists, as I have shown, often adopt a very broad definition of money.

[95] Varro *Ling.* 7.105: *liber, qui suas operas in servitutem pro pecunia quam debebat <nectebat,> dum solveret nexus vocatur, ut ab aere abaeratus.*

[96] Varro *Rust.* 1.17.2: *Omnes agri coluntur hominibus servis aut liberis aut utrisque: liberis, aut cum ipsi colunt, ut plerique pauperculi cum sua progenie, aut mercennariis, cum conducticiis liberorum operis res maiores, ut vindemias ac faenisicia, administrant, iique quos obaerarios nostri vocitarunt et etiam nunc sunt in Asia atque Aegypto et in Illyrico complures.*

longer present in Italy but when did they go away? Varro could be referring to the early Republic but it is also possible, given the post-Caesarian composition date of the *De re rustica*, that the Italian *obaerarii* were freed much more recently, as part of Caesar's debt relief measures in the early 40s.[97] However, if Caesar had freed an entire class of debtors rather than just eased the debt crisis with the less radical reforms that are attested (e.g. the remission of rents and the institution of *cessio bonorum*), it is likely that some source would mention the fact. Since no source mentions such an act, it is probable that *obaerarii* had long since disappeared from Italy by the late Republic.

The *obaerati*, another class of indebted individuals, may have also disappeared from Italy well before the end of the Republic, at least in the sense of persons in a state of quasi-servitude. Varro seems to equate the term *obaeratus* with *nexus*,[98] and Cicero states that Servius Tullius freed the *obaerati*.[99] Suetonius, however, describes Caesar as *obaeratus* early in his career—obviously not a case of debt-bondage.[100] Most likely *obaeratus* initially referred specifically to someone in debt-bondage but eventually acquired the more general meaning of 'indebted.' An analogous class of people seems to have existed in Gaul since Caesar describes Orgetorix as gathering "all his clients and *obaerati*" in order to protect himself from prosecution.[101]

The only debt-bondsmen clearly present in late Republican Italy were the *addicti*. *Addictio* was a legal procedure whereby debtors were placed in the power of their creditors,[102] but the precise status of *addicti* is unclear. Cicero tells us that a certain Heraclides was an *addictus*, placed in his creditor's custody until he managed to repay his debt.[103] As I noted above, Heraclides paid off his debt by handing over slaves to his creditor but those without such resources probably had to work off their debts, no doubt on terms highly favorable to the creditor.[104] That

---

[97] Lo Cascio (1982a) 266, 273 considers the *obaerarii* a phenomenon of archaic Rome while de Neeve (1984) 221–4 makes a rather unconvincing argument for Caesar having been responsible.

[98] Varro *Ling.* 7.105.

[99] Cic. *Rep.* 2.21.38.

[100] Suet. *Iul.* 46.

[101] Caes. *B Gall.* 1.4.2.

[102] Finley (1976) 116; de Neeve (1984) 182.

[103] Cic. *Flac.* 46–50.

[104] Finley (1976) 110 and 116 suggested that many debt-bondsmen were tenants whose creditors forced them to work either through the use of *addictio* or the threat of its use.

we hear so little about the use of labor to make payments, under this circumstance and others, is no doubt due to the contempt in which elite Romans held all manual labor.[105] Nevertheless, labor must have been an important means of payment, at least for debts and rents, especially in rural areas where wealthy landowners could easily put tenants and indebted clients to good use.

4.3 Stores of Wealth

A store of wealth is a means of transferring wealth from the present to the future,[106] and thus is a fundamental attribute of money since, in any given monetary transaction, the party receiving money presumably wants to retain the value of the payment. However, an asset does not attain the status of money simply by virtue of being a store of wealth. Most things have at least some value but very few typically can be *readily used to make transactions*. Nevertheless, in order to understand the role of money in the Roman economy, it is vital to consider what other stores of wealth Romans wanted to hold. Coinage is just one type of asset, and is in competition with other commodities for the demand of individuals. The value of coinage changes based in part on the relative desirability of other assets. By asking what assets Romans liked to hold, we can better gauge the impact on the economy of a change in the supply of coinage and how the demand for coinage itself might have changed. Though most goods have some value, I will focus here on those assets which Republican texts suggest were the most important: land, slaves, grain, wine, oil, livestock, furniture and tools.

Land was perhaps the ideal store of wealth in late Republican Italy. The virtues of land ownership were many. First and foremost, of course, land brought social respectability. From an economic standpoint land could usually be counted on to generate some sort of revenue, was difficult to steal or permanently damage and had low carrying-costs (although this varied depending upon what kinds of taxation the land was subject to and what kinds of crops, if any, were grown on it).

It is hardly a revelation to point out that the Romans valued land. What is worth emphasizing, though, is that the Romans recognized that land, as an asset, offered certain advantages, such as respectability and

[105] Cicero *Off.* 1.150–1 indicates extreme distaste for any labor that appears servile.
[106] Mankiw (1994) 141; Fischer et al. (1988) 142.

security, which could trump the greater returns that money offered. Cato the Elder, for one, carefully weighed the social and economic advantages offered by land ownership against those of coinage. At the beginning of the *De Agri Cultura* he concedes that trade and moneylending can bring high profits but praises the greater social respectability and lower risk associated with farming.[107] An anecdote that Cicero relates about Cato in the *De Officiis* reflects the same concerns. When asked the most profitable ways to invest money Cato listed pastoralism and agriculture, two land-intensive professions, but dismissed moneylending as immoral and did not even mention commerce.[108] Plutarch reports that Cato's most successful investments came from his real-estate purchases: "he bought ponds, hot springs, districts given over to fullers, pitch factories, land with natural pasture and forest, all of which brought him in large profits, and 'could not,' to use his own phrase, 'be ruined by Jupiter.'"[109] Cato sought out those types of land which promised high rents or profits and carried the least risk. Furthermore, even when Cato engaged in moneylending to finance long-distance trade, he made sure that his investment was secured by land rather than ships and cargo.[110]

Roman buyers considered a large number of factors when attempting to estimate the price of land,[111] but the question of expected returns dominated their thinking. While Cato was apparently most interested in the security of his possessions, Cicero, Varro and Atticus were more concerned with generating a return on their investments. Varro stated that "no sane man should be willing to undergo the expense and outlay of cultivation if he sees that it cannot be recouped."[112] Similarly Cicero, while discussing real estate in a letter to Atticus, remarks: "I know that

---

[107] Cato *Agr.* prologue.

[108] Cic. *Off.* 2.89: *Ex quo genere comparationis illud est Catonis senis; a quo cum quaereretur quid maxime in re familiari expediret, respondit 'bene pascere,' quid secundum: 'satis bene pascere,' quid tertium: 'male pascere,' quid quartum: 'arare.' Et cum ille qui quaesierat dixisset 'quid faenerari,' tum Cato 'Quid hominem' inquit 'occidere?'*

[109] Plut. *Cat. Mai.* 21.5: Ἁπτόμενος δὲ συντονώτερον πορισμοῦ τὴν μὲν γεωργίαν μᾶλλον ἡγεῖτο διαγωγὴν ἢ πρόσοδον, εἰς δ' ἀσφαλῆ πράγματα καὶ βέβαια κατατιθέμενος τὰς ἀφορμὰς ἐκτᾶτο λίμνας, ὕδατα θερμά, τόπους κναφεῦσιν ἀνειμένους, ἔργα πίσσια, χώραν ἔχουσαν αὐτοφυεῖς νομὰς καὶ ὕλας, ἀφ' ὧν αὐτῷ χρήματα προσῄει πολλὰ μηδ' ὑπὸ τοῦ Διός, ὥς φησιν αὐτός, βλαβῆναι δυναμένων. See also Cic. *Paradoxa Stoicorum* 51.2: *...isti callidi rerum aestimatores prata et areas quasdam magno aestimant quod ei generi possessionum minime quasi noceri potest.*

[110] See section 3.3.3.

[111] de Neeve (1985) 77–109.

[112] Varro *Rust.* 1.2.8: *Nemo enim sanus debet velle impensam ac sumptum facere in cultura, si videt non posse refici.*

it is your custom to inquire in how many years you may recoup yourself of a purchase."[113] Although Cicero himself was not always so prudent, as his attempts to buy land on which to construct a shrine for Tullia show,[114] many of his remarks convey the same general attitude. For example, in the *Pro Caecina* he states that the most profitable investment for the *pecunia* that Caesennia inherited would be in land.[115] Communities as well as individuals chose to invest in land and relied on its returns to fund and maintain public and private properties.[116]

Though the Romans expected their lands to generate revenue, the land itself was a form of emergency money particularly in the rural monetary zone. It was in this respect that the role of land as a store of wealth was most important. If necessary, one could sell land to pay off debts and thereby maintain one's credit or generate the cash required for some emergency. For example, while discussing Catiline's supporters Cicero rhetorically asks them: "since you are so abundantly endowed with lands and residences, silver plate, slaves and every sort of material goods, what holds you back from selling some of your property to make yourselves solvent again?"[117] According to Cicero, P. Cornelius Sulla, acting as P. Sittius' agent, sold off many of that man's estates in order to pay his debts.[118] Cicero himself contemplated the same procedure in 48 BCE to get cash to pay part of Tullia's dowry to Dolabella.[119] One might also note a certain Dio who "borrowed money, called in his debts and sold his land" in a desperate attempt to raise funds to pay off

---

[113] Cic. *Att.* 9.9.4: *De Lanuvino, statim ut audivi Phameam mortuum, optavi, si modo esset futura res publica, ut id aliquis emeret meorum, neque tamen de te, qui maxime meus, cogitavi. sciebam enim te quoto anno et quantum in solo solere quaerere, neque solum Romae sed etiam Deli tuum diagamma videram.*

[114] See, for example, Cic. *Att.* 12.43.2–3.

[115] Cic. *Caecin.* 16: ...*pecunia Caesenniae ex illa hereditate deberetur, eam porro in praediis collocari maxime expediret*...

[116] See: Cic. *Fam.* 13.11 (which indicates that the municipality of Arpinum owned land in Gaul); *Fam.* 13.7.1 (concerning another community owning land in Gaul); *Leg. Agr.* 2.78 (where Cicero links farm revenue to the upkeep of luxury estates situated elsewhere); and *Fam.* 8.9.4 (which suggests that Roman *civitates* owned land in Cilicia). Of this last passage, however, Shackleton Bailey (1977) 1.395 states "*civitates* must not be understood as townships in Italy."

[117] Cic. *Cat.* 2.18: *tu agris, tu aedificiis, tu argento, tu familia, tu rebus omnibus ornatus et copiosus sis, et dubites de possessione detrahere, adquirere ad fidem?*

[118] Cic. *Sull.* 56: *Tum autem, illo profecto, Sulla procurante eius rem et gerente plurimis et pulcherrimis P. Sitti praediis venditis aes alienum eiusdem dissolutum <est>, ut, quae causa ceteros ad facinus impulit, cupiditas retinendae possessionis, ea Sittio non fuerit praediis deminutis.*

[119] Cic. *Fam.* 14.6.1: *Ex tuis litteris, quas proxime accepi, cognovi praedium nullum venire potuisse. Quare videatis velim, quomodo satisfiat ei, cui scitis me satisfieri velle.*

Verres.[120] Similarly, Terentia contemplated selling a *vicus* to get money during Cicero's exile.[121] Land was the store of wealth with which, when all other means failed, one sought cash for pressing debts and other emergencies.[122]

For a variety of reasons land was a highly desirable asset even if it did not promise the returns of moneylending. It must always have been an important part of the portfolios of those Romans wealthy enough to own some. The desirability of land could only be diminished if property rights were seriously threatened, but this is precisely what happened in the last century of the Republic. Beginning with the Gracchi's attempt to reclaim *ager publicus* and continuing with Sulla's proscriptions and the on-going challenge of settling veterans, real and perceived threats to land-ownership increased as the Republic fell. As I shall argue more fully in Chapter 6, the very factors that made land less desirable in this period, increased the demand for coinage.

Slaves were another key asset. Romans were very much aware of the fact that slaves were not just useful for labor and display but were also a store of wealth that could constitute a large portion of one's assets. Thus in the *De Legibus* Cicero prescribes that "the Censors shall assess slaves and money."[123] The state even accepted slaves as security.[124] Plutarch, in his discussion of the riches of Crassus, argues that "though he owned numberless silver mines, and highly valuable tracts of land... nevertheless one might regard all this as nothing compared with the value of his

[120] Cic. *Verr.* II 1.28: *reperiretur pecunias sumpsisse mutuas, nomina sua exegisse, praedia vendidisse.*

[121] Cic. *Fam.* 14.1.5: *Quod ad me, mea Terentia, scribis te vicum vendituram, quid, obsecro te—me miserum!—, quid futurum est? et, si nos premet eadem fortuna, quid puero misero fiet? Non queo reliqua scribere—tanta vis lacrimarum est—, neque te in eundem fletum adducam; tantum scribo: si erunt in officio amici, pecunia non deerit; si non erunt, tu efficere tua pecunia non poteris.*

[122] Rawson (1976) 86 notes that "Romans often preferred to own a number of smaller estates, rather than one great one" and (page 89) that "the Roman landowner's relation to his land was much less emotional than that of the English landed gentlemen." The former practice would allow a Roman landowner to make a more measured response to financial crisis since the sale of only some properties might generate sufficient revenue to deal with a particular situation. While one could certainly sell part of a large estate, such a sale might disrupt its overall operation. See also: Shatzman (1975) 45. Furthermore, if Romans tended not to form great emotional attachments to particular estates, they could part with them more easily.

[123] Cic. *Leg.* 3.7: *censoris populi aevitates, suboles, familias pecuniasque censento.*

[124] Plut. *Cat. Min.* 6.4: ἔνιοι δὲ καὶ χωρία καὶ θεράποντας αὐτοῦ διδόντος καὶ βεβαιοῦντος ὑπέθεντο πρὸς τὸ δημόσιον. It is unclear whether or not this was a regular practice but, given the existence of public slaves and a vigorous slave market, it may well have been.

slaves."[125] Crassus was not alone in having slaves form an important part of his wealth. Cicero describes one legacy as consisting of HS 30,000, a house, silver plate, tapestries and valuable slaves.[126]

Slaves, of course, were not kept solely or even primarily as a store of wealth. On the one hand, they had significant advantages over conventional stores of wealth like coins, bullion or grain because their labor produced value and ideally profit for their owners. Thus, like land but unlike most other assets, slaves could generate wealth for their owners even while remaining in their physical possession. Furthermore, a slave's value could increase dramatically if properly trained. Cato the Elder lent money to his slaves who "would buy boys with it, and after training and teaching them for a year, at Cato's expense, would sell them again."[127] On the other hand, like grain and other comestible forms of wealth, slaves might deteriorate in value over time (e.g. become old or sick) and required an expense of effort or, in this case, food, shelter and clothing (at a minimum) to be maintained (i.e. slaves had high carrying-costs). For this reason Cato the Elder would sell his slaves when they became old or sick and no longer generated any profit for him.[128] There was also, of course, the risk of flight. Though rarely used as a means of payment, it is important to recognize that slaves were not simply a source of labor and popular means of displaying one's wealth. They were also an investment which might yield great profit. Slaves, as a store of wealth, offered considerable advantages over coinage and, given the perennial vigor of Rome's slave market,[129] they could, no doubt, easily be converted into cash if necessary.

Foodstuffs could also be important stores of wealth. Forbes and Foxhall's ethnoarchaeological study of Methana demonstrates the

---

[125] Plut. *Crass.* 2.5: ὄντων δ' αὐτῷ παμπόλλων ἀργυρείων, πολυτιμήτου δὲ χώρας καὶ τῶν ἐργαζομένων ἐν αὐτῇ, ὅμως ἄν τις ἡγήσαιτο μηδὲν εἶναι ταῦτα πάντα πρὸς τὴν τῶν οἰκετῶν τιμήν.

[126] Cic. *Verr.* II 2.35: *Huic hereditas ad HS facile triciens venit testamento propinqui sui Heraclii, plena domus caelati argenti optimi multaeque stragulae vestis pretiosorumque mancipiorum.*

[127] Plut. *Cat. Mai.* 25.6.

[128] Plut. *Cat. Mai.* 4.4: καὶ τούτους δὲ πρεσβυτέρους γενομένους ᾤετο δεῖν ἀποδίδοσθαι καὶ μὴ βόσκειν ἀχρήστους. See also: Cato *Agr.* 2.7: *servum senem, servum morbosum, et siquid aliut supersit, vendat.*

[129] Harris (1999) 75 notes that Augustus "introduced (AD 7) a two-per-cent tax on slave sales (Dio 55.31), which means that he believed that hundreds of thousands of taxable slave sales (I once hypothesized 250,000) took place every year." Scheidel (2005) 78 estimates an average annual import of 15–20,000 slaves for the last two centuries of the Republic but that would, of course, constitute a minimum number of sales since many slaves already resident in Italy would change hands as well.

potential importance of food storage in the ancient Mediterranean. They note that Methanites often store large quantities of food, amounts well beyond their consumption needs, despite the inevitable deterioration in the quality and value of the stored food. Forbes and Foxhall offer several explanations for this behavior. They point out that the Methanites have a "lack of confidence in the ability of the state to maintain a stable currency" and that "[a]gricultural produce...is less prone to problems of devaluation due to inflation than ordinary currency."[130] Food is also much more difficult to steal than coins. Methanites apparently prefer to keep their wealth in the form of commodities and only sell it in anticipation of a major purchase.[131] Thus food storage is an important economic strategy designed to protect the farmer from currency fluctuations, inflation and theft as well as food crisis. Romans of the late Republic faced all of these potential problems, and so we might well expect them to use food storage strategies similar to those of modern Methanites. An examination of the Republican agricultural manuals supports just such a conclusion. As Forbes and Foxhall comment, "[i]t sounds almost as though Roman bailiffs were more comfortable dealing in commodities than in cash."[132]

Grain, useful in its own right and available for payments or conversion to cash, was the food best suited to be a store of wealth. Studies of modern agricultural communities show that a farmer's economic strategies often revolve around the storage of grain.[133] In the 70s and 80s, for example, Forbes found that the inhabitants of Methana tended to store grain until it was necessary to make a large purchase, distrusting the stability of cash and the ease with which it could be stolen.[134] This last consideration was particularly important for farmers of the late Republic when rural violence seems to have become endemic in Italy.[135] Varro specifically warns against 'unexpected bands of robbers.'[136]

Both the Roman farmer's interest in granaries and choice of grain-types testify to an abiding concern for the long-term storage of grain. Cato recommends that the farmer have a well-built *villa rustica* with

---

130 Forbes and Foxhall (1995) 81.

131 Forbes and Foxhall (1995) 75–6.

132 Forbes and Foxhall (1995) 81.

133 Forbes and Foxhall (1995) 75–6; De Garine and Harrison (1988).

134 Forbes and Foxhall (1995) 81.

135 Harris (1971b) 295; Lintott (1999) 129; Brunt (1971) 108–9, 291–3, 311 and 551–7.

136 Varro *Rust.* 1.12.4.

facilities for storing commodities,[137] and also mentions 'shifting grain' (*frumentum transferri*) in a passage concerning work to be done on rainy days.[138] This remark, if it refers to the transfer of grain from one storeroom to another, could imply that Cato expected a farm to have a substantial granary. He may also be referring to the airing of stored grain.[139] Varro writes much more extensively and explicitly on the issue of grain storage, describing the ideal granary, recommending the right kind of plaster to use on walls and floors in order to keep out insects and animals, and even discussing grain preservatives.[140] He notes approvingly the methods employed by the Carthaginians and the people of Osca in Tarraconensis whose grain, he claims, could survive in storage for 50 to 100 years. The types of grain grown by the Romans also demonstrate the importance of storage in their economic strategies. The decision made by most Roman farmers to cultivate hulled grains like emmer "represent[s] a trade-off between a lower value for the crop and reduced risks of storage losses over a period of years."[141] The husks of emmer wheat "gave protection from disease and insects"[142] but such 'hulled' grains required additional processing before they could be eaten and made less appetizing food than 'naked' grains.[143] In other words, Romans sacrificed both taste and short-term value for storability.

If the Romans stored grain only to consume it later or to preserve it as seed-grain for the following season, it would not be especially remarkable, but Varro makes it clear that grain storage was a financial strategy:

> As to the crops intended for market, care must be used as to the proper time for taking out each; thus one should take out and sell at once those which do not stand storage before they spoil, while you should sell those which keep well when the price is high. For often products which have been stored quite a long time will not only pay interest on the storage, but even double the profit if they are marketed at the right time.[144]

---

[137] Cato *Agr.* 3.2: *Patrem familiae villam rusticam bene aedificatam habere expedit, cellam oleariam, vinariam, dolia multa, uti lubeat caritatem expectare.*

[138] Cato *Agr.* 2.3.

[139] See Pliny *HN* 18.302 and 322.

[140] Varro *Rust.* 1.57: *Triticum condi oportet in granaria sublimia, quae perflentur vento ab exortu ac septemtrionum regione, ad quae nulla aura umida ex propinquis locis adspiret. Parietes et solum opere tectorio marmorato loricandi; si minus, ex argilla mixta acere e frumento et amurca, quod murem et vermen non patitur esse et grana facit solidiora ac firmiora...*

[141] Forbes and Foxhall (1995) 76.

[142] Braun (1995) 34–5.

[143] Forbes and Foxhall (1995) 76.

[144] Varro *Rust.* 1.69: *Quae vendenda videndum, quae quoque tempore oporteat promi; alia enim,*

Cato also mentions the virtues of storage with respect to profit. The ability to store commodities until prices are high, he writes, "will redound to [the farmer's] wealth, his self-respect, and his reputation."[145] Famine or food shortage could turn a full granary into a small fortune and, even if high prices did not appear, older grain could still be used (e.g. as feed for livestock) when no longer fit for human consumption.[146]

Little late Republican evidence exists for the use of wine and oil as stores of wealth but there are a few suggestive passages. Cato advises the estate owner to have "plenty of vats for oil and wine, so that he may hold his products for good prices."[147] Wine and oil, like grain, were stores of wealth which one might try to exchange at the most opportune moments in order to maximize profits. Cicero uses the dual functions of wine, as a store of wealth and as a means of intoxication, to good effect in his *Philippics*. Of Antonius Cicero declares:

> It is incredible, and almost portentous how in so few days—I do not say months—he poured out so much property. There was an immense store of wine, a very great weight of the finest silver, a costly wardrobe, much elegant and magnificent furniture in many places, the belongings of a man not indeed lavish but fully supplied.[148]

Cicero here is clearly implying that Antonius spent Pompey's silver and converted his furniture and clothing into cash. Antonius no doubt sold off the 'immense store of wine' as well, but Cicero uses the verb *effundere* to suggest that the notorious author of the *De Sua Ebrietate* drank it instead. Cicero uses essentially the same list of property (i.e. wine, furniture, clothing and silver) in a later speech to much the same effect.[149] Both lists indicate that wine could be an important store of wealth in elite households.

Cattle-raising was considered both extremely profitable and respectable. Cato the Elder states conclusively in his agricultural manual that

---

quae manere non possunt, antequam se commutent, ut celeriter promas ac vendas; alia, quae servari possunt, ut tum vendas cum caritas est. Saepe enim diutius servata non modo usuram adiciunt, sed etiam fructum duplicant, si tempore promas.

[145] Cato *Agr.* 3.2: *et rei et virtuti et gloriae erit.*

[146] Forbes and Foxhall (1995) 74.

[147] Cato *Agr.* 3.2.

[148] Cic. *Phil.* 2.66: *Incredibile ac simile portenti est, quonam modo illa tam multa quam paucis non dico mensibus, sed diebus effuderit. Maximus vini numerus fuit, permagnum optimi pondus argenti, pretiosa vestis, multa et lauta supellex et magnifica multis locis non illa quidem luxuriosi hominis, sed tamen abundantis.*

[149] Cic. *Phil.* 13.11: *Redimet hortos, aedes, urbana quaedam, quae possidet Antonius; nam argentum, vestem, supellectilem, vinum amittet aequo animo, quae ille helluo dissipavit.*

"there is nothing more profitable than to take good care of cattle."[150] Indeed, in a famous anecdote reported by Cicero, Cato supposedly remarked that even raising cattle poorly was more profitable than farming.[151] In Cicero's writings ranchers (*pecuarii*) regularly appear as a distinct class of wealthy or at least respectable people listed alongside businessmen, merchants, *publicani* and farmers.[152] Ranchers were wealthy in large part because of the cattle they owned (though their pasture lands and slave herdsmen would also be quite valuable) and, therefore, cattle obviously functioned as a store of wealth even though Roman writers seldom refer to livestock in ways that explicitly recognize that function.

Only occasionally do cattle appear in descriptions of wealth. In the *Verrine* orations Cicero mentions a certain Apollonius who had invested all his property in cattle as well as slaves, villas and loans. The context, however, indicates that cattle were not considered a particularly liquid form of wealth since Cicero's argument was that the nature of Apollonius' investments proved that he had little to gain and much to lose from fomenting civil unrest in Sicily.[153] Land, slaves and cattle were all especially vulnerable in wartime. Cicero does make clear, however, that livestock was a store of wealth to which a farmer might turn if in need of cash, stating that:

> for a farmer to have to pay with coins—which he cannot grow, nor his plough or his toil procure him—he must sell his oxen, his very plough, the whole of his gear and stock.[154]

In Cicero's countryside coinage is not readily available and livestock was among the most valuable assets to which a farmer had recourse. In the *Paradoxa Stoicorum*, furthermore, Cicero suggests that cattle were

---

[150] Cato *Agr.* 54.5: *Nihil est quod magis expediat, quam boves bene curare.*

[151] Cic. *Off.* 2.89: *Ex quo genere comparationis illud est Catonis senis; a quo cum quaereretur quid maxime in re familiari expediret, respondit 'bene pascere,' quid secundum: 'satis bene pascere,' quid tertium: 'male pascere,' quid quartum: 'arare.'*

[152] Cic. *Verr.* II 2.188: *mercator an negotiator an arator an pecuarius*; *Font.* 12: *ex tot negotiatorum, colonorum, publicanorum, aratorum, pecuariorum*; *Font.* 46: *omnes illius provinciae publicani, agricolae, pecuarii, ceteri negotiatores; Verr.* II 2.17: *si cuiquam ordini sive aratorum, sive pecuariorum sive mercatorum probatus sit*; and *Pro Cluentio* 198: *Iam qui in agro Larinati praedia, qui negotia, qui res pecuarias habent, honesti homines et summo splendore praediti.*

[153] Cic. *Verr.* II 5.20: *fortunas eius ita constitutas fuisse familia, pecore, villis, pecuniis creditis, ut nemini minus expediret ullum in Sicilia tumultum aut bellum commoveri.*

[154] Cic. *Verr.* II 3.199 (adapted from the Loeb translation): *Nummos vero ut det arator, quos non exarat, quos non aratro ac manu quaerit, boves et aratrum ipsum atque omne instrumentum vendat necesse est.*

conventionally viewed as a store of wealth when he declares "I for my part shall never say that anybody who has lost cattle or furniture has suffered a loss of goods."[155] While a philosopher might regard true wealth to be merely the lack of desire for material goods, for the less enlightened livestock could be an important asset.

For the rich even furniture (*supellex*), was an important store of wealth. In a number of passages Cicero places furniture on a par with silver plate, clothing and wine as a potential source of cash in an emergency. In July of 47 BCE he wrote to Atticus, asking his friend to raise some money for him through the sale of silver plate and furniture.[156] Twice in the *Philippics* Cicero lists furniture along with such goods when describing the irretrievably lost property of Pompeius Magnus.[157] Cicero does not tell us exactly what became of these objects but it is clear that, unlike his landholdings, Pompey's son would be unable to recover them. The passage from the *Paradoxa Stoicorum*, mentioned above, also links furniture to cattle, undoubtedly a form of *pecunia*.[158] Though it performed no other monetary function, furniture was a significant store of upper class wealth.

A farmer's tools (*instrumentum*) served some of the same purposes as a wealthy man's furniture. In the *Verrines* Cicero notes that when Verres demanded coinage rather than grain from some farmers, they could only pay him by selling their tools.[159] Cicero, who speaks at length concerning this injustice, concedes that the farmers in question could have paid Verres by selling various urban possessions but he seems intent on exciting pity in his audience by appealing to the image of the subsistence farmer with no outside resources to fall back upon. Although it has been argued that agricultural equipment cost little,[160] for a small farmer the expense may have been relatively large. To sell such tools would have been a last, but no doubt frequently necessary, resort. Both tools and furniture were objects whose primary, non-monetary func-

---

[155] Cic. *Paradoxa Stoicorum* 8: *neque ego umquam bona perdidisse dicam si qui pecus aut supellectilem amiserit.*

[156] Cic. *Att.* 11.25.3: *te oro, ut in perditis rebus si quid cogi, confici potest quod sit in tuto, ex argento, [ves]te (quae satis multa est), supellectile, des operam.*

[157] Cic. *Phil.* 2.66 and 13.11.

[158] Cic. *Paradoxa Stoicorum* 8.

[159] Cic. *Verr.* II 3.199: *Non enim debetis hoc cogitare, 'habet idem in nummis, habet in urbanis praediis.' Nam cum aratori aliquid imponitur, non hominis si quae sunt praeterea facultates, sed arationis ipsius vis ac ratio consideranda est, quid ea sustinere, quid pati, quid efficere possit ac debeat.*

[160] Macve (1985) 253.

tions almost always dominated their use. However their value and utility allowed them sometimes to serve a secondary role as a safeguard against economic disaster.

4.4 Media of Exchange

A medium of exchange is a means of indirect exchange[161] or "a convenient stepping stone in obtaining one type of goods for another."[162] While we have seen plenty of exchanges that did not involve coinage, no other asset discussed in this chapter seems to have achieved the status of a medium of exchange with the possible exception of grain. The government, traders and private individuals all made or accepted payments of grain in some circumstances. Though it cannot be proven, it is likely that, at least in the rural monetary zone where it could most easily be produced and most inexpensively stored, grain was a means of exchange.

4.5 Units of Account

A Unit of Account is a means by which prices are quoted (i.e. a standard of value),[163] accounts are kept or debts are recorded.[164] It is not necessary for units of account to correspond to any physical objects actually circulating in the economy.[165] The *sestertius* is a good example of this phenomenon. From the mid-second century onwards the Romans calculated prices and values in *sestertii* even though very few of these coins were ever minted.[166] Units of account can facilitate both trade in the absence of a medium of exchange (i.e., in a 'barter economy') and the administration of a redistributive system (i.e. staple-finance).[167] Romans kept accounts of a great many goods in addition to coinage. Though few traces of them survive, tax collectors, merchants, government officials

[161] Polanyi (1968) 201.
[162] R. Firth, s.v. 'Currency, Primitive,' in *Encyclopedia Britannica*,[14] quoted in Polanyi (1968) 180.
[163] Polanyi (1968) 192 and 194.
[164] See Mankiw (1994) 141; Fischer et al. (1988) 141.
[165] Fischer et al. (1988) 141.
[166] *Sestertii* appear as part of only 18 Republican issues and none were minted between c. 208 and 91 BCE or from 85 to 48 BCE. See Crawford (1974) *passim*.
[167] Polanyi (1968) 184 and 192–4.

as well as farmers all kept detailed accounts of the commodities in their possession or with which they dealt. However, record-keeping alone does not make something a unit of account. Only in the rural monetary zone do such commodities perhaps constitute units of account, but lack of evidence once again precludes proof. Cato lists grain and oil accounts in addition to cash accounts and suggests that debts might be recorded in these commodities and others.[168] Unfortunately no other references to such activities survive and neither prices nor general wealth are ever recorded in terms of these goods. As a standard of value, coinage again seems preeminent.

4.6 Conclusion

Many different assets performed monetary functions within the Roman economy but none approached the utility of coinage which was *the* unit of account and standard of value and probably unrivaled as a means of exchange. The absence of any significant alternative to coinage in the fulfillment of these roles demonstrates the considerable level of monetization achieved by the Romans in the late Republic. Farmers had the greatest number of alternatives to coinage as a means of payment and, in grain, may have had another medium of exchange. The government and merchants also used some commodities to perform monetary functions, though apparently less frequently and in different ways. Having set out the evidence for both Republican money and pecuniary assets here and in the preceding chapters, it is now necessary to explore the differences in money use within the Roman economy by looking at the monetary zones individually and considering the relative importance of coinage and other assets in each.

---

[168] Cato *Agr.* 2.5 and 5.3–4.

CHAPTER FIVE

MONETARY ZONES

5.1 Introduction

Late in 43 BCE news of the proscriptions reached Cicero at his estate in Tusculum. He and his brother Quintus set out for Astura from which they intended to sail to Macedonia and meet up with Brutus. But on the road Quintus became worried about his lack of funds (*aporia*) and decided to return home, 'pack up', and then rejoin Marcus. The brothers parted tearfully and, a few days later, betrayed by his servants, Quintus was captured and killed.[1] The lesson was clear: prominent men would be wise to keep large sums of money handy as a precaution. The future emperor Galba, during his retirement in the early years of Nero's reign, reportedly never went anywhere "without the escort of a second carriage containing 10,000 gold pieces."[2]

Even when not in danger of proscription or prosecution, politicians needed cash to function effectively. Farmers, however, had very different monetary needs. Their chief danger (and opportunity) was food shortage. Republican agricultural writers emphasize that the prudent farmer must always maintain stores of his produce. Cato declares that "it is well for the master to have a well-built barn and storage room...so that he may hold his products for good prices,"[3] while Varro notes that "products which have been stored quite a long time will not only pay interest on the storage, but even double the profit if they are marketed at the right time."[4] Given the nature of ancient agriculture, it was hardly a risky speculation for estate owners to anticipate an eventual rise in the price of basic foodstuffs. Fear of famine would prompt smallholders to follow a similar storage strategy. Furthermore, since some commodities could easily take the place of cash in certain

---

[1] Plut. *Cic.* 47.
[2] Suet. *Galba* 8.
[3] Cato *Agr.* 3.2.
[4] Varro *Rust.* 1.69.1.

transactions,[5] coinage was not as important in the rural economy as elsewhere.

It is no great revelation to observe that people in different professions had different monetary needs. Many scholars of monetary history have proposed methods for distinguishing between various types of money-use within a given economy or have observed that types of money tend, in practice, to be segregated according to their functions. Max Weber wrote of 'economic zones' in which "different sorts of services rendered correspond to specific sorts of goods which mediate the payment function, so that different species of money exist side by side."[6] In studying Pelew money, Karl Polanyi observed that "each type of money has its own use, a circle within which it moves."[7] Richard Thurnwald's scheme, which categorized all kinds of exchange as reciprocal, redistributive or commercial, has had a particularly broad influence.[8] Similarly Keith Hopkins proposed "conceptualising the Roman economy as operating on five intersecting planes: the natural economy, bronze coinage, silver coinage, gold coinage and credit."[9]

For late Republican Rome these means of categorization are of limited utility. There was no one-to-one correlation between assets and monetary functions. The monetary system as a whole was characterized by great versatility in which one could accomplish all types of exchange (i.e. reciprocal, redistributive and commercial) with a number of different assets. In light of these difficulties it seems best to analyze the Roman monetary system by considering how people used money in different economic situations or contexts.

As I explained in Chapter 1, the Roman economy is best viewed as consisting of four 'monetary zones,' i.e. four separate though interconnected environments in which the characteristics of money-use differed significantly. These are the rural, urban, governmental and commercial monetary zones. The Governmental Monetary Zone consists of the sphere of monetary activity undertaken by the Roman government in, for example, taxation, public contracts and the payment of soldiers. The Commercial Monetary Zone comprises the economic activity of

---

[5] Cato suggests that the lending and borrowing of agricultural commodities was common in rural areas (*Agr.* 5.3–4). He also indicates that the *vilicus* might pay for part-time agricultural labor with a share of the produce rather than coinage (*Agr.* 136).

[6] Weber (1927) 237.

[7] Polanyi (1968) 200.

[8] See, for example, Finley (1975) 117; Einzig (1948) 338.

[9] Hopkins (1995/96) 61.

merchants and traders engaged in medium- and long-distance trade. The Urban Monetary Zone consists of the private monetary activity of urban dwellers except merchants, while the Rural Monetary Zone is the agricultural/pastoral sector of the economy and comprises the monetary behavior of farmers and estate managers, those directly engaged in agriculture. While rural areas were to a certain extent monetized in the late Republic, it is clear that rural dwellers could more readily use assets other than coinage for money and that monetary behavior was qualitatively different for urban dwellers. In this chapter I will examine in turn each of these zones with regard to the nature of the demand for money within it. I have two main goals. The first is to gauge the level of monetization within each zone, i.e. the extent to which coinage was used for payments, exchange and so forth.[10] Obviously it is impossible to provide a quantitative analysis of Roman monetization, but literary and archaeological evidence do indicate *relative* levels of money use. My second goal is to consider the extent to which other forms of money and assets with monetary functions reduced the demand for coinage in these zones. It is only by examining this issue that we can hope to understand the effect on the Roman economy of the vast increase in the supply of coins in the late Republic.

One point, however, must be immediately emphasized: I employ the concept of monetary zones simply as a tool to model the Roman monetary system, in the words of Keith Hopkins, as "a simplification of a complex reality, designed to show up the logical relationships between its constituent parts."[11] It should be readily apparent that these monetary zones do not perfectly describe that system. The *publicani* and urban market gardens are obvious examples of institutions and practices that do not fit neatly into this scheme.

5.2 The Governmental Monetary Zone

It is widely believed that the Roman government was highly monetized and relied heavily on coinage to conduct it affairs in the late Republic.[12] While there is some truth to these propositions, as the state's massive production of coinage suggests, that reliance should not be exaggerated.

---

[10] Chandavarkar (1977) 655.

[11] Hopkins (1995/96) 41. See also: Finley (1985) 182.

[12] This view is implicit in many works, e.g.: Crawford (1974); (1985); Harl (1996). Jones (1974) 189 states "Ancient governments operated upon a strictly cash basis."

While the government and its officials may have preferred to spend and receive coins, they nevertheless employed a variety of assets to make transactions. My discussion of the governmental monetary zone will evaluate the government's demand for money by considering the forms in which it received revenue and made payments as well as how money circulated among magistrates and provinces. The answers to these questions will help us determine how dependent the state was upon coinage and how sophisticated its monetary practices were.

5.2.1 *Government Revenues*

The government and individual magistrates acquired revenue in a variety of forms and from a wide array of sources. Though the spoils of war feature most prominently in our sources and taxation may have provided the largest and most regular source of income, indemnities, fines, fees, sales, rents, levies, corvées and other exactions also supplied the Roman government with money.

Table 5.1 provides a list of known revenue sources other than spoils and indemnities for which there is evidence from the late Republic.

Table 5.1 Known Late Republican Sources of Revenue

Region	Type of Revenue	Form of Payment	Source
Africa	*vectigal certum stipendiarium*	coinage?	Cic. *Verr.* II 3.12; 2.3.27; *CIL* I[2] 585
	φόρος ἐπι τῇ γῇ καὶ ἐπὶ τοῖς σώμασιν, ἀνδρὶ καὶ γυναικὶ ὁμοίως	in kind and coinage?	App. *Pun.* 135
	multae	in kind and coinage	Caes. *B Afr.* 97
Asia	*decumae*	in kind?	App. *B Civ.* 5.4; Cic. *Leg. Man.* 15
	scriptura	coinage?	Cic. *Leg. Man.* 15
	vectigal	*pecunia*, coinage and in kind	Cic. *Verr.* II 1.89; II 3.27; *Q Fr.* 1.1.26; *Leg. Man.* 15
	portorium, vectigal ex portu	coinage?	Cic. *Att.* 2.16; *Leg. Man.* 15
Carthage	*stipendium*	*argentum*	Livy 32.2
Cilicia	φόρος (1%)?	coinage?	App. *Syr.* 50
Cyrene	*scriptura*	coinage?	Plin. *HN* 19.40

Table 5.1 (*cont.*)

Region	Type of Revenue	Form of Payment	Source
Gaul	*stipendium*	pecunia	Cic. *Font.* 13 and 26
	requisitions	*frumentum* and *equitatus*	Cic. *Font.* 13 and 26
	stipendium	coinage	Suet. *Iul.* 25
	corvée	road building	Cic. *Font.* 17
	vectigal	in kind?	Cic. *Verr.* II 3.27
Greece	*aurum coronarium*	*pecunia*	Cic. *Pis.* 90
	vectigal	coinage?	Cic. *Q.Fr.* 1.1.33; *CIL* I² 585
Illyria	*vectigal*	?	Livy 45.26.14
Italy	*portorium*	coinage?	Cic. *Q.Fr.* 1.1.33; Suet. *Iul.* 43; Vell. Pat. 2.6.3
	vectigal vicensimum	*aurum*	Cic. *Att.* 2.16; Livy 27.10.11
	columnarium	coinage?	Cic. *Att.* 13.6.1; cf. Caes. *B Civ.* 3.32
	sumptuary fines	coinage?	Cic. *Att.* 12.35; Plut. *Cat. Mai.* 18
	market fines	*pecunia*	Livy 38.35.5
	pastoral fines	pecunia	Livy 35.10.12; Ov. *Fast.* 5.279–294
	tributum[13]	coin?	Plut. *Aem.* 38.1; Plin. *HN* 33.56
	vectigal	in kind?	Cic. *Verr.* II 3.27, *Leg. Agr.* 1.20–21, *Att.* 2.16; Suet. *Iul.* 20.3; *CIL* I² 585
Judaea	φόρος	in kind	Joseph. *AJ* 14.201–203 and 206
	φόρος τῶν σωμάτων?	coin?	App. *Syr.* 50
Macedonia	*vectigal* (mines)	coinage?	Livy 45.29.11; Plut. *Aem.* 28.6
	tributum	?	Livy 45.18.7, 29.4
	portoria	?	Cic. *Pis.* 87
	vectigal	in kind?	Cic. *Verr.* II 3.27
Sardinia	*vectigal*	in kind?	Cic. *Verr.* II 3.27

[13] Until 167 and after 44 BCE.

Table 5.1 (*cont.*)

Region	Type of Revenue	Form of Payment	Source
	conlationes	*frumentum*	Livy 23.32.9; 23.41.6
	tributum	coin?	Livy 23.32.9
	stipendium	coin?	Livy 23.41.6
	decumae and *octavae*	in kind	Caes. *B Afr.* 98
Sicily	*decumae vini, olei et frugum minutarum*	in kind	Cic. *Verr.* II 3.18, 112
	scriptura	coin?	Cic. *Verr.* II 2.169
	portorium (5%)	coin	Cic. *Verr.* II 2.176 and 185
	vectigal	*frumentum* and *pecunia*	Cic. *Verr.* II 3.137
Spain	*vectigal certum stipendiarium*	*pecunia*	Cic. *Verr.* II 3.12; II 3.27; *BHisp.* 42
	vicensimae	coin?	Livy 43.2.12
	exactiones publicae	*numerata pecunia, aurum* and *argentum*	Cic. *Fam.* 10.32.1
	mining revenue	bullion?	Polyb. 34.9.8–11
Syria	φόρος (1%)?	coin?	App. *Syr.* 50

This table highlights several problems. First of all, there is the fact that our evidence is so incomplete. It is likely, for example, that the use of *corvée* labor for road-building occurred in many places, not just Gaul. Similarly the Romans probably exacted *portoria* (tolls) and *scripturae* (pasture taxes) in most provinces but we only hear of them in a few places.

The poor quality of the evidence leads to a second major problem: how to determine in what form the taxes were paid. In only a few cases can we be fairly sure whether a tax or other type of revenue was paid in coin or in kind. It seems reasonable to assume that *portoria*, for example, were paid with coinage (if only because traders would presumably have access to coins), but only one late Republican source explicitly states that some government revenue, from Spain, took the form of *pecunia numerata*.[14] Suetonius reports that Julius Caesar imposed a large annual *stipendium* on Gaul,[15] and this tax, apparently, was paid in coin.[16] Livy

[14] Cic. *Fam.* 10.32.1: *magna numerata pecunia, magno pondere auri, maiore argenti coacto de publicis exactionibus.*

[15] Suet. *Iul.* 25: *eique $\overline{cccc}$ in singulos annos stipendii nomine inposuit.*

[16] Brunt (1981) 161–2 has doubts, noting that even in the first century CE "very

states that the Romans exacted a *stipendium* and payment of grain from certain Sardinian cities, again suggesting the *stipendium* was paid with coinage.[17]

Does the use of the term *stipendium* indicate payment in coin while *vectigal* denotes a payment in kind?[18] Richard Duncan-Jones has justly criticized this view.[19] On two occasions Cicero seems to suggest that some *vectigalia* were paid with coinage.[20] The fact that Cicero refers to certain African and Spanish taxes as "fixed tributary taxes" (*'vectigal... certum, quod stipendarium dicitur'*) indicates that a *stipendium* is a kind of *vectigal*.[21] It is possible that these taxes were paid in coin rather than in kind,[22] but more likely that a *stipendium* was merely a *fixed* tax (i.e., a set quantity due) rather than a tax requiring a fixed amount of *coinage*. Since, as both T. R. S. Broughton and Duncan-Jones have pointed out,[23] the Romans could and did fix taxes in grain,[24] the form of the African and Spanish taxes cannot ultimately be determined. Thus it appears that one can draw no definite conclusions concerning the form of tax payments from the use of the words *stipendium* or *vectigal*.

While there is little evidence pointing unambiguously to taxation in coinage, there are a number of sources indicating taxation in kind. The most detailed reports come from Sicily, where, Cicero reports, Rome

---

little money circulated in parts of Gaul... the government could hardly have obtained payment in cash." However, Duncan-Jones (1980) 217 suggests that this tribute derived from "Gallic gold-mines or gold stocks." Furthermore, as Nash (1978) 14 observes: "By the time of the Roman conquest... all the civitates of Central Gaul produced, or had the use of, at least one precious metal coinage, and in many cases also a small-value currency usually in bronze or potin."

[17] Livy 23.41.6: *Deinde aliae quoque ciuitates quae ad Hampsicoram Poenosque defecerant obsidibus datis dediderunt sese; quibus stipendio frumentoque imperato pro cuiusque aut uiribus aut delicto Carales exercitum reduxit.*

[18] See, for example, Lewis and Short (1879) s.v. *stipendium*; Lintott (1993) 71.

[19] Duncan-Jones (1990) 196–7.

[20] Cic. *Leg. agr.* 1.11: *Numquisnam tam abstrusus usquam nummus videtur, quem non architecti huiusce legis olfecerint? Provincias, civitates liberas, socios, amicos, reges denique exhauriunt, admovent manus vectigalibus populi Romani*; and *Q.Fr.* 1.1.26: *Quantum vero illud est beneficium tuum, quod iniquo et gravi vectigali aedilicio, cum magnis nostris simultatibus, Asiam liberasti! etenim si unus homo nobilis queritur palam te, quod edixeris, ne ad ludos pecuniae decernerentur, HS $\overline{cc}$ sibi eripuisse, quanta tandem pecunia penderetur, si omnium nomine, quicumque Romae ludos facerent, quod erat iam institutum, erogaretur?*

[21] Cic. *Verr.* III 3.12.

[22] Duncan-Jones (1990) 188.

[23] Duncan-Jones (1990) 192. Broughton (1929) 65 notes that "the stipendiary people in Africa had paid a set tribute per capita and a tax on their land; the payment however must necessarily have been made in kind."

[24] Josesph. *AJ* 14.206.

collected "tithes of wine, oil and minor crops" as well as a tax in grain.[25] Asia also paid some taxes in kind. Appian has Antony declare to a crowd at Ephesus in 42 BCE that the Romans, after taking control of the kingdom of Pergamum, had required the inhabitants "to contribute a portion of [their] yearly harvest in order that [the Romans] might share...the vicissitudes of the seasons."[26] In 46 BCE Caesar raised Sardinia's in kind tax from a tenth to an eighth of their produce.[27] This too seems to be a tax in kind, given the use of the word *decuma*. Gold and silver bullion may have been collected as mining revenue, as *aurum coronarium* ('crown gold'), and for other taxes in Spain, Macedonia, Gaul and Italy.[28]

The role of the *publicani* further complicates the question of the nature of Roman revenue. Thanks to them, what was paid to the government in taxes was not necessarily the same as what the government eventually received. The Romans auctioned off the right to collect some taxes, typically for five-year periods. This practice held several advantages for the government. First, it relieved the state of the burden of maintaining its own tax-collecting bureaucracy. Secondly, it allowed them to receive a steadier and more secure stream of revenue since the *publicani* shouldered the risks and uncertainties of tax-collection over a number of years and provided security for payments. Thirdly, by using the *publicani* as middlemen the state could easily convert in kind revenue to cash. If the *publicani* owned the produce they collected, they would need to market it in order to pay the sums they had promised the government.[29] Epigraphic evidence from Asia Minor reveals that the government provided incentives for the produce collected there by the *publicani* to be sold at Rome.[30] By employing the commercial monetary zone, in the form of the *publicani*, to mediate the extraction of revenue from the

---

[25] Cic. *Verr.* II 3.18: *vini et olei decumas et frugum minutarum*; and *Verr.* II 3.137 where Cicero describes *rem frumentariam omnem* as part of the Sicilian *vectigalia*.

[26] App. *B Civ.* 5.4: ἐπεὶ δὲ ἐδέησεν, οὐ πρὸς τὰ τιμήματα ὑμῖν ἐπεθήκαμεν, ὡς ἂν ἡμεῖς ἀκίνδυνον φόρον ἐκλέγοιμεν, ἀλλὰ μέρη φέρειν τῶν ἑκάστοτε καρπῶν ἐπετάξαμεν, ἵνα καὶ τῶν ἐναντίων κοινωνῶμεν ὑμιν.

[27] Caes. *B Afr.* 98: *HS C multat et pro decumis octavas pendere iubet.*

[28] Cic. *Att.* 2.16; Livy 27.10.11; Cic. *Fam.* 10.32.1.

[29] Of course the *publicani* also collected some taxes in cash and in some cases did not own the commodities they collected, merely facilitating their collection (e.g. the Sicilian grain revenue). See Lintott (1993) 75–8.

[30] See Nicolet (1991) 470–80 for discussion of *Monumentum Ephesenum* 1.73–4 as well as Engelmann and Knibbe (1989) and Nicolet (1994b) 224.

rural monetary zone, the Roman government had hit upon an efficient means to ensure itself a regular flow of coins.

Despite the ambiguity created by the sources and the role of the *publicani*, the Roman government and its agents did receive some in kind income from every province—though not necessarily as tax revenue *per se*. Provincial governors had the right to receive grain for their upkeep[31] and to requisition food, labor and transportation.[32]

The state of the evidence prevents us from forming a detailed picture of Roman revenues but enough information survives to make certain generalizations. Duncan-Jones put it best when he observed that the Roman state tended to extract revenue from people in the kinds of money available to them.[33] This statement echoes Cicero's words in the *Verrines* where he argues that a farmer should not be forced to pay something he cannot grow.[34] Except for some notable exceptions during the civil wars,[35] the Romans did not, as far as we can tell, make unrealistic demands on the provinces. North Africa provides two examples of the Romans adapting their demands for taxes to fit local conditions. After defeating Carthage in the Third Punic War, Rome instituted land and head taxes presumably to be paid in grain.[36] This decision may have been prompted by the realization that, in the absence of Carthage, the region could not support a substantial coin or bullion-based tax. Caesar's African settlement of 46 BCE provides a much more vivid and unambiguous example of the same tendency. The fines and new taxes imposed on certain communities varied considerably. While many were required to pay cash fines, Leptis had to pay a fixed amount of olive oil by weight each year and the inhabitants of Thysdra "on account of the insignificance of the city" were fined a quantity of grain.[37]

---

[31] Cic. *Verr.* II 3.188: *ex senatus consulto et ex legibus frumentum in cellam ei sumere liceret.*

[32] Roth (1999) 141–6 collects the evidence for "involuntary seizure" and "forced purchase" of food, other supplies and animals for transport. He also notes, page 110, that "The Roman army...routinely requisitioned civilians to carry supplies."

[33] Duncan-Jones (1990) 198: "taxes which by their nature were levied in money (indirect taxes) fell on monetised sections of the economy...Where there is any evidence, the land-tax visibly remained a tax in kind in a number of provinces. This apparently recognised the limited extent to which money could be extracted from an agricultural population in which ownership of money was sporadic."

[34] Cic. *Verr.* II 3.199.

[35] See, for example, App. *B Civ.* 5.4–6.

[36] App. *Pun.* 135: τοῖς δὲ λοιποῖς φόρον ὥρισαν ἐπι τῇ γῇ καὶ ἐπὶ τοῖς σώμασιν, ἀνδρὶ καὶ γυναικὶ ὁμοίως. See also: Garnsey (1988) 197.

[37] Caes. *B Afr.* 97: *Thapsitanis HS XX, conventui eorum HS XXX, itemque Hadrumetinis HS XXX, conventui eorum HS L multae nomine imponit...Leptitanos...XXX centenis milibus*

The Romans did more than just tailor their revenue demands to local conditions. It appears likely that taxpayers could, in some instances, choose how they paid their taxes. Cicero states that, at least with respect to the grain due their governors, provincials could pay the cash value of the grain rather than physically deliver it to the governor.[38] *Adaeratio*, the commutation of in kind payments to cash, would relieve the taxpayer of transit costs or other inconveniences.[39] Governors often abused this system by demanding that grain be delivered to whatever place in their province it was most expensive so as to receive a larger amount of money than they might have otherwise.[40] Cicero suggests that this practice took place in Sicily, Spain, Asia and other provinces.[41] One of the charges against Marcus Fonteius, that he accepted money in lieu of road construction from some communities in Gaul, suggests that such practices were not necessarily confined to commodity exactions.[42] The much more plentiful Imperial evidence indicates that *adaeratio* was common and widespread.[43] Septimius Severus seems to have banned *adaeratio* with respect to Egyptian grain taxes, perhaps because the conversion worked too much to the taxpayer's advantage.[44] It is reasonable to suppose—though there is little direct evidence—that *adaeratio* was a regular part of taxation in the late Republic, no doubt especially when the *publicani* were involved.

Although no explicit testimony for the practice exists, it is conceivable that conversions also operated in the other direction, i.e. commodities being used to pay a nominally cash-based tax. *Aestimatio*, the substitution of commodities for cash in making payments, was a familiar practice.

pondo olei in annos singulos multat... Thysdritanos propter humilitatem civitatis certo numero frumenti multat.

[38] Cic. *Verr.* II 3.191: *cum iis, credo, qui benignitate adducti per beneficium et gratiam civitatibus concesserunt ut nummos pro frumento darent.*

[39] Cic. *Verr.* II 3.191: *video Philomeliensibus expedire, quanti Ephesi sit frumentum, dare potius in Phrygia quam Ephesum portare aut ad emendum frumentum Ephesum pecuniam et legatos mittere.*

[40] Cic. *Verr.* II 3.192: *hoc enim magistratus in provincia adsequi potest, ut ibi accipiat ubi est carissimum.* Verres, of course, did much more than just this.

[41] Cic. *Verr.* II 3.192: *ideo valet ista ratio aestimationis in Asia, valet in Hispania, valet in iis provinciis in quibus unum pretium frumento esse non solet.* See also: Cic. *Verr.* II 1.95; *Pis.* 86; Livy 43.2.12.

[42] Cic. *Font.* 17: *Obiectum est etiam quaestum M. Fonteium ex viarum munitione fecisse, ut aut ne cogeret munire aut id, quod munitum esset, ne improbaret.*

[43] Jones (1966) 173; Wallace (1938) *passim.*

[44] Oliver (1989) 254–8, n. 235: Διοσκώρῳ Ἡφαιστίωνος καὶ Πιεσῆϊ Ὀσίριος καὶ ἄλλοις: ἀργύριον ἀντὶ πυροῦ καταβάλλιν ὑμᾶς ἐκω λύσαμεν. See also: Rathbone (1997) 198.

Caesar employed *aestimatio* to help ease a debt crisis in the 40s.[45] His measure allowed debtors to pay their creditors with goods instead of cash at a state-imposed price level. Evidence for the use of *aestimatio* in taxation (though not Roman taxation) comes from a second century BCE inscription recording the decision of Quintus and Marcus Minucius who arbitrated a dispute between the inhabitants of Genua and the Veiturii.[46] As part of the settlement the brothers decided that the Veiturii were to pay 400 *victoriati* to the Genuates each year as a *vectigal* for certain land. If the Veiturii failed to pay this sum, the Genuates could require them to hand over a twentieth of the grain crop and a sixth of the wine produced on the land in question. Though payment in coin was obviously preferable, the option of a payment in kind was a pragmatic alternative especially if a region was not fully monetized. Cicero reports that some cities in Asia built ships for the Romans *ex pecunia vectigali populi Romani*.[47] Though the term *aestimatio* is not applied to these contributions, it is likely that the ships were provided in lieu of cash. Obviously in this case low levels of monetization would not have been the motive behind the conversion. Presumably the Romans needed the ships to combat piracy. If no explicit references to the use of *aestimatio* in taxation exist, it may be due to the predominance of commodity-based taxation in the Republic or to the government's ability to tailor tax demands to taxpayers.

5.2.2 *Government Expenses*

Equally important for understanding the governmental monetary zone is the question of how and in what form expenditures were made. To what extent did the state rely on coinage to make payments? Although here again the quantity and quality of our evidence precludes definitive statements, it is relatively clear that the state and its agents made payments both in kind and in coin.

The main expenditures of the Roman government in the late Republic were the army, the *annona*, public works and magistrates' allowances.

[45] Caes. *B Civ.* 3.1: *cum fides tota Italia esset angustior neque creditae pecuniae solverentur, constituit, ut arbitri darentur; per eos fierent aestimationes possessionum et rerum, quanti quaeque earum ante bellum fuisset, atque hae creditoribus traderentur.* See also: Suet. *Iul.* 42 and Cicero *Fam.* 9.18.4

[46] *CIL* I^2 584.

[47] Cic. *Verr.* II 1.89: *Decem enim naves iussu L. Murenae populus Milesius ex pecunia vectigali populi Romani fecerat, sicut pro sua quaeque parte Asiae ceterae civitates.*

The *annona* was obviously a payment in kind,[48] but how did Rome pay for the other big budget items, especially the army? Although Frier has cast doubt on Crawford's argument (at least on the basis of the evidence he provided) that army costs correlate closely with annual emissions of coinage,[49] coins undoubtedly formed a major portion of military expenses. Polybius states that military salaries were paid in coin, while both Cicero and Livy link the soldiers' *stipendium* to coinage.[50] Sallust has Marius, addressing a Roman audience, note how difficult it was to prepare for war while sparing the treasury.[51] On paper, the annual cost in salary for one Roman legion might have been half a million *denarii*,[52] and a number of sources indicate that armies required large quantities of cash.[53] However, there are good reasons to suppose that a soldier typically received far less than his nominal salary in cash. Polybius tells us that sums were deducted from a soldier's salary for his food and equipment.[54] Although Gaius Gracchus apparently tried to abolish the clothing deductions, it is unclear whether or not he succeeded.[55] Evidence concerning the practices of the Imperial army suggest the ways in which army paymasters might have 'economized' on coinage. Duncan-Jones notes:

> There were very heavy clawbacks for food, clothing, etc. illustrated in surviving financial statements of soldiers serving in Egypt in the first century which show the soldier as retaining in cash less than half the payment nominally due to him (there was also a compulsory savings scheme).[56]

In addition, as William Metcalf has pointed out, since many of the military's requirements could be and were met locally, "the area of

---

[48] Though as the *annona* expanded, the state resorted to purchasing some of the necessary grain. See, for example, Cic. *Q.Fr.* 2.5.1.

[49] Crawford (1974) 694. Frier (1981) 293 argues that "Crawford's statistics do not prove the existence of this relationship to more than an exceptionally modest extent" though Frier concedes his "strong suspicion, a priori, that there is a considerable positive relationship, though perhaps not one of the character and degree favored by Crawford."

[50] Polyb. 6.39; Cic. *Font.* 13, *Pis.* 88, *Fam.* 10.32.1; Livy 23.48.5; 40.35.4.

[51] Sall. *Iug.* 85.3: *Bellum parare simul et aerario parcere... asperius est.*

[52] This is a conservative estimate, assuming a legion of 4,200 and an annual salary of HS 450. Roth (1999) 20 notes, however, that there was "no regulation size for the republican legion, and its strength varied from year to year." Crawford (1974) 695 suggests 1.5 million *denarii*.

[53] E.g. App. *B.Civ.* 5.5; Cic. *Font.* 13; Dio Cass. 42.49.

[54] Polyb. 6.39. See also: Roth (1999) 224.

[55] Plut. *C. Gracch.* 5.

[56] Duncan-Jones (1990) 44.

financial obligation most likely to have been met non-monetarily is the military one."[57] References to foraging, requisition, plunder and 'voluntary' or forced contributions from allies and enemies indicate that much of the army's needs for food, clothing, fodder, shelter, transportation and other supplies and services could be met without the outlay of cash.[58] Furthermore, Rome's allies and provincial governors sometimes sent supplies directly to Roman armies.[59] Cicero, for example, reports that Marcus Fonteius, while governing Transalpine Gaul, "requisitioned large troops of cavalry to serve in the wars then being waged... large sums of money to provide these with pay, and enormous quantities of corn to enable us to carry on the war in Spain."[60] We even hear of generals who are able to conduct military operations without receiving either money or grain from Rome. Livy reports, for example, that in 180 BCE messengers from Quintus Fulvius Flaccus in Spain told the Senate that his army did not need money or food sent to them.[61] Furthermore, though Cicero voted to provide Caesar's army in Gaul with money, the orator stated in the *De Provinciis Consularibus* his belief that booty could have supplied all that army's needs.[62] Bonuses, rewards and discharge payments provide further proof that soldiers regularly received assets other than coinage in compensation for their service.[63] As retirement 'bonuses' the government frequently distributed land to veterans. The Roman army required large amounts of cash to operate effectively but it is likely that in kind revenues sometimes financed a significant fraction of the state's largest budget item.

Two areas of expenditure where the government likely did rely quite heavily on coinage are public works and allowances to magistrates. The immense amount of public and quasi-public building at Rome in the second and first centuries BCE required vast quantities of labor

---

[57] Metcalf (1995) 146.

[58] Roth (1999) 117–55 provides ample documentation but notes (page 143) that Roman armies rarely requisitioned housing for troops.

[59] For contributions made by allies see Roth (1999) 227–30.

[60] Cic. *Font.* 13: *magnos equitatus ad ea bella, quae tum in toto orbe terrarum a populo Romano gerebantur, magnas pecunias ad eorum stipendium, maximum frumenti numerum ad Hispaniense bellum tolerandum imperavit.*

[61] Livy 40.35.4: *nec stipendio quod mitti soleret nec frumento portato ad exercitum in eum annum opus esse.*

[62] Cic. *Prov. Cons.* 28: *Illum enim arbitrabar etiam sine hoc subsidio pecuniae retinere exercitum praeda ante parta et bellum conficere posse*

[63] Suetonius, for example, reports that Caesar distributed slaves to his soldiers (*Iul.* 26). See also Shatzman (1972) 177–205.

and building material, but there is no evidence (except in the case of road-building and maintenance)[64] to suggest that the Romans acquired them through requisition or *corvée*. Polybius refers to public works as the largest part of the state budget.[65] The activities of various censors also show that they relied chiefly on money to finance public building. The sums granted them are often described as a fraction or multiple of a year's revenue,[66] while the costs of public works are recorded in terms of coinage.[67] Fenestella indicates the potential size of such expenditures, reporting that 180 million *sesterces* were granted to the urban praetor Q. Marcius Rex for the construction and repair of aqueducts in 144 BCE.[68] In 209 BCE the Senate used several hundred pounds of gold to pay contractors to supply clothing to the army operating in Spain, suggesting that the state may have employed bullion to pay for large contracts.[69] *Manubiae* (money derived from the sale of booty), fines and, on at least one occasion, *aurum coronarium* also helped financed public building.[70] There is little indication, however, concerning when and how the government disbursed funds to those who won public contracts.[71]

Magistrates both at Rome and in the provinces were also given cash to facilitate the performance of their duties. We rarely hear much concerning these allowances unless they were misused or the unused portion was returned to the treasury. Cicero returned a million *sesterces* to the

---

[64] *CIL* I² 593.17–9; Cic. *Font.* 17.

[65] Polyb. 6.13.

[66] Livy 40.46.16; 44.16.9. Livy (24.18.2) attributes the vigor with which the censors of 214 BCE pursued the regulation of morals to the emptiness of the treasury which prevented them from letting contracts for public building: *censores, uacui ab operum locandorum cura propter inopiam aerarii, ad mores hominum regendos animum aduerterunt castigandaque uitia quae, uelut diutinis morbis aegra corpora ex sese gignunt, eo enata bello erant.*

[67] For example, *CIL* I² 809, part of an early 1st century BCE contract, provides costs in *sesterces* per foot for road repairs at Rome. *CIL* I² 808 also records sums in *sesterces* for work on various stretches of the Via Caecilia.

[68] Quoted by Frontin. *Aq.* 17.

[69] Livy 27.10.11–3.

[70] E.g.: Servius Fulvius financed the construction of a wall with *manubiae* (*CIL* I² 635). The *aediles* of 193 BCE used *pecunia* from fines imposed on grazers to build two porticos and a wharf (Livy 35.10.12) and the following year's *aediles* also built a portico with money from fines (Livy 35.41.10). Domitius Calvinus used *aurum coronarium* to rebuild the *Regia* (Dio Cass. 48.42.4–5). See De Ruggiero (1925) 213–9 for other examples.

[71] Strong (1968) 98 suggested that those who won contracts for building maintenance would receive the money immediately, while for new works half the money would be paid right away and half when the work was done (on the model of *CIL* I² 125, which records a building contract from Puteoli). De Ruggiero (1925) 200 hypothesized that there was no standard practice and that the matter was left to the decision of the magistrate who let the contract.

treasury after governing Cilicia, though his staff had hoped to receive a share of the money.[72] Other magistrates apparently left their allowances to earn interest either at Rome or with the *publicani*.[73] Magistrates responsible for games received some state funds, though increasingly in the late Republic they used their personal fortunes and provincial contributions to supplement the allotted sums.[74] It is unclear how much money the state provided but Cicero gives us some idea of how much a magistrate might receive from a province. In a letter to his brother in 60 BCE Cicero praises Quintus for freeing Asia from an "unjust and heavy *vectigal*" imposed on behalf of the *aediles*.[75] Quintus, while governing the province, had banned awards of *pecunia* for games. Cicero reveals that an *aedile* might expect to receive as much as HS 200,000 from the province and that this had become a regular practice for those giving games at Rome. Dio reports that in 43 BCE the treasury was so empty that "not even the festivals... were celebrated, except some minor ones for form's sake."[76] This suggests that such events, while certainly not as expensive as the army, could still be a significant drain on the state's supply of cash.

The Roman government required large quantities of money in order to operate effectively. While coinage was probably used extensively to meet government obligations in most instances, the Romans were able to use other assets at least partially to fund the army and the *annona*, two very substantial portions of the budget. Minting levels reflect the state's demand for money and it is clear that the mint's output rose dramatically in the late Republic. It remains unclear, however, whether the proportion of the state's obligations met with coinage also increased.

5.2.3 *Internal Circulation*

A major characteristic of Rome's state financial system is decentralization. Magistrates and generals had relatively independent control

[72] Cic. *Att.* 7.1.6.

[73] Cic. *Leg. Man.* 37 and *Verr.* II 3.168–9 (Cicero here indicates that taking interest from the *publicani* was exceptional behavior).

[74] Cic. *Q. Fr.* 1.1.26; Plut. *Caes.* 5.8–9. See also the *Lex Colonia Genetivae* (*CIL* I[2] 594, Tablet b, Col. I, lines 20–9) which may reflect practices at Rome, and Mommsen (1894) vol. 4, 216–7.

[75] Cic. *Q. Fr.* 1.1.26.

[76] Dio Cass. 46.31.4: τοσαύτη γὰρ ἀχρηματία τὸ δημόσιον τότε ἔσχεν ὥστε μηδὲ τὰς πανηγύρεις τὰς ἐν τῷ καιρῷ ἐκείνῳ γενέσθαι ὀφειλούσας ἐπιτελεσθῆναι, ἔξω βραχέων τινῶν ὁσίας ἕνεκα.

of many kinds of revenues and expenditures. Governors as well as communities could and did mint their own coins. Furthermore, public money was stored not just at Rome but in both public and private hands throughout the provinces. Thus it is necessary to consider briefly the circulation of money and pecuniary assets within the governmental monetary zone. Such internal circulation did not, of course, involve market transactions, but it does shed light on the government's attitude towards and use of money.

A considerable amount of public money was deposited with the *publicani* and seems to have earned no interest (at least not for the state).[77] Other sums were in the hands of generals and provincial governors and might pass between them. Thus Cicero reports that Fonteius transferred to Spain money acquired in Gaul.[78] Similarly, money acquired by Lucullus in the Mithridatic war was apparently transferred directly to Pompey in order to finance the war against the pirates.[79] Roman generals often held large sums of money, acquired in the course of war, but, as J. Bradford Churchill has persuasively argued, these funds remained public property.[80] Such money could be spent on buildings, feasts, games or the general's own soldiers and staff but whatever remained was legally due to the *aerarium*.[81] Plutarch's account of the delayed triumph of Lucullus indicates that, although the general had turned over some money to the treasury and transferred other amounts to Pompey, he retained control of a substantial sum for several years.[82]

Roman officials seem to have regularly transported large quantities of coinage over long distances. In fact, nearly every surviving reference to the shipment of money concerns public rather than commercial funds.[83] Despite having at their disposal the financial networks of the *publicani* as well as recourse to *permutatio*, magistrates physically brought much revenue into and away from Rome. They were clearly aware of the dangers involved in such activity. Cato the Younger invented special

[77] Cic. *Verr.* II 3.168.
[78] Cic. *Font.* 13.
[79] Plut. *Luc.* 37.
[80] Churchill (1999) 109. Cf. Shatzman (1972) 176.
[81] As Churchill (1999) 101–9 argues, partly on the basis of the charges brought against Pompey concerning the *manubiae* his father acquired from Asculum in 89 BCE (Plut. *Pomp.* 4.1–3).
[82] Plut. *Luc.* 37.
[83] Plut. *C. Gracch.* 6; *Luc.* 37; *Cat. Min.* 38.1; Cic. *Fam.* 2.17; Livy 27.10.11–3, 40.35.4; App. *B Civ.* 3.11

containers so that money in his charge could be recovered in case of shipwreck,[84] while Cicero insured "from the danger of transport" the money he returned to Rome.[85] The fact that the state had to move coinage from region to region suggests that their financial institutions were insufficiently developed.

The decentralization of the government's finances was in many respects a source of strength since it allowed individual commanders and governors to solve problems without having to wait for supplies, money or permission from Rome. The system, however, did have some drawbacks. With its funds dispersed throughout the Mediterranean the senate could determine only with great difficulty the monetary resources available to it at any given time. This would severely impair the government's ability to plan for the future. Decentralization also facilitated embezzlement and fraud. Furthermore, by allowing funds to remain in private hands without due compensation or in the hands of generals indefinitely, the government failed to maximize revenues and manage its finances as efficiently as possible.

5.2.4 *Conclusion*

The Roman government minted large numbers of coins annually throughout the late Republic. This alone demonstrates that the state was highly monetized and had a considerable demand for coinage. However, my analysis of Roman revenues and expenditures shows that the government's need for coinage did have limits. In its interactions with other monetary zones the Roman state did not arbitrarily demand coinage. Instead the government taxed each zone through the assets most readily available to it. By means of intermediaries such as the *publicani* some of those assets were then converted into coinage. Similarly Roman expenditure took the form of both cash and commodities. The government made many payments without using coinage and others at least partially in kind. In fact, the government and its agents made use of nearly every kind of asset or financial instrument for which we have evidence. Like Cato's *vilicus* the Roman state had many different *rationes* and used them all. The government displayed great flexibility and versatility in its management of both money and other assets. Coinage was

---

[84] Plut. *Cat. Min.* 38.1

[85] Cic. *Fam.* 2.17.

very important but not all-important. Government demand for coinage was high but the use of other assets could mitigate that demand.

5.3 The Commercial Monetary Zone: Coinage in Long-distance Trade

The volume of long-distance trade grew dramatically in the late Republic as Roman and Italian traders spread throughout the Mediterranean basin in the wake of Roman imperialism. Gaul was packed with Roman traders,[86] who, along with their Italian counterparts, also formed substantial communities at Delos[87] and in North Africa.[88] Such was the importance of these merchants and ship-owners, according to Cicero, that the Romans had often gone to war to protect their interests.[89] Keith Hopkins writes of "the commercialization of the Roman economy"[90] noting that "the number of dated wrecks found from the last two centuries BCE is three times greater than in the previous two centuries"[91] and observing "the growth of specialist intermediaries."[92] Certainly bankers and other financial professionals are increasingly apparent.[93] The Roman elite probably invested in trade,[94] using networks of slaves and freedmen to manage their ventures.[95] In the second century BCE we also begin to see evidence for *collegia* of Italian traders in both Italy and the East.[96] Geoffrey Rickman dates the development of substantial commercial quarters at Rome to this same period.[97]

Hopkins saw coinage as the main engine of this commercialization, arguing that "an increase in the volume of inter-regional trade depended upon an increase in the volume of money to finance it. Mer-

---

[86] Cic. *Font.* 11: *Referta Gallia negotiatorum est, plena civium Romanorum.*

[87] Frank (1935) 276; Rauh (1993) 339.

[88] Sall. *Iug.* 64.5: *negotiatores, quorum magna multitudo Uticae erat.*

[89] Cic. *Leg. Man.* 11: *Maiores nostri saepe mercatoribus aut naviculariis nostris iniuriosius tractatis bella gesserunt; Verr.* II 5.149: *Quot bella maiores nostros et quanta suscepisse arbitramini, quod cives Romani iniuria adfecti, quod navicularii retenti, quod mercatores spoliati dicerentur?*

[90] Hopkins (1980) 105. See also: Verboven (1997) 40–1.

[91] Hopkins (1980) 105.

[92] Hopkins (1980) 102.

[93] Barlow (1978) 233; Andreau (1999) 132.

[94] Veyne (1979) 261–80; Gabba (1980) 91; Gianfrotta (1980) 103; Nash (1987) 90; Rauh (1993) 340.

[95] D'Arms (1981) 145; Brunt (1983) 314; Kirschenbaum (1987) *passim.*

[96] Frederiksen (1959) 118; Rauh (1993) 30–4.

[97] Rickman (1971) 121.

chants and their customers needed money to buy what was traded."[98] Similarly Claude Nicolet refers to money as the most important "technical underpinning" of commerce in antiquity.[99] By 'money' in these contexts both scholars were referring to coinage. But to what extent did Roman and Italian traders use coinage? The answer might appear rather self-evident, but it is worth recalling the many ancient peoples, such as the Phoenicians, who, despite conducting extensive long-distance trade, were nevertheless quite slow to adopt coinage.[100] Given the fact that Roman merchants used some assets other than coinage to facilitate transactions, it is necessary to evaluate the evidence for commercial monetization.

As with public funds,[101] little information survives concerning the transportation of private funds for commercial purposes. Silver coinage, which Keith Hopkins described as "the most important element in financing long-distance trade,"[102] has failed to turn up in any quantity in shipwrecks. This may be due to the extraordinary care with which large sums of money were transported but, if this is the case, why is Roman coinage so late in arriving in areas known to have been Rome's major suppliers of slaves and other luxury goods? The *denarius* appeared in Asia Minor, Southern Greece and Syria only at the very end of the Republic or in the early Empire.[103] Gaul provides a clear-cut example. As Crawford observed, "If Roman coinage barely penetrated southern Gaul before Caesar, the same cannot be said of Italian pottery and amphorae."[104] Italian traders were exchanging wine for Gallic slaves well before *denarii* arrived in the region in substantial numbers. The zone of circulation of Roman coinage did expand in the late Republic but this cannot be attributed entirely to traders.[105] If Roman traders can turn up well before Roman coins, clearly these merchants did not need Roman coinage in order to conduct their business.

What of gold? As I discussed in Chapters 2 and 3, the evidence for the use of gold bullion or foreign gold coins is slim. Nevertheless,

---

[98] Hopkins (1980) 106.

[99] Nicolet (1994a) 630.

[100] Kraay (1964) 88; Snell (1995) 1496.

[101] Andreau (1999) 117.

[102] Hopkins (1980) 106. Under the Empire gold coinage took over this role. See Hopkins (1995/6) 61–3.

[103] Kinns (1987); Price (1987); Baldus (1987).

[104] Crawford (1985) 168.

[105] Travaglini (1988) 76 attributes the monetization of Apulia in part to Gracchan colonization.

Cicero's reference to bans on the export of gold and silver from Italy,[106] and, in particular, his description of the behavior of the quaestor Publius Vatinius at Puteoli in 63 BCE[107] strongly suggest an important, if unquantifiable, role for bullion in long-distance trade.[108] Obviously gold's compactness and high value relative to weight would have made it an ideal choice for commercial exchange but underwater archaeology has thus far failed to turn up much evidence for the use of gold in long-distance trade. Despite Cicero's ship full of gold,[109] neither gold coinage nor bullion has emerged from Roman shipwrecks in any significant quantity.[110] If bullion was a critical commercial tool, it has thus far failed to reveal itself in the archaeological record.

While it is undeniable that coinage and bullion were sometimes transported over long distances in the Mediterranean, religious, military and governmental considerations account for the bulk of the transfers of which we hear. Many generals, of course, brought gold and silver back to Rome as booty and many communities sent gold as *aurum coronarium.* According to Cicero every year Jews exported gold from Italy and every other province as contributions to the Temple in Jerusalem, not for the purpose of commerce.[111] The need to pay soldiers must have prompted the movement of considerable amounts of coinage. Livy reports that in 180 BCE Quintus Fulvius Flaccus informed the senate that his army in Spain did not require "the pay which was customarily sent."[112] This suggests that, at the time, Rome usually sent coinage to Spain to cover military salaries. In his account of the war with Jugurtha, Sallust twice mentions the transport of pay (*stipendium*) for the army from Italy to North Africa.[113] Furthermore Velleius Paterculus refers to quaestors who

---

[106] Cic. *Flac.* 67: *Exportari aurum non oportere cum saepe antea senatus tum me consule gravissime iudicavit.*

[107] Cic. *In Vatinium* 12.

[108] As a number of scholars have suspected, e.g.: Crawford (1977b) 52; Harl (1996) 50; Verboven (1997) 67; (2003) 62.

[109] Cic. *Paradoxa Stoicorum* 20: *Auri navem evertat gubernator an paleae, in re aliquantulum, in gubernatoris inscitia nihil interest.*

[110] Parker (1992) 17 and 30. Presumably, however, shippers would have expended much greater effort to recover such a cargo.

[111] Cic. *Flac.* 67: *cum aurum Iudaeorum nomine quotannis ex Italia et ex omnibus nostris provinciis Hierosolymam exportari soleret.*

[112] Livy 40.35.4: *Hi cum duo secunda proelia, deditionem Celtiberiae, confectam provinciam nuntiassent, nec stipendio quod mitti soleret nec frumento portato ad exercitum in eum annum opus esse.*

[113] Sall. *Iug.* 86.1; 104.3.

convey *pecunia* to Rome from the eastern provinces in the forties BCE.[114] Although χρήματα, like *pecunia*, can have a range of meanings beyond simply 'money' or 'coinage,'[115] descriptions in Greek sources of Romans transporting χρήματα may also refer to coinage. For example, Plutarch reports that Lucullus sent χρήματα to Pompey in Spain in 74 BCE,[116] while Appian mentions soldiers in Octavius's company in 43 BCE who were "engaged in conveying... money to the army in Macedonia, or bringing other money and tribute... to Brundisium."[117] On only one occasion is the long-distance movement of coinage attributed to trade and in that instance we are explicitly told that the coins functioned as a commodity (*loco mercis*).[118]

The *tesserae nummulariae* provide some evidence for the movement of coinage. These small tags, it is now generally agreed, were attached to bags of coins to certify that they had been tested and counted.[119] There is do doubt that certified bags of money would save time and lower transaction costs when large payments were being made but, unfortunately, it is far from certain who used the *tesserae* and for what purpose. If businessmen or bankers used the *tesserae*, as some suppose,[120] then their distribution must reflect some aspect of the commercial movement of coinage. But, as Andreau suggests,[121] the *publicani* might be responsible for the *tesserae*, using them for transactions with the state and within or among tax-farming companies. In this case, the *tesserae* would not provide any useful information for the study of Roman commerce. Whoever used these tags—and there seems to be no compelling reason to believe that their use was exclusive to one particular group of

---

114 Vell. Pat. 2.62: *pecunias etiam, quae ex transmarinis provinciis Romam ab quaestoribus deportabantur.*

115 Seaford (2004) 16.

116 Plut. *Luc.* 5.2: συνέπραξεν ὁ Λούκουλλος προθυμότατα πεμφθῆναι τὰ χρήματα, and *Pomp.* 20.1: ἔσπευσεν ἀποσταλῆναι τὰ χρήματα.

117 App *B Civ.* 3.11: καὶ ἕτεροι στρατιῶται σὺν αὐτοῖς, οἱ μὲν ἀποσκευὰς ἢ χρήματα φέροντες ἐς τὴν Μακεδονίαν, οἱ δὲ ἕτερα χρήματα καὶ φόρους ἐξ ἐθνῶν ἄλλων ἐς τὸ Βρεντέσιον. See also Dio Cass. 45.3.2: ... καὶ μάλισθ' ὅτι καὶ χρήματα πολλὰ καὶ στρατιώτας συχνοὺς συμπροπεμφθέντας εἶχεν. Other examples: Plut. *C. Gracch.* 6; *Cat. Min.* 38.1; *Ant.* 67.5–6 and *Brut.* 23.4–5.

118 Plin. *HN* 33.46: *is, qui nunc victoriatus appellatur, lege Clodia percussus est; antea enim hic nummus ex Illyrico advectus mercis loco habebatur.*

119 Herzog (1919); Couch (1929) 105–7; Crawford (1970) 45; Barlow (1978) 117; Verboven (1994) 120; Andreau (1999) 88–9; Bogaert (2000) 52.

120 Couch (1929) 107; Barlow (1978) 117–8; Bogaert (2000) 53.

121 Andreau (1999) 89.

professionals—they are rarely found outside of Italy and thus indicate, at best, medium-distance coin movement.[122]

The lack of evidence for the movement of coinage in the service of Roman commerce does not prove that merchants made little use of coins. It does, however, suggest that coinage was most useful at the end points of trade, in the markets where goods were bought and sold. The finds of coins in the excavations of market places and the references to coins as a means of exchange and unit of account in Roman texts establish the substantial role that coinage played in commerce. When Cicero describes the magnitude of Roman commerce with Gaul he declares that "not a penny changes hands in Gaul without the transaction being recorded in the books of Roman citizens."[123] Coins facilitated trade in Gaul and elsewhere, but, if most trade was reciprocal, those coins need not come from or return to Rome. It seems likely, on the basis both of ancient descriptions of trade and simple economic rationality, that most ancient trade was reciprocal.

It is noteworthy that ancient writers seem to conceive of long-distance trade as being a balanced exchange of commodities between cities or regions. It is not that they see such exchange as *barter* but merely that both regions have commodities to offer. According to Diodorus, for example, the Romans brought wine to Gaul with which they acquired slaves.[124] Polybius describes trade at Byzantium in similar terms:

> the most plentiful supplies and best qualities of cattle and slaves reach us from the countries lying round the Pontus, while among luxuries the same countries furnish us with abundance of honey, wax, and preserved fish, while of the superfluous produce of our countries they take olive-oil and every kind of wine. As for corn there is a give-and-take, they sometimes supplying us when we require it and sometimes importing it from us...[125]

For Polybius long-distance commerce seems to involve the exchange of surplus produce. Both parties have commodities to offer for sale. Coinage could, of course, be present to facilitate transactions but it was mer-

---

[122] Crawford (1970) 45.

[123] Cic. *Font.* 11: *nummus in Gallia nullus sine civium Romanorum tabulis commovetur.*

[124] Diod. Sic. 5.26.3.

[125] Polyb. 4.38: πρὸς μὲν γὰρ τὰς ἀναγκαίας τοῦ βίου χρείας τά τε θρέμματα καὶ τὸ τῶν εἰς τὰς δουλείας ἀγομένων σωμάτων πλῆθος οἱ κατὰ τὸν Πόντον ἡμῖν τόποι παρασκευάζουσι δαψιλέστατον καὶ χρησιμώτατον ὁμολογουμένως, πρὸς δὲ περιουσίαν μέλι κηρὸν τάριχος ἀφθόνως ἡμῖν χορηγοῦσιν. δέχονταί γε μὴν τῶν ἐν τοῖς παρ' ἡμῖν τόποις περιττευόντων ἔλαιον καὶ πᾶν οἴνου γένος. σίτῳ δ' ἀμείβονται ποτὲ μὲν εὐκαίρως διδόντες ποτὲ δὲ λαμβάνοντες.

chandise that flowed back and forth between markets, not coins. The same process can be observed in Varro's discussion of estates and their access to transportation. It is not simply the case that roads and rivers allow goods to be taken away from an estate to be sold for money; they also allow goods to reach the estate from outside.[126] Although the evidence is admittedly slight, it seems that the Romans considered unidirectional trade to be unusual. Thus Caesar notes that the Germans "give access to traders rather to secure purchasers for what they have captured in war than to satisfy any craving for imports."[127] Even when coinage is mentioned in long-distance exchange, it appears only as an option, not the sole or regular means of acquiring goods. So, in a discussion of the island of Aethaleia and its iron mines, Diodorus notes that merchants purchased ingots there "in exchange either for money or for goods."[128] It seems as though even those who apparently make a distinction between purchase and barter accept as commonplace the use of commodities to acquire other commodities. So, for example, when Pliny the Elder reports that Gaius Hirrius *lent* 6000 eels to Caesar for triumphal banquets, he explains that this was because Hirrius refused to accept money or goods in exchange for them ('*nam permutare quidem pretio noluit aliave merce*').[129] Why use the phrase '*aliave merce*' unless the use of commodities instead of cash to make purchases was a common and reasonable practice?

Finally, one must consider what strategy might provide merchants with the most profits and least risk. Did a command economy move goods from the provinces to Rome and the Roman armies or from far-flung estates to their wealthy owners? Did traders move, as Gary Reger put it, "back and forth between production centers and customers?"[130] Given the fact that producers and consumers were scattered throughout the Mediterranean basin, it was almost certainly more efficient and profitable to acquire a new cargo at any given destination to replace the one just sold off instead of merely shipping back the proceeds of one's

[126] Varro *Rust.* 1.16: *Quae vicinitatis invectos habent idoneos, quae ibi nascuntur ubi vendant, et illinc invectos opportunos quae in fundo opus sunt, propter ea fructuosa. Multi enim habent in praediis, quibus frumentum aut vinum aliudve quid desit importandum; contra non pauci, quibus aliquid sit exportandum.*

[127] Caes. *B Gall.* 4.2: *Mercatoribus est aditus magis eo, ut quae bello ceperint quibus vendant habeant, quam quo ullam rem ad se importari desiderent.*

[128] Diod. Sic. 5.13.2: ταῦτα συναγοράζοντες ἔμποροι καὶ μεταβαλλόμενοι.

[129] Plin. *HN* 9.171.

[130] Reger (1997) 62.

sales.[131] Such an approach gave the merchant twice the opportunity for profit.[132] Based on a combination of both archaeological and literary evidence Filippo Coarelli, for example, has suggested that ships exporting Italian wine to the east returned with Greek art and other luxury goods.[133] Olive oil and ceramics also would have played a role in balancing trade;[134] central Italian products, as Greg Woolf has observed, were notably successful in the late Republic.[135] A. J. Parker has observed "Roman traffic was balanced between 'bulk' cargoes and compound cargoes."[136] This is to be expected since different regions would be able to offer traders and shippers goods of different size and value to fill their holds. How many empty shipwrecks have been discovered? How many shipwrecks just contained coins being sent to buy goods at some destination? Late Republican sources demonstrate both that the Romans recognized the risks involved in transporting coinage and had viable alternatives to the physical transportation of currency. If regional trade imbalances existed, bankers, *publicani* and well-placed friends could help merchants and traders move money by means of *permutationes* and *nomina*.[137]

Much of the movement of Roman coinage was probably due to the needs of Roman armies and the requirements of provincial government, not trade. It was in the interest of merchants and shippers to keep their holds full whenever they sailed. Empty vessels earned no shipping fees for their owners and brought in no profit. Transporting coinage was risky and alternatives were readily available. Coinage certainly facilitated trade but there were ways to do business without coins or, at least, minimize one's dependence on them. While the growth in the Roman coin supply is often seen as a major factor in the increase

[131] A number of scholars assume that this was standard practice in Roman commerce. Nash (1987) 101 claims that "Most of the Mediterranean goods which were given in exchange for slaves were perishable." Duncan-Jones (1990) 49 asserts that "traders whose ships carried foodstuffs in one direction still needed goods for the return voyage." As Parker (1992) 30 states: "coinage was apparently not often carried on board for trading purposes." See also: J.-M. Carrié's 'intervention' in Pekáry (1980) 116.

[132] As Howgego (1995) 92 argues: "even when cargoes were sold for money, it will have been preferable in most circumstances to purchase another cargo for the return journey, on which a profit could also be made."

[133] Coarelli (1983) 45–53.

[134] Verboven (1997) 58–9.

[135] Woolf (1992) 289.

[136] Parker (1992) 20–1.

[137] See Chapter 3.

of trade,[138] the role of financial instruments and institutions was probably greater. The expansion of Roman banking[139] and the creation of business networks throughout the Mediterranean[140] in the late Republic were the two primary developments allowing for the growth of trade. The role of coinage in long-distance trade was important but primarily confined to the endpoint markets where goods were bought and sold. As commercial goods circulated throughout the Roman Empire and beyond, coinage did not need to accompany them since merchants had access to bankers, social networks and religious associations[141] which could provide them with credit and facilitate the long-distance movement of profits. Thus while the Commercial Monetary Zone was highly monetized, traders used financial instruments and institutions to reduce their demand for coinage.

5.4 The Urban Monetary Zone

There is broad consensus among scholars over the importance of coinage in urban areas of the Roman Empire. Crawford describes coinage as "essential to the life of the cities at all social levels,"[142] while Howgego asserts it was "the normal form of exchange for goods, at least in the towns."[143] Duncan-Jones speaks of "urban locations where cash was plentiful" and Keith Hopkins claims that "everyday purchases were made in silver or bronze."[144] Burnett argues that this high level of monetization began around 200 BCE when "there was a full range of denominations small enough to be useful for the everyday needs of retail trading."[145] In this section I will review the evidence in favor of urban monetization but also the practices and institutions that alleviated some of the demand for coinage in Roman cities.

The events surrounding the edict of Gratidianus of the mid-80s BCE constitute the best literary evidence for monetization at Rome. As I noted in Chapter 2, the precise aim of his edict remains uncertain but it

[138] Hopkins (1980) 106.
[139] Barlow (1978) 233.
[140] D'Arms (1981) 145.
[141] See, for example, Rauh (1993); Andreau (1999); Verboven (2002).
[142] Crawford (1970) 42.
[143] Howgego (1992) 29.
[144] Duncan-Jones (1990) 194; Hopkins (1995/96) 61.
[145] Burnett (1987b) 95.

is clear that Gratidianus acted in response to a lack of public confidence in Roman coins.[146] Whether the edict addressed counterfeits, debasement or exchange rates, it certainly restored confidence in Roman coinage or at least in some kinds of Roman coinage. The edict obviously helped the plebs because, as both Cicero and Pliny report, it was so pleased with the measure that it erected statues in honor of Gratidianus throughout the city.[147] Cicero says that no one was ever more popular with the multitude.[148] The incident demonstrates that the lower classes had a great interest in the stability of the coinage and this in turn points to a high level of monetization at Rome.

The urban plebs needed money for a variety of purposes. Dio Chrysostom's description of the monetary needs of the poor urban dweller applies to the Republican period just as well as to the early Empire:

> the poor... have to pay house-rent and buy everything they get, not merely clothes, household belongings, and food, but even the wood to supply the daily need for fire, and even any odd sticks, leaves, or other most trifling thing they need at any time, and when they are compelled to pay money for everything but water, since everything is kept under lock and key, and nothing is exposed to the public except, of course, the many expensive things for sale.[149]

Let us begin by examining the evidence from the late Republic for the role of money in the housing market. Cicero clearly indicates that *tabernae* and *insulae* generated substantial revenues for some wealthy Romans.[150] Plutarch attributes a significant portion of Crassus's wealth to his ownership of real estate at Rome.[151] As Frier has shown, by leasing buildings to middlemen at a discount, wealthy Romans could assure themselves of a regular annual cash income and avoid the risks and difficulties of

---

[146] Cic. *Off.* 3.80.

[147] Cic. *Off.* 3.80: *Et ea res, si quaeris, ei magno honori fuit; omnibus vicis statuae, ad eas tus, cerei; quid multa?* Plin. *HN* 33.132: *igitur ars facta denarios probare, tam iucunda plebei lege, ut Mario Gratidiano vicatim tota statuas dicaverit.*

[148] Cic. *Off.* 3.80: *nemo umquam multitudini fuit carior.*

[149] Dio Chrys. 7.103–7.

[150] Cic. *Fin.* 2.83 (a general reference to the profit derived from *insulae* and *fundi*); *Att.* 14.9 and 14.11 (*tabernae* which Frier (1978/79) 2 says "were presumably lodging houses," Cicero reports an income of HS 100,000 from these buildings); *Att.* 12.32.2 and 16.1.5 (Cicero uses the rents from *insulae* on the Argiletum and Aventine to supply his son with money while staying in Athens); Nepos (*Att.* 14.3) notes that Atticus received all his income from Epirote and urban properties.

[151] Plut. *Crass.* 2.1–6: ὥστε τῆς Ῥώμης τὸ πλεῖστον μέρος ὑπ' αὐτῷ γενέσθαι.

direct management.[152] Whether they received their money directly from tenants or through middlemen, it is reasonably certain that the tenants paid in cash. When Caesar remitted rents in the 40s, the remissions were expressed in terms of coinage.[153]

It is likely that coinage played an important role in supplying the urban poor with food. The plebs was greatly concerned with the price of grain in the city and late Republican politicians curried favor with the masses by selling grain below market cost.[154] As Garnsey notes, "that many Romans had to buy grain is clear from... [texts] describing the popular reaction when wheat prices rose."[155] Conversely great fame could accrue to those who provided grain at low prices.[156] Cicero reports that during his quaestorship he believed himself to be the talk of Rome for having sent a considerable amount of grain to the city when prices were very high.[157]

It is also important to consider the broader food market. Garnsey estimated that "25% of the food energy requirement was derived from sources other than cereals."[158] The state did not subsidize meat, fish, olive oil and wine (except at occasional public banquets), and demand for these foods must have drawn a large group of consumers into the markets. Plutarch records that even Cato the Elder had recourse to the food markets for the "thirty *asses*' worth" of fish or meat he was accustomed to purchase.[159] Varro's *De Re Rustica* reveals the size and importance of the market for foodstuffs in the first century BCE. *Collegia* and other groups or individuals giving banquets and feasts relied on the markets for their supplies.[160] Pliny notes that there was an

---

[152] Frier (1978/79) 1–6.

[153] Dio Cass. 42.51: καὶ τὸ ἐνοίκιον ὅσον ἐς πεντακοσίας δραχμὰς ἦν ἐνιαυτοῦ ἑνος ἀφείς. Suet. *Iul.* 38: *Annuam etiam habitationem Romae usque ad bina milia nummum, in Italia non ultra quingenos sestertios remisit.*

[154] Rickman (1980b) 49.

[155] Garnsey (1991) 82. See Sall. *Hist.* 2.45.

[156] Cic. *Off.* 2.58: *Ne M. quidem Seio vitio datum est, quod in caritate asse modium populo dedit; magna enim se et inveterata invidia nec turpi iactura, quando erat aedilis, nec maxima liberavit.*

[157] Cic. *Planc.* 64: *Vere mehercule hoc dicam: sic tum existimabam, nihil homines aliud Romae nisi de quaestura mea loqui. Frumenti in summa caritate maximum numerum miseram.*

[158] Garnsey (1991) 82.

[159] Plut. *Cat. Mai.* 4.4: ...ὄψον δὲ παρασκευάζεσθαι πρὸς τὸ δεῖπνον ἐξ ἀγορᾶς ἀσσαρίων τριάκοντα.

[160] Varro *Rust.* 3.2.16: *Sed ad hunc bolum ut pervenias, opus erit tibi aut epulum aut triumphus alicuius, ut tunc fuit Scipionis Metelli, aut collegiorum cenae, quae nunc innumerabiles excandefaciunt annonam macelli. Reliquis annis omnibus si non hanc expectabis summam, spero, non tibi decoquet ornithon; neque hoc accidit his moribus nisi raro ut decipiaris. Quotus quisque enim est annus, quo non videas epulum aut triumphum aut collegia non epulari?*

"outcry of the common people" against a market tax.[161] Cicero received a large cash income from the lease of a minor garden.[162] The appearance in Rome of bakeries, dated by Pliny to the early second century, indicates increased reliance on the market for food and the preparation of food.[163] *Tabernae*, which included cook shops and wine bars, became much more evident in the late Republic as well and were "the basic source of daily staples."[164] At Rome and in other cities those residents without their own food preparation facilities relied on the cookshops and food vendors' stalls.[165] Purcell calls Rome "a city of shops, its people a nation of shopkeepers."[166] The importance of the market is also reflected in the role of the aediles who punished those who hoarded grain and artificially raised prices.[167] This concern can also be clearly seen in the *Lex Iulia de annona*.[168]

If the urban poor paid for food and shelter (not to mention clothing and other supplies) with coinage, where did it come from? Some obviously were artisans and shopkeepers who earned money by running their own businesses but this can only account for a small proportion of the population. Many must have earned cash from wage labor. Seasonal labor on farms around Rome (or other Italian cities) certainly provided some income for the poor,[169] but obviously would have to be supplemented during other parts of the year. As Brunt argued, "the common people in the city of Rome had to earn much of their

---

161 Plin. *HN* 19.56: *itaque, Hercules, nullum quam macelli vectigal maius fuit Romae clamore plebis incusantis apud omnes principes donec remissum est portorium mercis huius*. It is unclear when this incident took place.

162 Cic. *Fam.* 16.18.2: *Parhedrum excita, ut hortum ipse conducat. Sic holitorem ipsum commovebis. Helico nequissimus HS ∞ dabat, nullo aprico horto, nullo emissario, nulla maceria, nulla casa. Iste nos tanta impensa derideat? Calface hominem, ut ego Mothonem. Itaque abundo coronis.*

163 Plin. *HN* 18.107–8: *Pistores Romae non fuere ad Persicum usque bellum annis ab urbe condita super DLXXX. ipsi panem faciebant Quirites, mulierumque id opus maxime erat... artoptas iam Plautus appellat in fabula quam Aululariam inscripsit, magna ob id concertatione eruditorum an is versus poetae sit illius, certumque fit Ateii Capitonis sententia cocos tum panem lautioribus coquere solitos, pistoresque tantum eos qui far pisebant nominatos; nec cocos vero habebant in servitiis, eosque ex macello conducebant.*

164 Purcell (1994) 665.

165 Frayn (1993) 161.

166 Purcell (1994) 659.

167 Livy 38.35.5: *Et duodecim clipea aurata ab aedilibus curulibus P. Claudio Pulchro et Ser. Sulpicio Galba sunt posita ex pecunia qua frumentarios ob annonam compressam damnarunt; et aedilis plebi Q. Fulvius Flaccus duo signa aurata uno reo damnato—nam separatim accusaverant—posuit.*

168 *Dig.* 48.12.2. This law could be Augustan.

169 Purcell (1994) 664; Garnsey (1991) 68.

living in casual employment, partly...in the unloading and porterage of goods...partly in the building trade."[170]

Building projects were an established means of distributing largess to the people.[171] Construction and related activities such as the maintenance of buildings and roads channeled substantial quantities of coinage to the Roman lower classes. Although Crassus' force seems to have been composed of slaves,[172] there is good reason to believe that free workers typically provided most construction labor. After all, Cicero considers the construction of walls, harbors, aqueducts, theaters, temples and other buildings in the context of a discussion of generosity by means of *pecunia*.[173] Although explicit testimony concerning the status of Roman builders is lacking, Brunt was surely right that "free labour was extensively employed on public works at Rome."[174] A considerable amount of new construction occurred in and around Rome in the late Republic. Popular politicians financed many of these building projects and must have thereby provided employment for poorer Roman citizens.

Porterage too may have regularly offered a living to a great many able-bodied Romans. As Purcell notes, this is the type of activity "most easily overlooked" but was "the very pulse-rate of a huge conurbation like Rome."[175] The loading and unloading of goods, particularly those entering the city by river, and delivery of such goods within a city with narrow streets and restricted vehicular traffic were "activities actually generated by the city and part of its day-to-day existence."[176] In a city the size of Rome such activities must have consumed an enormous amount of labor. There is, however, little direct evidence for the organization of such work and we cannot exclude the possibility that slaves formed a substantial portion of the labor force.

Coin finds, counterintuitively, may not be an especially good indication of the nature or level of monetization. At Cosa, for example, excavators found 393 coins dating to the town's Republican period of

[170] Brunt (1980) 81.
[171] Brunt (1980) 98.
[172] Plut. *Crass.* 2.4: ...ἐωνεῖτο δούλους ἀρχιτέκτονας καὶ οἰκοδόμους. εἶτ' ἔχων τούτους ὑπὲρ πεντακοσίους ὄντας.
[173] Cic. *Off.* 2.60: *Atque etiam illae impensae meliores, muri, navalia, portus, aquarum ductus omniaque, quae ad usum rei publicae pertinent.*
[174] Brunt (1980) 84.
[175] Purcell (1994) 670.
[176] Purcell (1994) 670.

occupation, more stray finds than any villa can boast, but this amounts to only two coins per year of the settlement's existence.[177] It hardly seems enough for a town that experienced "a kind of Golden Age"[178] in the late Republic and must have served a local population of several thousand.[179] Certainly, stray finds are much more common in urban than rural excavations, but that is what you would expect to see, even if levels of monetization were uniform across city and country. Concentrated settlement would lead to the loss of more coins simply because there were more people around to lose them. Indeed, Greene even suggests "an abundance of coins from a site is likely to indicate bad economic circumstances rather than good" because "site finds are merely the coins which people could afford to lose."[180] Site finds do indicate some degree of monetization, of course, but cannot accurately reflect the composition of the coin stock once circulating there.[181]

The evidence for markets at Rome and elsewhere is more convincing proof of substantial urban monetization. Large cities had permanent structures designed for daily markets while smaller cities and villages had periodic markets and fairs.[182] Many urban residences also featured commercial space for the sale of goods and services.[183] At Rome there was a substantial increase in the development of commercial space starting at the beginning of the second century BCE.[184] Aediles oversaw the markets at Rome and similar officials are attested from other Roman towns.[185] Their existence and role in market regulation indicates that urban markets were becoming increasingly important. Garnsey suggests that the state first became interested in the regulation of markets and traders in the late Republic.[186] Varro clearly indicates that urban markets were the ultimate source of the cash revenue that astute villa

177 Brown et al. (1993) 238.

178 McCann et al. (1987) 176.

179 Rathbone (1981).

180 Greene (1986) 56.

181 As Greene (1986) 57 notes, "small denominations are more easily lost than large ones." Crawford (1970) 43 points out that, while the Roman forum was "littered with coins," they were "mostly bronze."

182 de Ligt and de Neeve (1988) 401–2; Frayn (1993) 4; MacMullen (1970) 337.

183 Garnsey (1976) 130.

184 Frank (1935) 203–4; Rickman (1980b) 19.

185 Frayn (1993) 123; Cic. *Leg.* 3.6: *Suntoque aediles curatores urbis, annonae ludorumque sollemnium.*

186 Garnsey (1988) 215.

owners might collect.[187] He emphasizes the importance of owning farms near cities or at least near transportation to cities in order to sell surplus or specialty produce.[188] Urban demand for clothing or at least the raw materials of clothing should also not be underestimated. Those in larger cities would have recourse to the market for wool and wool-products.[189]

The presence in Rome and other Italian cities of professionals whose work specifically involved the storing, testing, exchange and lending of money is also compelling evidence for the monetization of urban areas in the late Republic. Cicero's writings reveal the presence of bankers, auctions conducted through credit,[190] the long-distance transfer of money from city to city, and the "excellent men who sit *ad Ianum medium*" who knew more about money management than any philosopher.[191] Professional bankers, *argentarii*, appeared in the Roman Forum in the late fourth century,[192] and were followed in the late Republic by *nummularii* who tested and changed money.[193] These professionals spread to other important Italian towns as well. Bankers are known from Tarquinii, Tarentum, Naples, Puteoli and Syracuse.[194] Finds of *tesserae nummulariae* attest to the presence of *nummularii* at Pompeii, Tarquinii, Faesulae, Capua and elsewhere in Italy.[195]

In the Roman west, it is much more difficult to get a sense of the level of urban monetization. While bankers had long been active in the Greek east, there is very little evidence for them in the western provinces before the imperial period.[196] The profusion of local issues in Spain in

---

187 Varro *Rust.* 2.3.10 and 3.2.15–7.

188 Varro *Rust.* 1.16: *Multi enim habent in praediis, quibus frumentum aut vinum aliudve quid desit importandum; contra non pauci, quibus aliquid sit exportandum. Itaque sub urbe colere hortos late expedit, sic violaria ac rosaria, item multa quae urbs recipit, cum eadem in longinquo praedio, ubi non sit quo deferri possit venale, non expediat colere.*

189 Barker (1989) 13.

190 Cic. *Caecin.* 16.

191 Cic. *Off.* 2.87: *Sed toto hoc de genere, de quaerenda, de collocanda pecunia, vellem etiam de utenda, commodius a quibusdam optimis viris ad Ianum medium sedentibus quam ab ullis philosophis ulla in schola disputatur.*

192 Andreau (1999) 30; Bogaert (2000) 44–5.

193 Crawford (1970) 45; Bogaert (2000) 50. Herzog (1919) 6 and Barlow (1978) 70 consider *nummularii* to have been the slaves of *argentarii*. Andreau (1999) 86 argues that the *tesserae*, while certainly the product of coin assayers, are not the work of *nummularii*. Even under this interpretation, however, the *tesserae* remain important evidence for the need for expert coin testers in urban areas in the late Republic.

194 Barlow (1978) 247–58.

195 Herzog (1919) 14; Barlow (1978) 247–58.

196 Howgego (1992) 15: "No inscription records a banker in any western province before the first century A.D." A *tessera nummularia* (*ILLRP* #1023), however, was found

the second and first centuries BCE certainly indicates monetization but, in the absence of literary and epigraphic evidence, it is difficult to determine in what manner the coins were used.[197] Some issues could have facilitated urban trade but others may been minted primarily to pay soldiers or taxes.[198] Coastal areas, influenced by Greeks and Carthaginians, may have already attained a high degree of urban monetization before the arrival of the Romans. In the interior urban monetization no doubt accompanied the gradual Romanization of the provinces.[199]

5.5 Redistribution: Limits to Urban Monetization

The evidence and arguments for urban monetization in the late Republic and early Empire are such that it is easy to forget that public and private redistribution could supply city residents with many different goods and thereby completely bypass markets and coin-based transactions. Government redistribution, private munificence and patronage all contributed to the circulation of goods. Such activities do not alter the thesis that towns were highly monetized but they do moderate it somewhat. Alternate means of distribution existed which complemented and supplemented market exchange. The best known, albeit exceptional, example is the state's role in supplying grain to Rome in the period before 58 BCE. The government used its redistributive powers to collect grain which it transported to Rome and sold below the market price. Although Romans still had to buy the grain, it arrived at least partially by means of a redistributive network.[200]

---

at Arelate in Gallia Narbonensis and Barlow (1978) 257 suggests that L. Titius Strabo might have worked as a banker in Gaul.

[197] Knapp (1987) and Burnett et al. (1992) discuss the various Spanish issues and the problems involved in determining their use.

[198] Crawford (1977b) 52 and Lintott (1993) 73 link the 'Iberian *denarii*' to Roman taxation. Knapp (1987) 20 suggests that "we should assume that native silver issues had either a fiscal or a social purpose... [But] most later bronze issues will have been for financial reasons," i.e. "to supply a local population with small change in order to expedite market transactions." Burnett et al. (1992) 114 suggests that Bolskan minted some issues "to finance Sertorius' military expenditure." Howgego (1995) 58 also notes the "ambiguity" of the Spanish numismatic evidence.

[199] Knapp (1987) 24 observes differences between the coast and the interior of Spain in the late Republic: "The areas along the Ebro were evidently in need of small change, while the interior was not."

[200] See Garnsey, Gallant and Rathbone (1984) 30–44; Rickman (1980) 49.

From 58 BCE a *lex Clodia* provided free grain to as many as 250,000 Roman citizens.[201] This appears to be the only continuously operating and fully public redistribution program of the late Republic. Under the Empire, of course, the *annona* came to include many other foodstuffs. But Clodius's grain law did not support the food requirements of the entire populace. In 46 less than a third of the population of Rome received free grain;[202] the markets and 'internal supply' (i.e. distribution within the *familia*) had to supply the rest. Private and semi-public distributions of food would occasionally supplement these sources. Victorious generals and ambitious politicians often feasted the inhabitants of the city or gave away money to woo the populace.[203] Crassus, for example, gave every Roman provisions (σιτηρέσιον) for three months and Lucullus gave away more than a hundred thousand jars of wine.[204] Varro tells us that such events were not infrequent. When a character in his dialogue observes that "rarely is there a year in which you do not see a banquet or a triumph, or when the clubs do not feast," another replies that "it may fairly be said that there is a banquet every day within the gates of Rome."[205] While this passage indicates that redistributions of food occurred frequently,[206] it does not change the overall picture of Rome as highly monetized. The whole point of Varro's exchange is that banquets, feasts and triumphs make certain kinds of villa production extremely profitable. Rich men and victorious generals did not feed the populace with homegrown produce; they purchased the food in the markets at Rome. As Purcell put it: "the *epulum* would not have been possible without the *taberna*."[207]

Private redistribution might bypass markets altogether if it occurred within the *familia* or through a patron's network of clients. In the first case, one can easily imagine that many wealthy urban households fed

---

[201] Brunt (1962) 69–70; Virlouvet (1994) 25.

[202] Purcell (1994) 648.

[203] Cic. *Off.* 2.58: ...*et si quando aliqua res maior atque utilior populari largitione adquiritur, ut Oresti nuper prandia in semitis decumae nomine magno honori fuerunt.*

[204] Plut. *Crass.* 2.2: ...τρεῖς δὲ μῆνας ἑκάστῳ Ῥωμαίων σιτηρέσιον ἐκ τῶν αὐτοῦ παρασχών; and Plin. *HN* 14.96: *ipse cum rediit ex Asia, milia cadum congiarium divisit amplius centum.*

[205] Varro *Rust.* 3.2.16: *Quotus quisque enim est annus, quo non videas epulum aut triumphum aut collegia non epulari? Sed propter luxuriam, inquit, quodam modo epulum cotidianum est intra ianuas Romae.*

[206] Except perhaps with respect to the feasts of the *collegia.*

[207] Purcell (1994) 685.

their children, relatives and slaves with the produce of various rural properties, supplemented by small urban gardens.[208] Many upper class Romans took pride in eating their own food and drinking their own wine,[209] and, according to Cicero, some Romans bought farms to supply the *familiae* of their expensive seaside villas with foodstuffs.[210] While it is unclear to what extent the wealthy preferred their own produce to that acquired on the market, they certainly grew themselves at least some of what they consumed.[211] Non-market food distribution might even take place outside of the elite. As Garnsey points out:

> the existence of family links between inhabitants of the city and countryside...might have been characterized by a regular or sporadic inflow of food into ordinary Roman households, especially those of recent immigrants from rural communities not far from Rome.[212]

In smaller towns it is likely that a larger proportion of urban residents worked nearby plots of land themselves and so had less need to purchase goods in markets. Nevertheless, reciprocity and gift giving must have played at least a small role in supplementing the diet of most Romans.[213]

Patronage also served as a mechanism for the distribution of goods outside of the marketplace. At the morning *salutatio* a patron would give gifts of food to his supporters, though by the early Empire a cash sum came to replace the food.[214] We know little about the role of patronage in food distribution, but it is unlikely that such activities greatly diminished the demand for money or the level of monetization. Clients could not survive for very long on one meal a day. They also required clothing and shelter.

[208] On the importance of small urban gardens see Plin. *HN* 19.51–7.

[209] Rawson (1976) 93. See Hor. *Epist.* 2.2.160 ff.

[210] Cic. *Leg. agr.* 2.78: *at videmus, ut longinqua mittamus, agrum Praenestinum a paucis possideri. Neque istorum pecuniis quicquam aliud deesse video nisi eius modi fundos, quorum subsidio familiarum magnitudines et Cumanorum ac Puteolanorum praediorum sumptus sustentare possint.* See also: D'Arms (1970) 16.

[211] See Frayn (1993) 59. Peacock and Williams (1986) 61 argue that "we must think in terms of a two-tier system with market exchange playing an important role among the lower echelons of society, while in the larger towns and among the aristocracy, reciprocity and redistribution would have played a more dominant part."

[212] Garnsey (1991) 83.

[213] See: Frayn (1993) 160; Peacock and Williams (1986) 61. Martial's *Xenia* and *Apophoreta* include many poems describing such gifts of food.

[214] Verboven (2002) 195.

It is difficult to estimate the significance of government redistribution, private distributions, patronage and reciprocity for the level of monetization of Roman towns. Only the government could have conducted redistributive operations on a scale large enough to radically reduce market demand but government distribution of foodstuffs was clearly quite limited in the late Republic. Joan Frayn has argued that even the more extensive Imperial distributions of bread, wine and pork did not "affect severely the general trade in these commodities."[215] Wealthy Romans occasionally made massive gifts of food or money to the people of Rome but none undertook to support the population indefinitely. Theirs were grand but limited gestures designed to win popularity and political support. When Crassus undertook to support each citizen of Rome for three months, it was clearly an exceptional undertaking.[216] It is likely that the significance of different types of redistribution varied from city to city and over time. Cities with large populations engaged in non-agricultural activities probably relied much more heavily on markets than smaller towns whose hinterlands could more easily support them. Rome's large population of freedmen and descendants of freedmen had few connections to rural agriculture and had no choice but to rely on the market. Some, of course, might have patrons who could supplement their food supply but they can hardly be expected to have furnished it entirely.[217] It is probably best to think of the market, public and private redistribution, patronage and reciprocity as partially redundant networks providing security in times of crisis. The larger the city, the more likely it would be that the market dominated and the more vulnerable the lower-classes became. Thus, while Whittaker is right to point out that 'internal supply' can account for a significant part of urban demand, it is unlikely that it accounted for a static percentage.[218] Every Roman who did not starve to death probably received some food (or occasional shelter, clothing etc.) from a friend, relative, owner, patron, general or the government. The wealthy may have been more likely to rely on their own estates for much of their food but even Cato bought food in the market and Republican sumptuary laws indicate that

---

[215] Frayn (1993) 159.

[216] Plut. *Crass.* 2.2.

[217] Verboven (2002) 114 argues that "the poorest in Roman society did not generally have a patron to protect them" and suggests that clients typically were not wholly dependent on the generosity of their patrons except in times of crisis.

[218] Whittaker (1985) 60.

wealthy Romans demanded many products that they could not produce themselves.[219]

Aristotle considered the self-sufficient city-state ideal, but even he was aware that every city needed to import some goods.[220] While there is considerable evidence for redistribution and 'internal supply,' no one has suggested that such activity extended beyond basic foodstuffs for the general populace and only the largest and wealthiest *familiae* could supply all their needs without recourse to the market. Redistribution, 'internal supply' and reciprocity certainly met some of the needs of some people but, given the literary and archaeological evidence for urban money use, the market must have supplied most of the needs of most people. Rome's population grew rapidly in the second and first centuries BCE,[221] and it is important to consider the impact of such growth on its demand for goods and services. Larger cities probably relied more heavily on the market and monetary transactions in the marketplace since large cities had greater specialization and inhabitants would be more cut off from the productive hinterland. These considerations suggest that the level of monetization and the demand for coinage increased as urbanization progressed during the late Republic. The availability of banks and credit as well as bullion would moderate this urban demand for coinage somewhat, but the urban monetary zone was certainly as monetized as the commercial zone, and, like the commercial zone, it was growing rapidly.

5.6 The Rural Monetary Zone

As we saw in the previous chapter, those engaged in agriculture had access to a variety of assets with which to make payments and store wealth. Now it is necessary to consider the relative importance of coinage in the rural monetary zone. To do so one must begin by confronting the issue of rural autarchy, that is, the notion that Roman farmers preferred to avoid market exchange as much as possible by producing

---

[219] The *lex Fannia* of 161 BC and its successors the *lex Didia* and *lex Licinia* sought to limit spending on meals and control what was served at them. See Macrob. *Sat.* 3.17.1–13.

[220] Arist. *Pol.* VII 5.1; 6.4. Finley (1985) 125 elaborates on this point: "there is scarcely a city which is self-sufficient in timber, metals, salt, spices, not to mention slaves, hides, semi-precious stones and other commodities that have become necessary amenities for civilized society."

[221] Morley (1996) 39.

for themselves as much of what they consumed as possible. There is a broad scholarly consensus that the Romans advocated self-sufficient agricultural practices,[222] and considerable support for the idea that by choice or necessity farmers tended to follow such recommendations,[223] though some have dissented.[224] This consensus stems from a number of passages in Roman sources but there has yet to be a systematic analysis of the relevant material. Obviously, if Roman farmers were by and large self-sufficient, their demand for and use of coinage would be minimal.[225] In this section I will argue that, although the Romans neither advocated nor practiced self-sufficiency and some coinage did penetrate into the countryside, Roman farmers nevertheless had less need for coins than urban dwellers, merchants or government officials.

Let us begin by considering the Republican sources that have been thought to reflect (and promote) the ideal of self-sufficiency. Cato laid down the most well known rule of thumb: "a *paterfamilias* should be a seller, not a buyer."[226] Finley used this to back up his claim that "the

---

[222] For example: White (1970) 394; Duncan-Jones (1974) 37–8; Percival (1976) 161; Rawson (1976) 93; Knapp (1977) 13; Frayn (1979) 27; D'Arms (1981) 82; Whittaker (1985) 58; Dyson (1985) 77; Meijer (1990) 14–5; de Ligt (1993) 131; Morley (1996) 76; Laurence (1998) 139; Paterson (1998) 165; Horden and Purcell (2000) 151.

[223] What self-sufficiency entailed or on what level it operated tends to vary from scholar to scholar. Some see self-sufficiency as being pursued on the level of the individual farm [for example, Toynbee (1965) 104; Maróti (1976) 109; Finley (1985) 138; Duncan-Jones (1994) 3; Erdkamp (2005) 319] while others view it as a local or regional phenomenon [for example, Brunt (1972) 156; Frayn (1979) 150; Hopkins (1995/96) 61; Campbell (1996) 91]. Partial self-sufficiency is envisioned on the bi-sectorial estate [Carandini (1983) 195], with respect to the production requirements of particular cash crops [Lirb (1993) 268] and for the peasant's diet [de Ligt (1990) 55]. Whittaker (1985) 58, writing of the early Empire, also notes "self-sufficiency with a twist," i.e. the collective self-sufficiency of an individual's scattered estates. As for the motivations behind self-sufficiency, Evans (1981) 441 attributes it to "the inadequacy of Roman land transport," while Halstead (1987) 86 calls it "very hard-headed economic rationality indeed." According to Macve (1985) 253 "the idea of self-sufficiency was largely an economic necessity." See also: Duncan-Jones (1974) 38; Morley (1996) 76.

[224] Veyne (1979) remains the only extended discussion of which I am aware concerning self-sufficiency in the late Republic but many others—though often accepting that some Romans advocated it—have expressed doubts about the *practice* of autarchy at least in some circumstances, particularly on the basis of the archaeological record and the evidence concerning rural markets. See, for example, Frederiksen (1970) 336; de Ligt (1990) 25; (1991) 45–6; (1993) 149; Laurence (1998) 139; Garnsey (1998) 148; Paterson (1998) 158; (2001) 370; Horden and Purcell (2000) 151; Temin (2001) 178; Andreau (2002a) 116–7; Rosenstein (2004) 15. Martin (1971) 253–4 even argues against seeing the late Republican agricultural writers as advocates of self-sufficiency.

[225] Burnett (1987) 96; Duncan-Jones (1994) 3.

[226] Cato *Agr.* 2.7 [translation: Finley (1985) 110]: *Patrem familas vendacem, non emacem esse oportet.*

landowners of antiquity" relished their "independence [both] from the market as buyers, [and] from reliance on others for their own necessities."[227] Varro provides similar remarks. "Who has not heard," he asks, "our fathers called him lazy and extravagant who hung in his storeroom a side of bacon which he had purchased from the butcher rather than got from his own farm?"[228] In another passage Varro emphasizes the ideal productive capacity of the farm:

> Nothing should be bought which can be raised on the place or made by the men on the farm, in general articles which are made of withes and of wood, such as hampers, baskets, threshing-sledges, fans, and rakes; so too articles which are made of hemp, flax, rush, palm fibre, and bulrush, such as ropes, cordage, and mats.[229]

The message seems clear: as much as possible the farm should provide its owner with the food and equipment he might need.

Agricultural manuals are not the only places where seemingly autarchic sentiments appear. In his second speech on Rullus's agrarian law Cicero declared: "he is a luxurious rake—who sells his forests before his vineyards."[230] The point, apparently, is that a forest helps an estate owner remain self-sufficient by providing many materials vital to the operation of the farm while a vineyard can be a considerable drain on an estate's resources. Later in the same speech Cicero mentions that a few people own "the whole district of Praeneste" and speculates that the owners want "farms to assist them in maintaining enormous households and bearing the expenses of country houses at Cumae and Puteoli."[231] Since there certainly were more profitable ways of investing money, the implication seems to be that the owners of the *ager Praenestinus* wanted productive estates that could supply their luxury villas with food they had grown themselves as well as other supplies.

---

[227] Finley (1985) 110.

[228] Varro *Rust.* 2.4.3: *qui non audierit patres nostros dicere ignavum et sumptuosum esse, qui succidiam in carnario suspenderit potius ab laniario quam e domestico fundo?*

[229] Varro *Rust.* 1.22.1: *Quae nasci in fundo ac fieri a domesticis poterunt, eorum nequid ematur, ut fere sunt quae ex viminibus et materia rustica fiunt, ut corbes, fiscinae, tribula, valli, rastelli; sic quae fiunt de cannabi, lino, iunco, palma, scirpo, ut funes, restes, tegetes.*

[230] Cic. *Leg. agr.* 2.48: *Ut in suis rebus, ita in re publica luxuriosus nepos, qui prius silvas vendat quam vineas.*

[231] Cic. *Leg. agr.* 2.78: *at videmus, ut longinqua mittamus, agrum Praenestinum a paucis possideri. Neque istorum pecuniis quicquam aliud deesse video nisi eius modi fundos, quorum subsidio familiarum magnitudines et Cumanorum ac Puteolanorum praediorum sumptus sustentare possint.*

Passages such as the ones quoted above seem to make a reasonably good case at least for an ideal of self-sufficiency, if not for actual practice, but there are good reasons to be skeptical. It is not clear to what extent one can rely on Cato and Varro's knowledge of agricultural practice,[232] and, assuming they are reliable, what conclusions one can draw from them for any farmers outside their presumably elite audience.[233] More importantly, is it correct to interpret their recommendations as encouraging farmers to practice autarchy? A look at the context in which the supposed encouragement appears suggests that it is not.

Let us consider, for example, the context of Cato's recommendation that the *paterfamilias* be a seller not a buyer. The passage describes a whole range of activities to be conducted on the farm:

> Run over the cash accounts, grain accounts, and purchases of fodder... what has been sold, what collected... Give orders that whatever maybe lacking for the current year be supplied... whatever work should be let out be let... Look over the live stock and hold a sale. Sell your oil if the price is satisfactory... Sell worn-out oxen, blemished cattle, blemished sheep, wool, hides, and old wagon, old tools, an old slave, a sickly slave, and whatever else is superfluous. The master should have the selling habit, not the buying habit.[234]

Though there are ample references to selling in this passage, Cato also recommends purchases of fodder, supplies and labor. Cato was concerned about *excess* expenditure, not expenditure *per se*. The point is to use the resources of the farm to maximum advantage. That is why Cato lists, for example, the various jobs slaves can do on festival days or during stormy weather,[235] and why he recommends the sale of superfluous goods. Idle slaves and old livestock must still be fed and so

---

232 As Martin (1971) 81–2 points out, even Varro, while acknowledging the great Cato, found his book to be "très insuffisant." See Varro *Rust.* 1.2.24–8. White (1970) 20 remarks that "Apart from the defects in presentation, there are numerous errors and several examples of sheer fatuity in Cato." Of Varro, Frederiksen (1970) 335 argues that he is "useful only where he draws on his own direct experience; otherwise he is often derivative, muddled or simply fanciful." Spurr (1986) x, however, argues that "the Roman agricultural writers... present reliable information about an Italy they knew well."

233 Martin (1971) 89–90. Cato's ideal farm (*Agr.* 1.7) is 100 *iugera* in size. By contrast, according to Plutarch (*Crass.* 2.7–8) Marius' veterans each received about 23 *iugera*. P. Servilius Rullus proposed 10 *iugera* allotments of Campanian land for his colonists in 64 BCE (Cic. *Leg. agr.* 2.78).

234 Cato *Agr.* 2.5–7.

235 Cato *Agr.* 2.2–4 and 39.

constitute a drain on the estate's resources. Cato states that "a farm is like a man—however great the income, if there is extravagance not much will remain"[236] and "even though work stops, expenses run on nonetheless."[237] Cato accepts that some purchases are necessary and provides a long list of items that the estate owner must buy and where to buy them:

> Tunics, togas, blankets, smocks, and shoes should be bought at Rome; caps, iron tools, scythes, spades, mattocks, axes, harness, ornaments, and small chains at Cales and Minturnae; spades at Venafrum; carts and sledges at Suessa and in Lucania; jars and pots at Alba and at Rome; and tiles at Venafrum...[238]

Lucius Tunnius and Gaius Mennius, we are soon informed, "make the best press-ropes."[239] It is true that many of the purchases Cato recommends, such as the tools mentioned above or the mills for sale at Suessa and Pompeii,[240] are one-time outlays for the construction and set up of a farm, but part-time labor and fodder at least were annual expenses.[241] Furthermore, as has already been noted, Cato does not prohibit the *vilicus* from making purchases or indeed from lending and borrowing but instead advises the *vilicus* not to purchase anything without the knowledge of his master and limit his lending and borrowing to transactions with no more than two or three other households.[242] The neighbors play an important part in Cato's household economy. He states:

> If you are popular in the neighbourhood it will be easier for you to sell your produce, easier to let out your work, easier to secure extra hands. If you build, the neighbours will help you with their work, their teams, and their materials.[243]

Other households, then, provide an estate owner not only with a market for his produce but also supplemental workers whom he can hire

[236] Cato *Agr.* 1.6: *scito idem agrum quod hominem, quamvis quaestvosus siet, si si sumptvosus erit, relinqui non multum.*

[237] Cato *Agr.* 39.2: *cogitato, si nihil fiet, nihilo minus sumptum futurum.*

[238] Cato *Agr.* 135.1: *Romae tunicas, togas, saga, centones, sculponeas; Calibus et Minturnis cuculliones, ferramenta, falces, palas, ligones, secures, ornamenta, murices, catellas; Venafro palas. Suessae et in Lucanis plostra, treblae; Albae, Romae dolia, labra; tegulae ex Venafro.*

[239] Cato *Agr.* 135.3.

[240] Cato *Agr.* 22.3.

[241] Cato *Agr.* 5.4: *operarium, mercennarium, politorem diutius eundem ne habeat die.*

[242] Cato *Agr.* 5.3–4.

[243] Cato *Agr.* 4: *si te libenter vicinitas videbit, facilius tua vendes, opera facilius locabis, operarios facilius conduces; si aedificabis, operis, iumentis, materie adiuvabunt.*

and supplies he may purchase. It is hard to reconcile Cato's remarks concerning the purchase of tools and supplies, the importance of neighbors, and the hiring of labor with the claim that his "entire handbook smacks of" self-sufficiency.[244] It is probable, however, that the coinage necessary for starting up a new farm greatly exceeded that required for the farm's regular operation. Cato makes it clear that part time agricultural labor might receive payment in kind but city-based merchants and workers likely expected cash.[245]

While Varro's interest in the profits of agriculture have long been recognized,[246] his views on the necessary expenses associated with it have received less attention. Like Cato, Varro emphasized the avoidance of excess expenditure rather than of expenditure *per se.* He also stressed the importance of cultivating good relations with neighbors in order to secure access to labor and supplies. Immediately after listing all the items that should be made or grown on the farm, Varro concedes that some items can be bought "if purchased with a view to utility rather than for show... [and] if care is taken to buy them where they can be had of good quality, near by and at the lowest price."[247] Varro presumably condemns the purchase of bacon because it is easy and inexpensive for a farmer to raise his own pigs. On more than one occasion Varro suggests that autarchic behavior could actually be financially ruinous. Wine was a staple of the Roman diet, so one might assume that its production would have to form part of a farmer's basic strategy for self-sufficiency. Varro, however, notes that "there are those who claim that the cost of upkeep [of a vineyard] swallows up the profits."[248] Clearly the outlays involved in the operation of a vineyard were substantial. If even market-oriented vineyards found it difficult to make a profit, surely it would be hard to incorporate wine production into a self-sufficient estate unless it was quite large.

Varro makes clear that the availability of transportation was vital to a farm's profitability since it allowed goods to reach market,[249] but he

---

[244] White (1970) 51.

[245] Only in his discussion of the purchase and assembly of mills does Cato (*Agr.* 21–2) mention prices in *sesterces*, listing the cost of materials, transportation and assembly.

[246] See, for example, D'Arms (1981) 85–6.

[247] Varro *Rust.* 1.22.2: *Quae e fundo sumi non poterunt, ea si empta erunt potius ad utilitatem quam ob speciem, sumptu fructum non extenuabunt; eo magis, si inde empta erunt potissimum, ubi ea et bona et proxime et vilissimo emi poterunt.*

[248] Varro *Rust.* 1.8.1: *contra vineam sunt qui putent sumptu fructum devorare.*

[249] Varro *Rust.* 1.16.6: *eundem fundum fructuosiorem faciunt vecturae, si viae sunt, qua plaustra agi facile possint, aut flumina propinqua, qua navigari possit.*

also stresses importance of having local access to certain products and specialists:

> if there are towns or villages in the neighbourhood, or even well-furnished lands and farmsteads of rich owners, from which you can purchase at a reasonable price what you need for the farm, and to which you can sell your surplus, such as props, or poles, or reeds, the farm will be more profitable than if they must be fetched from a distance; sometimes, in fact, more so than if you can supply them yourself by raising them on your own place. For this reason farmers in such circumstances prefer to have in their neighbourhood men whose services they can call upon under a yearly contract—physicians, fullers, and other artisans—rather than to have such men of their own on the farm; for sometimes the death of one artisan wipes out the profit of a farm.[250]

Under some circumstances self-sufficiency was neither virtuous nor profitable. Only on big, remote estates, according to Varro, did it make sense to staff specialists.[251]

Cato and Varro did not advocate self-sufficiency but rather a strategy of reducing unnecessary expenditure and cultivating a network of mutual support within the local community. They understood and accepted the fact that a farmer could not meet all his needs solely by means of his own property and dependents. Moderation was the point, not extreme self-reliance. Indeed, if there was an ideal of self-sufficiency, Varro may have been warning against it.

Cicero's remarks hardly provide any better evidence for a self-sufficient ideal or autarchic practice. He is interested in depicting his opponents as greedy and corrupt, not describing household management techniques. The image of the rake who sells his forest before his vineyards could derive some of its power from the fact that the possession of woods was far more conducive to self-sufficiency, but Cicero's main goal in likening the authors of the agrarian bill to this hypothetical rake was

---

[250] Varro *Rust.* 1.16.3–4: *si ea oppida aut vici in vicinia aut etiam divitum copiosi agri ac villae, unde non care emere possis quae opus sunt in fundum, quibus quae supersint venire possint, ut quibusdam pedamenta aut perticae aut harundo, fructuosior fit fundus, quam si longe sint importanda, non numquam etiam, quam si colendo in tuo ea parare possis. Itaque in hoc genus coloni potius anniversarios habent vicinos, quibus imperent, medicos, fullones, fabros, quam in villa suos habeant, quorum non numquam unius artificis mors tollit fundi fructum.*

[251] Varro *Rust.* 1.16.4: *Quam partem lati fundi divites domesticae copiae mandare solent. Si enim a fundo longius absunt oppida aut vici, fabros parant, quos habeant in villa, sic ceteros necessarios artifices, ne de fundo familia ab opere discedat ac profestis diebus ambulet feriata potius, quam opere faciendo agrum fructuosiorem reddat.*

to portray them as equally extravagant, more interested in luxury than state revenues. This rhetorical strategy continues with his discussion of the *ager Praenestinus.* Cicero was trying to convince his audience that Rullus, who proposed sending five thousand colonists to Capua, intended to distribute the land so that his friends could acquire large parcels. It may well have been the case that the men who owned large estates near Praeneste sought to be more self-sufficient by using those properties to supply their Campanian villas, but Cicero probably mentioned them in order to tie Rullus and his backers to the unpopular beneficiaries of Sulla's proscriptions and remind them of a recent, unfair land distribution. He mentions the Campanian villas in order to suggest that the men who will come to possess the territory of Capua are already excessively wealthy and not simple, honest folk like Cicero's audience.[252] These two passages from the *De lege agraria*, like Cato and Varro's agricultural writings, suggest that extravagance was a bad trait for an estate owner but not that estate owners necessarily did or should practice self-sufficiency. They do not, furthermore, provide much guidance in determining a general level of rural demand for coinage.

An anecdote from the *Verrines* may be somewhat more helpful in establishing the role of coinage in the countryside. Cicero reports that, instead of paying Sicilian farmers the 4 *sesterces* per *modius* of maintenance grain specified by the senate, Verres had demanded that *they* pay *him* twice that amount.[253] As this measure followed the excessive exaction of a grain tithe and the purchase of a second tithe for which the farmers actually received very little in payment,[254] the farmers had neither the cash to pay Verres nor enough grain to sell in order to raise the requisite sums. Under these circumstances, Cicero claims, farmers were forced to sell their tools and livestock because they could not grow coins.[255] Cicero apparently believed that his audience would consider it plausible that few coins passed through farmers' hands and used this to generate further sympathy for his Sicilian clients. This impression is immediately reinforced when, after pointing out that a farmer cannot grow coins, Cicero insists that his listeners "must not argue...that this same man

[252] Cic. *Leg. agr.* 2.77: *num vobis aut vestri similibus integris, quietis, otiosis hominibus in hoc numero locum fore putatis?*

[253] Cic. *Verr.* II 3.196–7.

[254] Cic. *Verr.* II 3.198.

[255] Cic. *Verr.* II 3.199: *nummos vero ut det arator, quos non exarat, quos non aratro ac manu quaerit, boves et aratrum ipsum atque omne instrumentum vendat necesse est.*

has the sum required in cash or in town property."[256] Regardless of an individual's other possessions, Cicero insists that they "consider the relative capacity of his farm in itself."[257] He expects his audience naturally to consider farms as independent units and ones unlikely to generate much revenue in coin. The lack of coinage in the countryside, however, does not necessarily imply that farmers pursued self-sufficiency.

The major Republican texts on agriculture do not support the idea that Roman farmers sought to be self-sufficient. Certainly, Cato and Varro caution against excess expenditure, and suggest that one way to avoid excess was through production or manufacture on the estate rather than purchase in the market but that amounts to a very minor and qualified kind of self-sufficiency. The most that can be said is that the agronomists' advice, if followed, would minimize the use of coinage by farmers, not eliminate it. As noted earlier, Cato implies that an estate owner had the most demand for coinage when building or stocking a farm. The year-to-year operations would still require some purchases but perhaps not as many and, again, some of these operational expenses could be met with assets other than coinage. Neighbors could help meet certain needs as well. This is a countryside not filled with self-sufficient villas but also not featuring a particularly strong demand for coinage.

It would be a mistake, however, to draw conclusions about rural monetization solely on the basis of elite literary sources. Archaeological and comparative evidence can also provide some guidance.

Over the past few decades surface survey and rural excavations have built up an increasingly detailed picture of Roman rural life. Some difficulties persist, such as the relative lack of excavation of smaller sites, the problem of determining how much and what kind of land pertained to a particular villa or farmstead, and the fact that different building material preferences almost certainly distort our view of settlement patterns.[258] Nevertheless, the excavation of rural sites offers some strong indications about rural monetization.

---

[256] Cic. *Verr.* II 3.199: *non enim debetis hoc cogitare, 'habet idem in nummis, habet in urbanis praediis.'*

[257] Cic. *Verr.* II 3.199: *nam cum aratori aliquid imponitur, non hominis si quae sunt praeterea facultates, sed arationis ipsius vis ac ratio consideranda est, quid ea sustinere, quid pati, quid efficere possit ac debeat.*

[258] On the challenges involved in archaeological survey and rural excavations as well as the interpretation of their results see, for example: Potter (1979) 123–5; Greene (1986) 98–109; Lloyd (1991) 236; Barker (1995) 224; Mattingly and Coccia (1995).

It was once assumed that relatively few coins circulated in the countryside because not many turned up in the excavation of rural sites.[259] In recent decades, however, the picture has changed.[260] Coins do turn up in villa excavations, albeit in small numbers (rarely more than a handful of stray finds) and not on every site. Republican era rural sites throughout Italy have yielded *denarii* or various Roman bronze denominations.[261] As I noted in my discussion of the urban monetary zone, stray coin finds are difficult to interpret. The three *denarii*, for example, found in the villa near Gravina di Puglia do not seem like much, given that the site was occupied for about a hundred years.[262] Still, we should not expect to find that many coins in places where the population density was so much lower than the typical town. That coins appear, if in low numbers, on villas indicates at the very least a low level of rural monetization. It is also possible that farmers tended to keep their coinage stored at their urban properties (if they had any) or on deposit with bankers in towns. Such practices, however, would only highlight higher urban demand for coinage.[263]

Even when rural sites do not yield coinage, they still show the implausibility of self-sufficiency and strongly imply the use of coinage. To illustrate, one need only consider two villas in northern Campania which were excavated in the 1960s. The Posto and San Rocco villas are similar in many respects; both were constructed around 100 BCE and remained in use through the end of the Republican period.[264] However, from neither site were any coins found dating to the Republican period of

[259] Burnett (1987) 96.

[260] Howgego (1992) 20 claimed that "the increasing number of careful excavations of more truly rural sites show that coins are to be found scattered in the countryside in quantity, and not just in 'developed' areas such as Italy." However, de Ligt (1993) 111 characterizes Howgego's view of rural monetization as "very optimistic." For the Republican era at least, I tend to agree with de Ligt's assessment.

[261] For example: Small (1974); Small et al. (1992); Barker (1995) 207; Gazzetti (1995); Visonà and Frey-Kupper (1996) 81.

[262] Small et al. (1992) 196–7.

[263] Of course, not all farmers lived in cities and only wealthier Romans could afford urban property. Survey and excavation suggest considerable local variation within Italy between isolated farmsteads and town or village-based farmers who did not permanently occupy their rural properties. Garnsey (1979) 19 notes: "The agro-town, the essential feature of which is the separation and alienation of the peasantry from the land, was not in my view an ancient phenomenon. In ancient Italy, the movement of agricultural workers took place in two directions, from an urban base, from a rural base." On rural settlement in Italy see also: Potter (1979); Jones (1980); Greene (1986) 98–109; de Ligt (1990); Lloyd (1991); Yntema (1992/93); Barker (1995); Curti et al. (1996).

[264] Cotton (1979); (1985).

occupation. Taken in isolation, this lack of coins might lead one to conclude that the farms had been self-sufficient. Such a conclusion might seem especially appealing for the Villa San Rocco which had a good sized *villa rustica* and was ideally situated with respect to the criteria in the agricultural manuals.[265] But it is dangerous to make arguments based on what was not found on a site and, in the case of these two villas, it is also unnecessary. While no coins were found, at both sites there was ample evidence for interaction with the market. Sherds of glass, iron nails, and non-local ceramics and building materials prove that these estates were not self-sufficient and they strongly imply the use of coinage. The picture is the same throughout Republican Italy for the large or moderately sized rural farms and villas that have been excavated. Whether or not coins appear, non-local remains show that these households were integrated into the larger economy. This state of affairs has always been recognized by archaeologists who, it is only fair to note, have been the least beguiled by the notion of Roman self-sufficiency. As Stephen Dyson put it, "the quality, quantity and standardization characteristic of Roman goods from amphorae and utilitarian pots to roof tiles [found on Roman estates] argue against too much autonomous production."[266]

What of smallholders? The dwellings of the poor have received less attention from archaeologists and may be much harder to discern. Survey archaeology does identify the remains of small rural structures and they are often quite numerous, but it can be impossible to determine whether they are the permanent residences of peasants or temporary housing for farmers living in towns or villages who needed shelter during periods of peak agricultural labor. Some smaller rural sites may be the property of relatively wealthy farmers who owned several widely scattered plots of land. Dispersed holdings were, after all, a good risk avoidance strategy. It is with the problem of Roman peasants or smallholders that comparative evidence can provide some guidance.

Keith Hopkins once remarked that comparative history should depend on systematic, not *ad hoc*, comparisons.[267] In line with such a systematic approach, two studies seem particularly relevant to the question of the economic behavior of Roman peasants. The first is Robert

---

265 Cotton (1985) 78.
266 Dyson (1985) 77.
267 Hopkins (1972) 193.

McC. Netting's broad examination of agricultural systems involving smallholders, whom he defined as "peasants with an intermediate technology of the plow and draft animals, living in a state, and subject to demands for tax or tribute from other elite groups."[268] Roman peasants clearly meet all these criteria. Furthermore, since Netting found many "commonalities of behavior and institutions"[269] among smallholders as diverse as Swiss Alpine dairy farmers, the Nigerian Kofyar and the Mexican chinampas, his findings may provide some insight into Roman peasant farming. Netting's conclusions with respect to the integration of smallholders into the broader economy are striking. Smallholders, he notes, "do not normally live in isolation from larger networks of economic exchange or political organization" and, in fact, the "greatest problem with modeling a viable system of rural population, land, technology, and labor has been the tendency to treat such systems as self-sufficient and independent."[270] Neither individually nor collectively, then, are smallholders likely to be autarchic.

A second study whose findings seem relevant is that of Johnson and Earle on *The Evolution of Human Societies*. By means of case studies of nineteen cultures from foraging, family-level groups like the !Kung to peasant communities within a regional polity such as the Javanese villagers of Kali Loro, the authors examine how societies evolve economically, politically and socially. They make two observations relevant to the economic situation of Roman peasants. The first is that even family-level foragers in economies far less complex than that of Republican Rome must engage in exchange to meet some of their needs.[271] The second observation concerns the economics of peasant communities, the other end of the spectrum of cultures studied. The general circumstances of these communities are broadly similar to those of Republican Italy in that they feature peasants practicing intensive agriculture within large, socially stratified states. "Peasant communities," they observe, "are integrated into large, hierarchically structured economic systems; and... despite a significant measure of household subsistence autonomy as compared to modern families, they are the least self-sufficient of all the peoples examined."[272]

---

268 Netting (1993) 7.
269 Netting (1993) 3.
270 Netting (1993) 15.
271 Johnson and Earle (2000) 50.
272 Johnson and Earle (2000) 363.

Comparative evidence can rarely be more than suggestive. It is always possible that Roman peasants were atypical smallholders or that Roman Italy was an unusual sort of agrarian state. Still, it is striking how well the conclusions of Netting, Johnson and Earle conform with what the literary and archaeological evidence suggests about rural monetization in late Republican Italy. While they cannot be conclusive, these comparative studies at least indicate that it would be quite remarkable if Roman peasants were self-sufficient and not dependent on markets. Taken together, the remarks of the Roman agronomists, the findings from excavations and the comparative evidence all make a compelling case against Roman agricultural self-sufficiency on any level.

It is clear that the countryside was monetized to some extent, but how important was coinage? Several considerations lead me to conclude that rural demand for coinage was quite low relative to that of urban areas, i.e., a farmer needed fewer coins to manage his economic affairs than a comparably wealthy urban dweller. A Roman who lived in a city and was not engaged in agriculture had to either buy or receive as a gift everything he or she needed to survive (except water). Farmers who worked their own land also had to make some purchases with cash but almost certainly far fewer, since they could grow some or probably most of the food they consumed. Farmers still had to buy at least some clothing, tools, equipment, supplies or building materials but, while some of these purchases would require coins, grain, oil, wine and labor could facilitate some of their transactions. This reduced the rural inhabitant's need for cash. It was more difficult for urban dwellers to make payments with assets other than cash, in part because the higher cost of urban real estate made it much more expensive to store bulk commodities in town. A storeroom full of grain was a potentially lucrative speculative investment in both city and country but involved greater carrying costs for the city dweller. He would either have to rent space to store the grain, if he did not own urban property, or forgo earning some rent, if he did. So not only did commodity-based transactions reduce the farmer's demand for coinage, but those other assets were also better investments for him. A farmer could offer grain in payment for something from another farmer and the grain was more likely to be accepted (or accepted with less of a discount) because the other farmer would not only be able to consume the grain but might also store it as an investment, use it as seed grain, feed it to livestock or employ it in other transactions to pay for goods or services. For farmers who wanted to take advantage of commodity price fluctuations, as Cato and Varro suggest they should, and who could easily and relatively inexpensively store produce, accepting commodities instead of cash might prove quite profitable.

Rural partnerships also diminished rural demand for coinage. For example, if several peasants took turns looking after their combined flocks, it obviated the need to pay or buy a shepherd.[273] This may have been a common solution among peasants,[274] and certainly fits in well with what the agronomists say about the importance of neighbors. Cooperation is not an autarchic strategy but it is also not a strategy that necessarily requires cash. Rural partnerships constitute joint investments of labor and so are means of economizing on money balances.

Cicero tried to generate sympathy for his Sicilian clients by emphasizing the inability of farmers to grow coins. He was likely accurate in his depiction of the countryside as being cash poor, but, barring the appearance an exceptionally rapacious governor, this was not a problem. Sicilian and Roman farmers (the latter group no longer even paying any *tributum* after 167 BCE)[275] simply had less use for coinage than others. The commodities they grew offered many advantages that coinage did not and fulfilled some monetary functions as well. In comparison with the other monetary zones, all of which exhibit signs of having achieved much higher levels of monetization, the rural monetary zone had relatively limited need for coinage.

---

[273] Lirb (1993) 273.

[274] Lirb (1993) 285.

[275] Plin. *HN* 33.56. Furthermore, as Crawford (1985) 187 notes, "with the enfranchisement of Italy in 88, all men were now Roman citizens and therefore paid no *tributum*." Of course, the remission of the tax would affect all Romans, farmers or otherwise, but it is nevertheless worth recalling since property taxes could otherwise be a significant factor in the creating rural demand for coinage. See Hopkins (1980); de Ligt (1993) 136.

CHAPTER SIX

THE DEMAND FOR ROMAN MONEY

6.1 Introduction

The Romans possessed a marketplace of monetary assets. Coins competed with bullion, financial instruments and other forms of *pecunia* which could in certain circumstances perform monetary functions. People relied on coinage to a greater or lesser degree depending on their particular needs and the advantages and disadvantages offered by these different assets. But this market was not static. As we have already seen, the supply of coinage grew dramatically in the late Republic. What does this suggest about the development of the Roman economy?

6.2 Quantity Theory

Those who have sought to understand the consequences of the increase in the supply of Roman coins have generally turned to Quantity Theory, which posits a close relationship between money supply and prices in an economy. While the general idea of such a relationship may go back to antiquity,[1] Quantity Theory owes its modern formulation to Irving Fisher and his equation, $MV = PT$, i.e., that the money supply (M) multiplied by its velocity (V) is equal to the price level (P) multiplied by the number of transactions (T). If Roman M grew rapidly in the last century of the Republic, it must have had a considerable effect on some or all of the other variables in this equation. Because it is hard to measure T, the number of transactions, it is usually replaced in the equation by Y (or Q), the total output of the economy.[2] Y is not equal to T since some transactions can involve no new output (e.g. selling used goods or land, financial transactions, etc.). Therefore V in this revised equation must become the "income velocity" rather than the "transactions velocity" of money.[3]

---

[1] Nicolet (1971) 1203–27.
[2] Mishkin (1992) 524.
[3] Mankiw (1994) 147.

M, *P* and *Y* can all be determined fairly easily for modern economies and can be estimated for some historical periods. *V*, however, presents certain problems and is difficult to measure except in terms of *M*, *P* and *Y*. Indeed, the exchange equation is often written $V = \frac{PY}{M}$ and is thus considered the definition of velocity.[4] However economist Richard Selden warns:

> The term 'velocity of money' is a misnomer if taken literally. Economists are interested not in the speed and direction of money as it moves through space but in a quite different idea—the frequency with which money is spent.[5]

The income velocity of money is best defined as "the number of times a [monetary unit] enters someone's income in a given period of time"[6] or "the number of times per year that the nominal money supply turns over in financing aggregate spending or income."[7] As we shall see, however, the nature of *V* in the exchange equation continues to cause difficulties for economic historians.

In "Taxes and Trade" Hopkins used Quantity Theory to explore the implications for the Roman economy of a large increase in the money supply. He assumed that the Roman money supply (*M*) increased greatly from 157 to 50 BCE but that prices (*P*) had remained steady. The price equation, he argued, tells us that under these circumstances something must have happened to either *V* or *Q* (or both) in order for equilibrium to be restored. That is, either the velocity of money dropped or the quantity of goods produced increased or, and this is Hopkins' conclusion, both occurred.

With respect to the velocity of money Hopkins reasoned as follows:

> the speed at which money circulated (*V*) probably slowed down in this period, for three reasons: the state treasuries must have kept huge sums in reserve and even stored money as treasure; so too did private individuals and professional bankers; thirdly, the greater distance which separated tax-payers and tax-spenders left considerable amounts of cash idle in transit.[8]

---

[4] Mishkin (1992) 605.
[5] Selden (1956) 234.
[6] Mankiw (1994) 148.
[7] Fischer et al. (1988) 303.
[8] Hopkins (1980) 109–10.

At the same time, however, Hopkins suggested that "money percolated into a myriad of transactions which had previously been embedded in the subsistence economy."[9] This statement seems to imply that the velocity of money increased in some respects since it had to "move faster" if it was to be used in all these new transactions. However Hopkins was almost certainly referring to the fact that monetization, "more people using [money] for more activities,"[10] causes Q to rise since only the goods and services paid for with money figure in the calculation of Q. That this was his intended meaning is clear from the fact that he couples the phenomenon of monetization with "the substantial rise in the volume of trade in an expanded area"[11] which also involves an increase in Q. Though he does believe V decreased, Hopkins seems to argue that the rise in M was chiefly counteracted by the rise of Q.

There are several difficulties involved in this (or any) application of Quantity Theory to the Roman economy. One involves the way in which the Roman money supply grew. Rome's conquests in the late Republic certainly caused an increase in the Roman money supply (M) since the taking of spoils and the imposition of taxes and indemnities on new provinces allowed Rome to mint more coins, but the total output of the Roman Empire (Q) would also rise even before one factored in the effects of an increase in M. To see why this is so, it is necessary to recognize that Roman expansion did not simply increase the Roman money supply, it caused monetary systems to *merge*:

$$M_{E2} = M_{E1} + M_P = \frac{P_E Q_E}{V_E} + \frac{P_P Q_P}{V_P}$$

In this equation M_{E1} represents an initial Roman money supply while M_{E2} represents that supply following the integration of some new province and its money, M_P, into the Roman monetary system. Assuming no difference in price levels or velocity between the Empire and its new territory (i.e., $V_E = V_P$ and $P_E = P_P$) then:

$$M_{E2} = \frac{P(Q_E + Q_P)}{V}$$

[9] Hopkins (1980) 109–10.
[10] Hopkins (1980) 110.
[11] Hopkins (1980) 110.

Thus, as the Empire grew, the aggregate output of new territories employing Roman coinage were added to Rome's initial *Q*, causing it to rise.

Of course, these equations simplify matters somewhat. Roman coinage did not immediately replace local coinage in every conquered territory. In some provinces local coinage persisted for decades or even centuries. In other provinces hybrid money supplies emerged. However, in the second and first centuries BCE the use of the *denarius* spread throughout Italy[12] as well as to Sicily (c. 200),[13] Africa (c. 146),[14] Macedonia (early first century),[15] Gaul (after 83),[16] Spain (c. 70),[17] Asia Minor (after 50)[18] and Southern Greece (40s).[19] In these regions and others small amounts of Roman coinage began to arrive even earlier. Hopkins was certainly aware of this issue. He concedes, for example, that "some part of the growth in Roman silver coins was simply a replacement for the coinage of the conquered," but insists that "there was a real increase in the money supply in the Republican period of imperial expansion in the western Mediterranean."[20] While this may be true, the only increases in *Q* of which we can be absolutely certain through the application of Quantity Theory must have occurred concomitantly with, rather than as a result of, the rise of *M*.[21]

Another issue concerns the role of non-Roman money-stocks circulating in the Mediterranean world.[22] Should such money be included in estimates of the Roman money supply? Can the volume of such issues be estimated to the same extent as Roman coins? What about uncoined silver and gold? Verboven claims that large payments were made with gold bullion and correctly observes that "we have no idea of how the supply of gold bullion evolved in the Late Republic."[23] Silver bullion poses similar problems.

---

12 Travaglini (1988) 76 argues that the *denarius* only became the principal means of circulation in Apulia during the first century BCE.

13 Crawford (1987) 43.

14 Burnett et al. (1992) 182.

15 Touratsoglou (1987) 54.

16 Crawford (1985) 165.

17 Hopkins (1980) 108; Knapp (1987) 23.

18 Kinns (1987) 113.

19 Price (1987) 99.

20 Hopkins (1980) 108.

21 When Hopkins revisited the topic of "Taxes and Trade" he dropped the argument based on Quantity Theory and declared that "the whole argument of coin circulation was not vital to my thesis." See Hopkins (1995/96) 54.

22 Verboven (1997) 44.

23 Verboven (1997) 67.

Finally there is the problem of velocity about which, as Hopkins noted, "we know virtually nothing"[24] since it is so difficult to measure. The concept of velocity is, furthermore, counterintuitive and thus prone to confusion and misuse.[25] In his article on the use and abuse of Quantity Theory Dennis Flynn advises historians to turn instead to the "demand-for-money-to-hold" concept which is the foundation of modern monetary reasoning.[26] Demand Theory, as I will show, offers a way around the problem of velocity.

6.3 The Demand for Money

Soon after Fisher developed his exchange equation, A. C. Pigou adapted it to create a new equation ($M^d = kPY$) defining the demand for money.[27] He replaced the idea of money's velocity of circulation with the variable *k* which represents "the proportion of resources" kept in the form of money.[28] Instead of talking about how many transactions are made within an economy, he looked at how much money people want to hold. It is true that *k* is merely the reciprocal of V ($V = \frac{1}{k}$), but it is much more convenient to think in terms of the demand for money than its velocity. This change in perspective provides a more useful theoretical framework for examining the process of monetization and the relationship between prices, output and the money supply in the late Roman Republic. Demand theory posits that money is just one of many forms in which wealth can be held and that an individual's demand for money will depend on the utility and potential returns offered by a range of

---

[24] Hopkins (1995/96) 62. Goldsmith (1987) 41–2 estimated on rather slender grounds a velocity of circulation for the Empire at the death of Augustus of 2.5 to 3.0. Harris (1993) 20–1 rightly noted: "As for the speed at which Roman money circulated, no one, so far, has demonstrated the truth of any general proposition." This is still the case.

[25] See discussions of velocity in Verboven (1997) 42; Flynn (1984) 403. Lockyear (1999) 242–3 illustrates the potential for confusion. Lockyear notes that according to the "classical economist's view of money" (which he rejects), the increase in the Republican money supply should have caused either inflation or a decrease in velocity. He argues that the "little evidence we have suggests neither happened, and thus we must be looking at a large-scale growth in the use of coinage in this period, and... that the functions of coinage in Roman Italy... must have expanded." But the growth in the use of money and the expansion of coin functions, by increasing demand for coinage, would both cause velocity to decrease!

[26] McCusker and Riley (1984) 270–1 and *passim*, examining a period with much better economic data, reached the same conclusion as Flynn.

[27] Note that the exponent in this equation should be understood to mean "the demand for" *M* rather than "to the *d* power."

[28] See Pigou (1917) 38–65.

assets. Note, however, that this theory makes no assumptions about *how* people choose to allocate their resources (which will obviously vary tremendously from culture to culture) but merely supposes that, given finite wealth and a market economy, those choices will have predictable effects on prices, supply and the demand for money.[29]

The theory of the demand for money, Milton Friedman noted in 1956, is "a general approach rather than a label for a well-defined theory."[30] Most of the problems discussed in modern monetary theory are either irrelevant or inapplicable to the Roman world, irrelevant in that they involve financial assets and institutions unknown to antiquity and inapplicable because we lack sufficient data to apply to the appropriate equations. However, money demand theory is, in essence, the study of the economic behavior of individuals and while we cannot quantify that behavior, our knowledge of their habits and practices with respect to coinage and commodities can help us speculate intelligently about Roman demand. Money demand theory provides us with a set of questions to ask about Roman assets and economic conditions. The answers to these questions will, in turn, allow us to gauge the level of demand for Roman coinage and how it changed in the late Republic.

The basic idea behind demand theory is as follows: individuals and firms decide how much money they want to hold or, more precisely, what proportion of their assets they wish to hold as money. Keynes divided the factors governing this decision into three categories: transactions, precautionary and speculative motives.[31]

The "Transactions Motive" for holding money rests on the function of money as a means of payment or exchange. It refers to the idea that people hold money (at least in part) in order to make transactions.[32] For example, "lunch money" is money held for a transactions motive

[29] Von Reden (2002) 142 claims that "modern economic and monetary theory is now regarded by most scholars as unhelpful for understanding money in the ancient world." If so, it is unfortunate. While many statistical and quantitative tools of modern economics are inapplicable to ancient economies, they can still serve as a guide, indicating likely parameters. Saller (2002) provides a good example of the way in which modern economic theory can inform the debate over growth in the Roman economy. Temin (2001) presents the most compelling argument for applying macroeconomics to the Roman economy: the Romans had a market economy. While Temin focuses primarily on the early Empire, there is plenty of evidence for variable prices, instrumental behavior and the role of supply and demand in forming prices from the late Republic as well.

[30] Friedman (1956) 3.

[31] Keynes (1936) 170–2.

[32] Mishkin (1992) 531.

(i.e. to buy one's lunch). The transactions demand for money is limited first and foremost by wealth. One's money holdings cannot exceed one's total resources. But within that limit, an individual's transactions demand for money is determined by his or her need to make money payments as well as the costs and benefits of holding money. Money makes it easier to purchase goods and services because, since it is a medium of exchange, its use incurs no (or fewer) transaction costs.[33] Holding money also makes purchasing more convenient by obviating the need to waste time converting other assets into money.[34] Thus money provides "transactions facilitating services."[35] However holding money also has its drawbacks: the "opportunity cost" of money, the interest you might have earned on other assets. Because of this opportunity cost, economists generally believe that the transactions motive is negatively related to interest rates since the higher interests rates are, the more income one loses by holding money.[36]

Since one cannot always predict one's level of expenditure, people also hold money for precautionary motives as "a cushion against unexpected need" or in case of unexpected opportunity.[37] Thus the precautionary demand for money refers to the "stock of money held to pay unpredictable expenses,"[38] so that one does not have to borrow or convert other assets into money in order to pay those expenses. Precautionary demand increases when "uncertainty about the level of future transactions grows."[39]

The speculative motive for holding money, finally, is closely related to money's role as a store of wealth.[40] As Apostolos Serletis notes, "people

---

[33] The concept of transaction costs should be understood as extending well beyond any actual fee charged by a party to a transaction. It includes the time one has to spend to accomplish the transaction, and the wear and tear it involves. See Laidler (1985) 61–2.

[34] Serletis (2001) 67.

[35] Serletis (2001) 78.

[36] Mishkin (1992) 538–9.

[37] Mishkin (1992) 532.

[38] Tucker (1997) 656.

[39] Mishkin (1992) 539 n. 9.

[40] Mishkin (1992) 532. Speculative demand, it should be noted, is the most controversial aspect of money demand theory. Some economists doubt the very existence of this motive or at least note that speculative demand analysis has not been a fruitful avenue of research [Laidler (1985) 152; Mishkin (1992) 541]. However part of the problem facing the modern study of speculative demand relates to financial assets which were not yet available in antiquity, suggesting that a speculative motive may have existed even if it no longer does today. Furthermore this approach to the demand for money has led directly to important ideas about portfolio diversification, the role of economic expectations and

hold money as part of their portfolio of assets and... the demand for money depends on the return and risk offered by money and by other assets that people can hold instead of money."[41] The basic idea behind the speculative demand for money is usually illustrated by supposing that there are only two kinds of assets: money and bonds. The proportion of one's total wealth that one chooses to hold in the form of money rather than bonds will depend on the expected risks and returns of these two assets. Money provides no return but has little risk attached to it while bonds can provide returns in the form of "the sum of the current yield and the expected rate of capital gain."[42] However, since it is possible for the price of bonds to fall, holding bonds is riskier than holding money. If people expect bond prices to rise, they will use their money to buy bonds since they will thereby increase their overall wealth. Conversely, if people expect bond prices to fall, they will choose to hold money instead in order to avoid capital losses.[43] Speculative demand, therefore, is money held either to exploit a potential decrease in the price of assets or as part of a risk buffering strategy.[44]

6.4 Demand in the Late Republic

Greek and Roman writers tell us at least as much about the assets individuals held or sought to hold as they do about their transactions. As I showed in Chapter 5, when combined with the archaeological evidence these literary sources allow us to make reasonable guesses about the *relative* levels of demand for coinage among rural and urban residents, traders and imperial and local government. Farmers, as I have already suggested, had the least demand for coinage for transactions.[45] The tendency for farmers to diversify production and rigorously exploit the resources of their own land limited the number of transactions they needed to make. Since some transactions could be made with the key commodities (grain, oil, wine etc.), the transaction costs of "in kind"

---

asset demand in general. The "Speculative Motive" seems, therefore, to be a legitimate rubric under which to discuss such issues and their effects on the demand for money.

[41] Serletis (2001) 79.

[42] Serletis (2001) 60.

[43] Serletis (2001) 60. As Tobin (1958) 85 and Mishkin (1992) 539–40 point out, this illustration of speculative demand is overly simplistic since it does not explain portfolio diversification (i.e. it assumes one would hold bonds or money, not both).

[44] Tobin (1958) 85; Mishkin (1992) 540.

[45] See section 5.6.

exchange must have been low. The "transactions facilitating" properties of money in rural areas were not much greater than those of the main agricultural commodities. Other drawbacks to holding coinage, such as the ease with which it could be stolen and the general lawlessness of rural Italy, must have also played a role in limiting demand.

At Rome and in other urban areas the demand for money for transactions must have been quite high relative to rural demand. The urban poor needed money to pay for food, shelter and clothing. Even those who received free grain from the state and had liberal patrons would need to buy some food and other goods.[46] The poor paid in advance and frequently for their lodgings.[47] While most wealthy Romans probably lived in their own houses and possessed rural estates which could provide them with food and some clothing, they also purchased many luxury goods in urban markets. Coinage was both a luxury good (in the "asset demand" sense)[48] and the chief means of acquiring other luxuries. There is, of course, ample evidence for a marked increase in the consumption of luxury goods in the late Republic.[49] For all urban dwellers, transactions balances must have constituted a relatively high proportion of total wealth.

More difficult to gauge is the level of transactions demand among those engaged in commerce. In some cases traders needed coinage to facilitate exchange in the marketplace (to buy and sell their wares), to pay *portoria*, harbor fees and no doubt also to rent storage space for their goods. But traders had access to financial instruments and institutions that would help limit their demand for coinage.[50] Traders were certainly the most financially sophisticated class and would have been the most comfortable (and adept) at making use of devices which limited their need for coinage. Studies of modern economies have shown that, while monetization initially leads to an increase in the demand for money, as people become more financially sophisticated, their demand for money

[46] Verboven (2002) 114 emphasizes the limits of patronage both in terms of the overall percentage of the population that might receive assistance and the extent of that assistance.

[47] Frier (1977) 34–5.

[48] Mishkin (1992) 96: "an asset is a luxury if its wealth elasticity is great than 1, and as wealth grows, the quantity demanded of this asset grows more than proportionally."

[49] For example, Macrobius *Sat.* 3.17.1–13; Plin. *HN* 14.95–96; 33.141–2. See also: Daube (1969) 124–5; Clemente (1981) I, 2.

[50] See Chapter 3.

actually decreases.[51] The same is likely to have been true of Roman traders if not to the same degree that it has been for modern western economies. Thus, commercial demand probably exceeded rural demand but would not have approached urban levels.

The transactions demand for coinage must have been quite high for both the Roman government and municipalities. Rome needed coins to pay soldiers, officials, and contractors while municipalities faced similar expenses. For cities there were many advantages to holding coinage and even more to actually producing it. Coinage made transactions and accounting easier while minting coinage provided profits (through the emission of fiduciary bronze coins) and prestige (to those who controlled the designs). Government transactions demand probably rivaled urban demand though the state did make some payments in kind.

In some circumstances the intervals at which income is received may also help indicate transactions demand. David Laidler suggests that "if the size of [transaction costs] is sufficiently great that the agent never finds that it pays to hold bonds, and if the payment period then lengthens, the agent's money holding will vary."[52] However Milton Friedman has argued that "institutional conditions," such as the frequency of payment, "are to be regarded as resultants of an economic equilibrating process, not as physical data."[53] In other words, individuals and firms will try to change the frequency with which they make payments to correspond with their desired level of money balances. Regardless of the direction of causation, there does appear to be some correlation between payment intervals and demand levels. There are a number of reasons to suppose that payment intervals were typically long in the Roman world except for urban wage laborers (whose transactions balances were likely to be low anyway). The phenomenon of *nundinae* and other period markets would cause money to be held for longer intervals. Increased urbanization, however, brought with it more permanent markets and therefore fewer restrictions on when and where one could buy and sell goods (i.e. transaction costs were reduced). Rents from agricultural land were probably paid on a yearly basis while the transport of stored produce to market may only have been cost-effective during slow

---

[51] Jonung (1978) 216; Bordo and Jonung (1981) 98–9.

[52] Laidler (1985) 61 n. 3.

[53] Friedman (1956) 13 notes: "Surely, the increase in the average cash balance over the past century in this country that has occurred for other reasons has been a factor producing a lengthening of pay periods and not the other way around."

periods in the planting cycle when one's labor force (human and animal) became available. The characters in Varro's *De re rustica* speak in terms of an estate's annual income even when that estate engaged in animal husbandry rather than the cultivation of crops.[54] For the very poor who received and paid out money for food and shelter on a daily basis, short payment intervals would have suppressed money demand. For wealthier urban inhabitants the payment interval must have been longer and was no doubt governed by the agricultural year, the limits of the sailing season or the use of middlemen. Though his tenants paid daily, Cicero received an annual lump sum from his urban properties.[55] The payment interval was long in the governmental monetary zone as well. Taxation of agricultural land was on an annual basis while the use of tax-farming corporations to bid for the right to collect even non-agricultural taxes may mean that the state received some income at even greater intervals. While there is some evidence concerning payment intervals for our period, it does not seem to be sufficient to help identify significant differences in money demand between the four monetary zones. Technological limitations (e.g. in communications and transportation) probably prevented most Romans from managing their assets as they would have preferred.

Because the precautionary demand for money is closely related to the transactions demand,[56] it seems likely that the same relative differences in demand existed between the different sectors of the Roman economy. Thus farmers will have had smaller precautionary balances than city dwellers, not because their income and expenses were more predictable but because the proportion of unexpected expenditure requiring coinage rather than other assets was smaller.[57] Similarly the level of precautionary demand from traders would have been higher than that of farmers though not as high as urban demand. The Roman government and elite may constitute exceptions to this scheme. Since the state always had the power to raise taxes, create new sources of revenue, confiscate property and, indeed, mint (or debase) its own coins, it did not necessarily have to keep precautionary money balances

---

[54] Varro *Rust.* 3.2.14–15: *in annos singulos plus quinquagena milia e villa capere dicebat... sexaginta milia ea pars reddiderit eo anno villae.*

[55] Frier (1978/79) 4–5.

[56] Laidler (1985) 64–9; Mishkin (1992) 538–9.

[57] Urban and rural dwellers undoubtedly faced *different* kinds of problems and uncertainties but there does not seem to be any reason to believe that life in one region was by nature more uncertain.

commensurate with its level of uncertainty. Nevertheless, the *aerarium sanctius* did seem to function as Rome's "precautionary treasury."[58] The elite, on the other hand, may have had considerable precautionary demand for coinage since, as Jongman has argued, they faced "the need to alleviate the complexities and unpredictability of property transfers from one generation to the next."[59]

Turning now to speculative demand, it is evident that, for farmers, diversified holdings of agricultural commodities held clear advantages over coinage. Such considerations undoubtedly limited rural demand. In the cities agricultural commodities had less of an advantage over coinage. The urban poor, of course, would not hold speculative balances since the primary limit to money demand is wealth. For others the higher cost of urban real estate meant that storing goods in the city was more expensive, diminishing the potential returns from price increases. Wealthy Romans did possess large stores of wine and other commodities but it is not clear that they were speculative economic (as distinct from social or political) investments.[60] Slaves and real estate were undoubtedly the most popular assets among the upper classes. Slaves were a somewhat risky investment but could be quite profitable.[61] Land, both urban and rural, would provide a regular and relatively predictable flow of rents and could easily be resold for a profit in Rome's vigorous real estate market. From the time of the Gracchi onwards, political, social and military instability caused the price of land to fluctuate wildly. Those in a position to take advantage of these fluctuations became quite wealthy.[62]

It is unlikely that the government had any speculative motives for holding money since it had far more effective means of gaining wealth (e.g. imperialism and taxation). Indeed, the Roman state willingly gave up opportunities to profit from the speculative use of coinage.[63]

Speculative motives, of course, formed the very foundation of the commercial enterprise, whether one thinks in terms of the lone trader moving from market to market or of large companies bidding for contracts to supply Roman armies. Traders profited from the opportuni-

[58] Barlow (1977) 290.
[59] Jongman (2003) 191.
[60] For large holdings of wine see: Plin. *HN* 14.95–6; Cic. *Phil.* 2.66.
[61] Plut. *Cat. Mai.* 21.7.
[62] For example Crassus and Chrysogonus: Plut. *Crass.* 2.3; Cic. *Rosc. Am. passim.*
[63] The state let *publicani* hold on to some of its cash balances without paying interest (Cic. *Verr.* II 3.168).

ties afforded them by price fluctuations or regional variations in supply and demand as well as, occasionally, artificial shortages of their own creation.[64] To take advantage of these opportunities presumably often required coinage. Thus the speculative demand for money must have been high among traders although, again, limited by access to financial devices and institutions.

6.5 Changes in Demand

The preceding discussion has suggested a general pattern of demand in the Roman world: relatively little demand for coinage in the rural areas and much higher (if varying) levels of demand elsewhere. Could the over-all level of demand have changed from the mid-second to the mid-first century as the supply of coinage increased? Several different factors might bring about such a change in demand: the level of demand in a particular sector of the economy might increase or decrease (e.g. as rural areas become more monetized, their demand for coinage grows),[65] the relative size of different sectors might change (e.g. a general shift of population from an area of low demand to one of high demand would increase aggregate demand),[66] or conditions affecting the demand motives might change (e.g. a slave revolt might cause precautionary balances to rise across the board).[67] In fact, all these factors must have contributed to a substantial increase in the aggregate level of Roman demand for coinage in the last century of the Republic.

Let us begin with the monetization of the countryside which drove up demand for money in the rural monetary zone. While scholars have thus far paid relatively little attention to the problem of change in monetization in the late Republic, two factors suggest that rural demand for coinage grew in this period. First, increased urban demand for foodstuffs must have contributed to the monetization of Italy as local

[64] E.g. Livy 38.35.5.

[65] Chandavarkar (1977) 706–7.

[66] Some modern studies of long-term changes in velocity/demand use urbanization or the proportion of the labor force engaged in non-agricultural pursuits as a proxy variable for monetization. See Bordo and Jonung (1981) 104–7; Jonung (1978) 224. For some reservations see Chandavarkar (1977) 674.

[67] Friedman (1956) 9 notes that periods of war increase the demand for money. Increased security, whether it is the result of peace, economic stability or welfare programs, has the opposite effect. See Bordo and Jonung (1981) 197; Jonung (1978) 228–9.

markets became integrated into Rome's supply network.[68] Secondly, the settlement on Italian land of veterans who had become accustomed to the regular use of coinage during their military service would also increase demand in the agricultural sector.[69]

Governmental transactions demand probably also rose dramatically in the late Republic, with payments in coin assuming a larger proportion of total expenses. This is one way to interpret the substantial expansion in the minting of Roman coins in this period.[70] The growing cost of the *annona*, whose needs could no longer be met solely through taxation in kind,[71] army pay raises,[72] as well as general increases in public building and other cash intensive activities, also indicate greater demand.

Changes in the relative sizes of different sectors of the economy also resulted in an overall increase in demand. Late Republican urbanization,[73] increased long-distance trade,[74] and the enlargement of the Empire and its administrative responsibilities would have driven up the aggregate demand of Roman cities, officials and merchants.

Finally, changes in political and military conditions had a direct impact on demand. These factors probably caused a huge increase in precautionary demand in the first century. It has long been recognized that the hoard evidence reflects the level of violence in the Roman world,[75] but hoards also reflect changes in the demand for coinage. The increase in the level of uncertainty in Italy from the second century to the first was enormous. Although the Romans were involved in many conflicts in the second century, Italy itself was relatively well insulated from them. For example, the violence surrounding the deaths of the Gracchi and the destruction of Fregellae was relatively brief and isolated. By contrast, in the first century Italy witnessed the Social War, the Civil War between

---

[68] See Morley (1996) 142 and 174.

[69] Hollander (2005) 229–39.

[70] Obviously the production of "free coinage" on any major scale would undermine this argument. Cic. *Att.* 8.7.3 remains the only Republican evidence for it but, as Verboven (2003a) 51 n. 10 points out, "Cicero was at this time proconsul with a military command in Campania, and so hardly qualifies as an ordinary citizen." See also Foraboschi (2003) 231–44.

[71] Rickman (1980b) 45; Meijer (1990) 14–23.

[72] For Caesar's pay raise: Suet. *Iul.* 26. Gaius Gracchus effectively increased soldiers' salaries by abolishing deductions for clothing: Plut. *C. Gracch.* 5.

[73] Morley (1996) 39 suggests that "in the last two centuries BC...the population of Rome grew from about 200,000 to about a million."

[74] Hopkins (1980) 105; Peacock and Williams (1986) 25; Parker (1992) 30; Woolf (1992) 289.

[75] Crawford (1969a) 76–81.

Marius and Sulla, the slave revolt of Spartacus, rampant piracy, the Catilinarian Conspiracy, the beginnings of the Civil War between Caesar and Pompey, proscriptions, confiscations and frequent talk of the cancellation of debts. When one's physical safety and property rights are both regularly threatened, the acceptability and ease of transport associated with coinage make it even more desirable as an asset. The violence and uncertainty of the first century must have brought about a dramatic increase in precautionary balances.

Overall speculative demand will also have risen considerably from the second century to the first. As coinage came to play a more important role in politics, one might easily earn substantial profits through high interest loans to candidates and defendants in need of cash with which to bribe voters or jurors.[76] The more important role of private wealth in financing armies, games and other public events and institutions gave new opportunities to bankers, elite financiers and traders. Client kings, embassies and provincial cities might also be desperate for cash.[77] Interest rates probably rose in the weeks leading up to an election as well as during other periods of political uncertainty.[78]

While there are many good reasons to suppose that the demand for coinage grew sharply in the late Republic, two factors that may have limited this growth need to be considered: the increasing presence of false coins in circulation; and the development and spread of more sophisticated financial institutions and practices.

The late Republic probably witnessed a substantial increase in the circulation of forged Roman coins, although difficulties related to the identification and dating of such coins make it impossible to pinpoint the beginning of the trend.[79] The existence of a significant quantity

[76] For a discussion of the elaborate machinery of electoral corruption involving *divisores, sequestres* and *sodales* see Lintott (1990) 1–16.

[77] There are many examples but it may suffice to mention that a *lex Gabinia*, possibly of 67 BCE, made it illegal to loan money to provincials (Cic. *Att.* 5.21.12 and 6.2.7).

[78] Cicero (*Att.* 4.15.7) reports in the summer of 57 BCE that *ambitus* had caused interest rates to double in a very short period of time: *ardet ambitus*... *faenus ex triente Id. Quint. factum erat bessibus.*

[79] Burnett (1987b) 97 dates the phenomenon to the first century BCE while Crawford (1970) 45 argues for the arrival of large quantities of plated coins in the second century BCE. Forgeries turn up quite frequently during excavations but rarely appear in hoards. See Burnett (1982) 136; (1987b) 100; Crawford (1968b) 55. This makes such coins harder to date though it suggests that Romans were quick to notice them. If the *nummularii* were involved in testing coins, their appearance in the late Republic may be no coincidence. Lo Cascio (1996) 275–6 links the rise in false coins to the state's own "large-scale monetary manipulations." As the intrinsic value of a coin diverges from its official value, there is more profit in forgery.

of false coins in circulation had serious consequences. First of all, it increased transaction costs since coins had to be tested. Secondly, the circulation of such coins would make many people feel uneasy about coined money in general. Forgers took advantage of those who were new to, and therefore more unfamiliar with, coinage. For them monetization meant more opportunities for fraud and deception. The state's own "monetary manipulations" (e.g. the progressive reduction in the weight of the *as*)[80] would also contribute to this unease and may have caused some to resist the trend toward monetization.[81]

The development and spread of financial institutions and instruments might have put a brake on the rising demand for money as well since they provided "methods of economizing on money balances."[82] Financial instruments permitted long-distance transactions without the physical transport of coinage,[83] while the presence of bankers at auctions facilitated exchange on a more local level.[84] The supply of banking services also grew in the late Republic.[85] But the Romans did not possess the more "advanced" financial devices such as credit cards and transmissible checks,[86] which some economists believe responsible for the decline in the demand for money in the U.S. and elsewhere in the latter half of the twentieth century.[87] Furthermore, it is not clear how far the use of Roman financial instruments extended beyond the sphere of traders and the very wealthy. Anand Chandavarkar has argued that rural populations are slow to take advantage of the opportunities afforded by new financial institutions:

> the short-run impact of monetization...is likely to be an increase in the demand for currency rather than increased bank deposits...because the transition from transactions in kind to transactions in currency is psychologically and institutionally easier than that from barter to bank money, which involves a quantum jump in institutional and behavior patterns.[88]

---

[80] As Crawford (1973) 50 notes, "the weight standard of the bronze coinage of the last two centuries of the Republic goes up and down like a yo-yo." The revaluation of the *denarius* from 10 *asses* to 16 around 141 BCE must also have disturbed some would-be users of coinage.
[81] See section 2.4.
[82] Bordo and Jonung (1981) 98.
[83] See section 3.3.1.
[84] Andreau (1999) 133.
[85] See section 3.4.
[86] Andreau (1999) 42–3.
[87] Bordo and Jonung (1981) 98.
[88] Chandavarkar (1977) 706–7.

On the whole, therefore, it is unlikely that the growth of banking and related professions in the late Republic did much to reduce the demand for coinage outside of the realm of traders and the elite.

6.6 Economic Growth?

The general trend of increased monetization and rising demand for coinage in the late Republic has important consequences for our understanding of how the Roman economy developed. To illustrate this, let us return to the problem posed by Hopkins in "Taxes and Trade." If, instead of working with $P = \frac{MV}{Q}$, we use the money demand function, $M^d = kPY$, and assume that demand for money equals supply,[89] the equation becomes $M = kPY$. M rose dramatically in the late Republic, perhaps to five or ten times its initial volume. What about prices? There is little evidence for prices in this period and, since commodities often experienced large short-term price swings and unusual prices were the ones most likely to be recorded, surviving prices must be used cautiously. Crawford suggests a "remarkably slow" inflation rate for the second century,[90] while Howgego points to "the progressive abandonment of small denominations" as a sign of "general, but not necessarily continuous" inflation.[91] Here I will follow Burnett who estimated that "from the second century BC to the first century BC prices approximately doubled."[92] Thus, if M rose by a factor of five to ten while P only doubled, then either k or Y or both had to rise.[93] This is almost exactly the problem Hopkins posed except that instead of velocity (V) we are considering k, the proportion of income people choose to hold in the form of money. Hopkins conceded that velocity decreased (i.e. k increased) but he seems to have underestimated the magnitude of its change (particularly with respect to precautionary motives). Based on the factors I have set out above, it is likely that k rose sharply in the late Republic.

---

[89] Even if there was no "free coinage," the phenomena of municipal and provincial mints suggest that this is a plausible assumption.

[90] Crawford (1985) 177.

[91] Howgego (1995) 122.

[92] Burnett (1987b) 108.

[93] Stiglitz (1997) 747: "What actually happens when the money supply is increased (assuming prices are fixed) is a combination of changed holdings of money and changed output."

How much did k increase? Let us explore a few possible scenarios, beginning with a conservative estimate for the increase in M of five times its initial volume and a doubling of Y (due to the merger of monetary systems as the zone in which the *denarius* circulated grew, not per capita growth).[94] Under this scenario an increase in k of only 25% would balance the equation. Given the strong reasons there are to suppose a considerable increase in k, there would seem to be no room in this scenario for any per capita growth in Y. Larger estimates for the growth of the zone of circulation (aggregate growth in Y) would actually require k to fall. So, for example, if Y increased threefold due to aggregate growth from 150 to 50 BCE, and during this period M grew by a factor of five and prices doubled, then k would have to drop 16%. In fact, only a scenario featuring a very optimistic estimate for the increase in the money supply combined with a very conservative estimate for aggregate growth of Y leaves any room for both the increase in k that must have occurred and some per capita economic growth. For example, if M grew by a factor of ten and Y doubled due to aggregate growth, then k could more than double and still accommodate a 10% per capita growth in Y over the century.[95] This does not, however, seem to be a likely set of circumstances, especially with respect to aggregate growth. After all, in the period in question, the use of the *denarius* spread to Africa and Macedonia as well as parts of Italy, Spain and Gaul.[96] Without much better data on coin circulation and economic conditions, it is hard to gauge the implications for aggregate growth of the incorporation of these regions into the zone of *denarius* circulation. A threefold increase in Y due to aggregate growth seems somewhat more plausible. Such an increase in Y coupled with a moderate estimate for increase in M of seven to eight times initial volume yields an increase in k ranging from 16–33%. Again, hardly any room remains for per capita growth.[97] In the early

[94] See section 6.2. This increase in Y is *aggregate* growth, i.e., the additional output of people in newly integrated regions of the empire now conducting transactions with *denarii* instead of their pre-conquest currency. It is not *per capita* growth. On the difference between the two, see Saller (2002) 258.

[95] Saller (2002) 259–60 suggests that a per capita growth rate of 0.1% per year is consistent both with Hopkins' arguments concerning Roman growth and the long-term estimates of Robert Lucas.

[96] See section 6.2.

[97] Saller (2002) 251–69 argues on other grounds against the possibility of such growth during this period, suggesting instead "less than 0.1% per year, and even that rate... not sustained." He points out the need for "sustained technological improvement" and "human capital investment" to achieve "sustained economic growth."

Empire, as the volume of coinage continued to rise and political turmoil receded (reducing precautionary balances), per capita growth may be somewhat more likely but that issue is beyond the scope of this work.

6.7 Conclusion

At the beginning of this book I emphasized the broad meaning of *pecunia* in ancient Rome. *Pecunia* embraced a wide array of assets and in the late Republic farmers, merchants and government officials all used several different kinds of *pecunia* to make transactions and store their wealth. Nevertheless, the unique properties of coinage made it especially desirable as an asset. The Roman monetary system was quite versatile and, if no asset was as readily usable as coinage for making transactions, many assets could and did take the place of coinage in certain circumstances. But perhaps it is best to view late Republican monetary history from a less anachronistic perspective and say that over the course of the second and first centuries BCE the *denarius* increasingly took the place of other assets as a means of payment and a store of wealth. The *denarius* system was certainly a success story but in the turbulent final decades of the Republic it was perhaps too successful. Beginning in the 70s when *denarius* production dipped slightly[98] and bronze denominations ceased altogether,[99] demand may have outstripped supply. Despite the huge growth in the supply of coinage from the mid-second century, we still find Cicero complaining of *inopia pecuniae* in 56 BCE.[100] The violence and uncertainty of the period led even farmers to hoard coinage.[101] Caesar's attempt in 49 BCE to limit legally an individual's holdings to sixty thousand *sesterces* reflects the same problem (admittedly exacerbated by civil war).[102] A better and more lasting solution came in 46 BCE when he began to mint substantial quantities of gold coinage.

---

[98] See section 2.2. However, Verboven (2003) 61 argues that "the numismatic evidence does not support the idea of a contraction of the money supply in the period 79–50." Of course, demand could still outstrip production even if the supply did not contract.

[99] See Table 2.1.

[100] Cic. *Q. Fr.* 2.5.1: *Sed eodem die vehementer actum de agro Campano clamore senatus prope contionali. Acriorem causam inopia pecuniae faciebat et annonae caritas.*

[101] Cic. *Att.* 8.13.2: *multum mecum municipales homines loquuntur, multum rusticani; nihil prorsus aliud curant nisi agros, nisi villulas, nisi nummulos suos.*

[102] Dio Cass. 41.37–8.

BIBLIOGRAPHY

Alexandropoulos, J., 1982. "La circulation monétaire en Afrique Proconsulaire de 146 avant J.-C. à la fin du règne de Tibére," *Revue des Études Anciennes* 84, 96–103.

Andreau, J., 1978. "Financiers de l'aristocratie à la fin de la republique," in Edmond Frézouls (ed.), *Le dernier siècle de la République romaine et l'époque augustéenne*, Strasbourg: A. E. C. R., 47–62.

——, 1982. "Brèves remarques sur les banques et le crédit au 1er siècle av. J.-C.," *Annali dell'istituto italiano di numismatica* 29, 99–123.

——, 1984. "Histoire des métiers bancaires et évolution économique," *Opus* 3, 99–114.

——, 1987. *La vie financière dans le monde romain: Les métiers de manieurs d'argent (IVe siècle av. J.-C.–IIIe siècle ap. J.-C.)*, Rome: École Française.

——, 1992. "L'argent à Rome: les rentes de l'aristocratie," in Roger-Pol Droit (ed.), *Comment penser l'argent? Troisième forum Le Monde Le Mans*, Paris: Le Monde Éditions, 161–172.

——, 1995. "Italy, Europe and the Mediterranean: relations in banking and business during the last centuries BC," in J. Swaddling, S. Walker and P. Roberts (eds.), *Italy in Europe: Economic Relations 700 BC–AD 500*, London: British Museum, 305–312.

——, 1997. "Deux études sur les prix à Rome: les 'mercuriales' et le taux d'intérêt," in J. Andreau, P. Briant and R. Descat (eds.), *Économie antique: Prix et formation des prix dans les économies antiques*, Saint-Bertrand-de-Comminges: Musée Archéologique Départemental, 105–120.

——, 1999. *Banking and Business in the Roman World*, Cambridge: Cambridge University Press.

——, 2002a. "Markets, Fairs and Monetary Loans: Cultural History and Economic History in Roman Italy and Hellenistic Greece," in P. A. Cartledge, E. E. Cohen and L. Foxhall (eds.), *Money, Labour and Land: Approaches to the Economies of Ancient Greece*, London: Routledge, 113–129.

——, 2002b. "Twenty Years after Moses I. Finley's *The Ancient Economy*," in W. Scheidel and S. von Reden (eds.), *The Ancient Economy*, New York: Routledge, 33–49.

Andreau, J., P. Briant, and R. Descat (eds.), 1994. *Économie antique: Les échanges dans l'antiquité; le rôle de l'état*, Saint-Bertrand-de-Comminges: Musée Archéologique Départemental.

——, (eds.), 1997. *Économie antique: Prix et formation des prix dans les économies antiques*, Saint-Bertrand-de-Comminges: Musée Archéologique Départemental.

Antonelli, C., 1998. "La circolazione monetale in età repubblicana ed imperiale nel sud del Piceno e in particolare nella Valle del Vomano," *Münstersche Beiträge zur antiken Handelsgeschichte* 17, no. 2, 1–11.

Archibald, Z. H., J. Davies, V. Gabrielsen, and G. J. Oliver (eds.), 2001. *Hellenistic Economies*, London: Routledge.

Aubert, J.-J., 1994. *Business Managers in Ancient Rome: A Social and Economic Study of Institores, 200 BC–AD 250*, Leiden: E. J. Brill.

——, 2001. "The Fourth Factor: Managing Non-Agricultural Production in the Roman World," in D. J. Mattingly and J. Salmon (eds.), *Economies beyond Agriculture in the Classical World*, London: Routledge, 90–111.

Aymard, A., 1947. "Les capitalistes romains et la viticulture italienne," *Annales E.S.C.* II, 167–265.

Backendorf, D., 1998. *Römische Münzschätze des zweiten und ersten Jahrhunderts v. Chr. vom italienischen Festland*, Berlin: Gebr. Mann Verlag.

Badian, E., 1965. "M. Porcius Cato and the Annexation and Early Administration of Cyprus," *Journal of Roman Studies* 55, 110–121.

——, 1972. *Publicans and Sinners: Private Enterprise in the Service of the Roman Republic*, Ithaca: Cornell University Press.

Bagnall, R. S., 1997. *The Kellis Agricultural Account Book (P. Kell.IV Gr.96)*, Oxford: Oxbow Books.

Bagnall, R. and R. Bogaert, 1975. "Orders for Payment from a Banker's Archive: Papyri in the Collection of Florida State University," *Ancient Society* 6, 79–108.

Baldus, H. R., 1987. "Syria," in A. M. Burnett and M. H. Crawford (eds.), *The Coinage of the Roman World in the Late Republic: Proceedings of a Colloquium Held at the British Museum*, Oxford: B.A.R., 121–152.

Balsdon, J. P. V. D., 1946. "Roman History, 65–60 BC: Five Basic Problems," *Journal of Roman Studies* 52, 134–141.

Barker, G., 1989. "The Archaeology of the Italian Shepherd," *Proceedings of the Cambridge Philological Society* 35, 1–19.

——, 1995. *A Mediterranean Valley: Landscape Archaeology and Annales History in the Biferno Valley*, London and New York: Leicester University Press.

Barlow, C. T., 1977. "The *Sanctius Aerarium* and the *Argento Publico* Coinage," *American Journal of Philology* 98, 290–302.

——, 1978. *Bankers, Moneylenders and Interest Rates in the Roman Republic*, diss. University of North Carolina at Chapel Hill.

——, 1980. "The Roman Government and the Roman Economy, 92–80 BC," *American Journal of Philology* 101, 202–219.

Billeter, G., 1898. *Geschichte des Zinsfusses im griechisch-römischen Altertum bis auf Justinian*, Leipzig: Teubner.

Bogaert, R., 1968. *Banques et banquiers dans les cités grecques*, Leyden: A. W. Sijthoff.

——, 1983. "Note su l'emploi du chèque dans l'Égypte ptolémaïque," *Chronique d'Égypte* 58, 212–221.

——, 2000. "Banking in the Ancient World," in H. Van der Wee and G. Kurgan-Van Hentenryk (eds.), *A History of European Banking*, Antwerp: Mercatorfonds, 13–68.

Bordo, M. D., and L. Jonung, 1981. "The Long Run Behavior of the Income Velocity of Money in Five Advanced Countries, 1870–1975: An Institutional Approach," *Economic Inquiry* 19, 96–116.

Boren, H. C., 1961. "The Sources of Cicero's Income: Some Suggestions," *Classical Journal* 57.1, 17–24.

Botrè, C., and E. Fabrizi, 1994/95. "La monetizaione aurea nella Roma repubblicana (250–50 a.C.)," *Rivista italiana di numismatica e scienze affini* 96, 37–45.

Braid, M., 1998. "Stake in the Future for Cape Wine Workers," *The Independent*, February 16th, 9.

Braun, T. 1995. "Barley Cakes and Emmer Bread," in J. Wilkins, D. Harvey and M. Dobson (eds.), *Food in Antiquity*, Exeter: University of Exeter Press, 25–37.

Broughton, T. R. S., 1929. *The Romanization of Africa Proconsularis*, Baltimore: The John Hopkins Press.

——, 1951. *The Magistrates of the Roman Republic*, Vol. 1, New York: American Philological Association.

Brown, Frank E., Emeline Hill Richardson, and L. Richardson, Jr., 1993. *Cosa III: The Buildings of the Forum: Colony, Municipium, and Village*, University Park: American Academy in Rome.

Brunt, P. A., 1962. "The Army and the Land in the Roman Revolution," *Journal of Roman Studies* 52, 69–86.

——, 1972. "Review of K. D. White, *Roman Farming*," *Journal of Roman Studies* 62, 153–158.

——, 1975. "Two Great Roman Landowners," *Latomus* 34, 619–635.

——, 1980. "Free Labour and Public Works at Rome," *Journal of Roman Studies* 70, 81–100.

——, 1981. "The Revenues of Rome," *Journal of Roman Studies* 71, 161–172.
——, 1983. "Review of J. H. D'Arms' *Commerce and Social Standing in Ancient Rome*," *Journal of Economic History* 43, 314–315.
——, 1987. *Italian Manpower, 225 BC–AD 14*, Oxford: Clarendon Press.
Burford, A. M., 1960. "Heavy Transport in Classical Antiquity," *Economic History Review* 13, 1–18.
Burnett, A. M., 1977a. "The Authority to Coin in the Late Republic and Early Empire," *Numismatic Chronicle* 137, 37–63
——, 1977b. "The Coinages of Rome and Magna Graecia in the Late Fourth and Third Centuries BC," *Revue suisse de numismatique* 56, 92–121.
——, 1978. "The First Roman Silver Coins," *Numismatica e antichità classiche* 7, 121–142.
——, 1982. "The Currency of Italy from the Hannibalic War to the Reign of Augustus," *Annali dell'istituto italiano di numismatica* 29, 125–137.
——, 1987a. "Africa," in A. M. Burnett and M. H. Crawford (eds.), *The Coinage of the Roman World in the Late Republic: Proceedings of a Colloquium Held at the British Museum*, Oxford: B.A.R., 175–185.
——, 1987b. *Coinage in the Roman World*, London: Seaby.
——, 1998. "The Coinage of the Social War" in A. M. Burnett, U. Wartenberg, and Richard Witschonke (eds.) *Coins of Macedonia and Rome: Essays in Honour of Charles Hersh*, London: Spink, 165–172.
Burnett, A. M., M. Amandry, and P. P. Ripollès (eds.), 1992. *Roman Provincial Coinage*, Vol. 1, London: British Museum Press.
Burnett, A. M., and M. H. Crawford (eds.), 1987. *The Coinage of the Roman World in the Late Republic: Proceedings of a Colloquium Held at the British Museum*, Oxford: B.A.R.
Buttrey, T. V., 1957. "On the Retariffing of the Rome Denarius," *American Numismatic Society Museum Notes* 7, 57–65.
——, 1973. "A Hoard of Republican Asses from Rome," *Numismatic Chronicle* 133, 44–51.
——, 1976. "The *Denarii* of P. Crepusius and Roman Republican Mint Organization," *American Numismatic Society Museum Notes* 21, 67–108.
——, 1987. "Crete and Cyrenaica," in A. M. Burnett and M. H. Crawford (eds.), *The Coinage of the Roman World in the Late Republic: Proceedings of a Colloquium Held at the British Museum*, Oxford: B.A.R., 165–174.
——, 1989a. "The Morgantina Excavations and the Date of the Roman *Denarius*," *Morgantina Studies* 2, 215–219.
——, 1989b. "Morgantina and the *Denarius*," *Morgantina Studies* 2, 220–226.
——, 1993. "Calculating Ancient Coin Production: Facts and Fantasies," *Numismatic Chronicle* 153, 335–351.
——, 1999. "The Content and Meaning of Coin Hoards," *Journal of Roman Archaeology* 12, 526–532.
Buttrey, T. V., and D. Cooper, 1994. "Calculating Ancient Coin Production II: Why it Cannot be Done," *Numismatic Chronicle* 154, 341–352.
Buttrey, T. V., and S. E. Buttrey, 1997. "Calculating Ancient Coin Production, Again," *American Journal of Numismatics* 9, 113–135.
Camodeca, G., 1999. *Tabulae Pompeianae Sulpiciorum (TPSulp): Edizione critica dell'archivio puteolano dei Sulpicii*, Rome: Edizioni Quasar.
Carandini, A., 1983. "Columella's Vineyard and the Rationality of the Roman Economy," *Opus* 2, 177–204.
Campbell, Brian, 1996. "Shaping the Rural Environment: Surveyors in Ancient Rome," *Journal of Roman Studies* 86, 74–99.
Carter, G. F., and R. S. Nord, 1991–92. "Calculation of the Average Die Lifetimes and the Number of Anvils for Coinage in Antiquity," *American Journal of Numismatics* 3–4, 147–164.
Cartledge, P. A. (ed.), 2002. *Money, Labour and Land: Approaches to the Economies of Ancient Greece*, London: Routledge.

Casson, L., 1980. "The role of the state in Rome's grain trade," in J. H. D'Arms and E. C. Kopff (eds.), *The Seaborne Commerce of Ancient Rome*, Rome: American Academy in Rome, 21–33.

——, 1990. "New Light on Maritime Loans: P. Vindob G 40822," *Zeitschrift für Papyrologie und Epigraphik* 84, 195–206.

Cerutti, S., 1993. "Brutus, Cyprus and the Coinage of 55 BC," *American Journal of Numismatics* 5–6, 69–87.

Chandavarkar, A. G., 1977. "Monetization of Developing Economies," *International Monetary Fund Staff Papers* 24.3, 665–715.

Churchill, J. Bradford, 1999. "*Ex qua quod vellent facerent*: Roman Magistrates' Authority over *Praeda* and *Manubiae*," *Transactions of the American Philological Association* 129, 85–116.

Clemente, G., 1981. "Le leggi sul lusso e la società romana tra III e II secolo a.C.," in A. Giardina and A. Schiavone (eds.), *Società romana e produzione schiavistica: Modelli etici, diritto e trasformazioni sociali*, Rome: Editori Laterza, 1–14.

Coarelli, F., 1977. "Public Building in Rome between the Second Punic War and Sulla," *Papers of the British School at Rome* 45, 1–23.

——, 1983. "Il commercio delle opere d'arte in età tardo-repubblicana," *Dialoghi di archeologia* 1.1, 45–53.

——, 1994. "Saturnino, Ostia e l'annona. Il controllo e l'organizzazione del commercio del grano tra II e I secolo a.C.," in *Le ravitaillement en blé de Rome et des centres urbains dès débuts de la République jusqu'au Haut Empire: Actes du colloque international organisé par le Centre Jean Bérard et l'URA 994 du CNRS; Naples, 14–1 février 1991*, Naples and Rome: Centre Jean Bérard and École Française de Rome, 35–46.

Cohen, E. E., 1992. *Athenian Economy and Society: A Banking Perspective*, Princeton: Princeton University Press.

Cornell, T. J., 1995. *The Beginnings of Rome: Italy and Rome from the Bronze Age to the Punic Wars (c. 1000–264 BC)*, London and New York: Routledge.

Cotton, M. Aylwin, 1979. *The Late Republican Villa at Posto, Francolise*, London: British School at Rome.

——, 1985. *The San Rocco Villa at Francolise*, London: British School at Rome and Institute of Fine Arts of New York University.

Couch, H. N., 1929. *The Treasuries of the Greeks and Romans*, Menasha: George Banta Pub. Co.

Crawford, J. W., 1994. *M. Tullius Cicero: The Fragmentary Speeches. An Edition with Commentary*, Atlanta: Scholars Press.

Crawford, M. H., 1968a. "The Edict of M. Marius Gratidianus," *Proceedings of the Cambridge Philological Society* 14, 1–14.

——, 1968b. "Plated Coins–False Coins," *Numismatic Chronicle* 8, 55–59.

——, 1969a. "Coin Hoards and the Pattern of Violence in the Late Republic," *Papers of the British School at Rome* 37, 76–81.

——, 1969b. *Roman Republican Coin Hoards, Royal Numismatic Society Special Publications*, London: Royal Numismatic Society.

——, 1969c. "The Financial Organization of Republican Spain," *Numismatic Chronicle* 9, 79–93.

——, 1970. "Money and Exchange in the Roman World," *Journal of Roman Studies* 60, 40–48.

——, 1971. "Le problème des liquidités dans l'antiquité classique," *Annales* 26, 1128–1233.

——, 1973. "Paestum and Rome—The Form and Function of a Subsidiary Coinage," *Supplement* to *Annali dell'istituto italiano di numismatica, La monetazione di bronzo di Poseidonia—Paestum, atti del III convegno del CISN, Napoli, 19–23 aprile, 1971, Roma* 18–19, 47–109.

——, 1974. *Roman Republican Coinage*, 2 vols. Cambridge: Cambridge University Press.

——, 1975. "Mint and Moneyer in the Roman Republic," *Journal of Roman Studies* 65, 177–179.
——, 1977a. "Republican *Denarii* in Romania: The Suppression of Piracy and the Slave-trade," *Journal of Roman Studies* 67, 117–124.
——, 1977b. "Rome and the Greek World: Economic Relationships," *Economic History Review* 30, 42–52.
——, 1978a. "Ancient Devaluations: A General Theory," in *Les 'dévaluations' à Rome: Époque républicaine et impériale*, Rome: École Française de Rome, 147–155.
——, 1978b. "Trade and Movement of Coinage across the Adriatic in the Hellenistic Period," in R. A. G. Carson and C. M. Kraay (eds.), *Scripta Nummaria Romana: Essays Presented to Humphrey Sutherland*, London: Spink and Son Ltd., 1–11.
——, 1979. "The Roman Republic," in R. Carson, P. Berhaus and N. Lowick (eds.), *A Survey of Numismatic Research 1972–1977*, Berne: International Numismatic Commission, 161–176.
——, 1982. "Unofficial Imitations and Small Change under the Roman Republic," *Annali dell'istituto italiano di numismatica* 29, 139–164.
——, 1985. *Coinage and Money under the Roman Republic. Italy and the Mediterranean Economy*, London: Methuen and Co. Ltd.
——, 1987. "Sicily," in A. M. Burnett and M. H. Crawford (eds.), *The Coinage of the Roman World in the Late Republic: Proceedings of a Colloquium Held at the British Museum*, Oxford: B.A.R., 43–52.
——, (ed.), 1996. *Roman Statutes*, London: Institute of Classical Studies.
Cribb, J. (ed.), 1986. *Money: from Cowrie Shells to Credit Cards*, London: British Museum.
Cullens, A. J., 1988. "A Recalculation of the Number of Grain Recipients in the Late Republic," *Liverpool Classical Monthly* 13.7, 98–99.
Curti, Emmanuele, Emma Dench, and John R. Patterson, 1996. "The Archaeology of Central and Southern Roman Italy: Recent Trends and Approaches," *Journal of Roman Studies* 86, 170–189.
D'Arms, J. H., 1970. *Romans on the Bay of Naples: A Social and Cultural Study of the Villas and Their Owners from 150 BC to AD 400*, Cambridge: Harvard University Press.
——, 1977. "M. I. Rostovtzeff and M. I. Finley: The Status of Traders in the Roman World," in J. H. D'Arms and J. W. Eadie (eds.), *Ancient and Modern: Essays in Honor of Gerald F. Else*, Ann Arbor: The University of Michigan, 159–179.
——, 1980. "Republican Senators' Involvement in Commerce in the Late Republic: Some Ciceronian Evidence," *Memoirs of the American Academy in Rome* 36, 77–90.
——, 1981. *Commerce and Social Standing in Ancient Rome*, Cambridge: Harvard University Press.
D'Arms, J. H., and E. C. Kopff (eds.), 1980. *The Seaborne Commerce of Ancient Rome: Studies in Archaeology and History*, Rome: American Academy in Rome.
Dalton, G., 1965. "Primitive Money," *American Anthropologist* 67, 44–65.
Daube, D. 1969. "The Protection of the Non-Tipper," in D. Daube (ed.), *Roman Law: Linguistic, Social and Philosophical Aspects*, Edinburgh: Edinburgh University Press, 117–128.
Davies, J., 1998. "Ancient Economies: Models and Muddles," in H. Parkins and C. Smith (eds.), *Trade, Traders and the Ancient City*, London and New York: Routledge, 225–256.
de Callataÿ, F., 1995. "Calculating Ancient Coin Production: Seeking a Balance," *Numismatic Chronicle* 155, 289–311.
De Cecco, M., 1985. "Monetary Theory and Roman History," *Journal of Economic History* 45, 809–822.
de Ligt, L., 1990. "Demand, Supply, Distribution. The Roman Peasantry between Town and Countryside. I: Rural Monetisation and Peasant Demand," *Münstersche Beiträge zur antiken Handelsgeschichte* 9.2, 24–56.
——, 1991. "Demand, Supply, Distribution. The Roman Peasantry between Town and

Countryside. II: Supply, Distribution and a Comparative Perspective," *Münstersche Beiträge zur antiken Handelsgeschichte* 10.1, 33–77.

——, 1993. *Fairs and Markets in the Roman Empire: Economic and Social Aspects of Periodic Trade in a Pre-Industrial Society*, Amsterdam: J. C. Gieben.

de Ligt, L., and P. W. de Neeve, 1988. "Ancient Periodic Markets: Festivals and Fairs," *Athenaeum* 66, 391–416.

de Neeve, P. W., 1984. *Colonus: Private Farm-Tenancy in Roman Italy during the Republic and Early Principate*, Amsterdam: Gieben.

——, 1985. "The Price of Agricultural Land in Roman Italy and the Problem of Economic Rationalism," *Opus* 4, 77–109.

De Ruggiero, Ettore, 1925. *Lo stato e le opere pubbliche in Roma antica*, Torino: Fratelli Bocca.

De Ruyter, P. H., 1996. "The *Denarii* of the Roman Republican Moneyer Lucius Julius Bursio, a Die Analysis," *Numismatic Chronicle* 156, 79–147.

Dean, E. (ed.), 1965. *The Controversy over the Quantity Theory of Money*, Lexington: D. C. Heath and Co.

Deniaux, E., 1994. "Le patronage de Cicéron et l'arrivée des blés de Sicile à Rome," in *Le ravitaillement en blé de Rome et des centres urbains dès débuts de la République jusqu'au Haut Empire: Actes du colloque international organisé par le Centre Jean Bérard et l'URA 994 du CNRS; Naples, 14–1 février 1991*, Naples and Rome: Centre Jean Bérard and École Française de Rome, 243–254.

Duncan-Jones, R. P., 1974. *The Economy of the Roman Empire: Quantitative Studies*, Cambridge: Cambridge University Press.

——, 1980. "The Wealth of Gaul," *Chiron* 11, 217–220.

——, 1990. *Structure and Scale in the Roman Economy*, Cambridge: Cambridge University Press.

——, 1994. *Money and Government in the Roman Empire*, Cambridge: Cambridge University Press.

——, 1995. "Change in the Late Republican *Denarius*," *The Numismatic Chronicle* 155, 109–117.

——, 1997. "Numerical Distortion in Roman Writers," in J. Andreau, P. Briant and R. Descat (eds.), *Économie antique: Prix et formation des prix dans les économies antiques*, Saint-Bertrand-de-Comminges: Musée Archéologique Départemental, 147–159.

Dyson, S., 1985. "The Villa of Buccino and the Consumer Model of Roman Rural Development," in C. Malone and S. Stoddart (eds.), *Papers in Italian Archaeology* IV, Oxford: BAR, 67–84.

Effenterre, H. van (ed.), 1979. *Points de vue sur la fiscalité antique*, Paris: Université de Paris.

Einzig, P., 1948. *Primitive Money in its Ethnological, Historical and Economic Aspects*. London: Eyre and Spottiswoode.

Ekelund, R. B., Jr., and R. F. Hébert, 1997. *A History of Economic Theory and Method*, 4th edition, New York: McGraw-Hill.

Engelman, H., and D. Knibbe, 1989. "Das Zollgesetz der Provincia Asia. Ein neue Inschrift aus Ephesos," *Epigraphica Anatolica* 14, 1–206.

Erdkamp, P., 1995. "The Corn Supply of the Roman Armies during the Third and Second Centuries B.C.," *Historia* 44, 168–191.

——, 1998. *Hunger and the Sword: Warfare and Foodsupply in Roman Republican Wars (264–30 BC)*, Amsterdam: J. C. Gieban.

——, 1999. "Agriculture, Underemployment, and the Cost of Rural Labour in the Roman World," *Classical Quarterly* 49.2, 556–572.

——, 2005. *The Grain Market in the Roman Empire: A Social, Political and Economic Study*, Cambridge: Cambridge University Press.

Étienne, Robert, 1979. "Tenos et L. Aufidius Bassus (*IG*, XII 5, 860)," *Zeitschrift für Papyrologie und Epigraphik* 36, 145–149.

Evans, J. K., 1981. "Wheat Production and Its Social Consequences in the Roman World," *Classical Quarterly* 31.2, 428–442.
Fallu, É., 1979. "Les règles de la comptabilité publique à Rome à la fin de la République," in H. van Effenterre (ed.), *Points de vue sur la fiscalité antique*, Paris: Le Centre, 97–112.
Finley, M. I., 1965–66. "Technical Innovation and Economic Progress in the Ancient World," *Economic History Review* 18, 29–45.
——, 1975. "Anthropology and the Classics," in M. I. Finley (ed.), *The Use and Abuse of History*, New York: Viking Press, 102–119.
——, 1976. "Private Farm Tenancy in Italy before Diocletian," in M. I. Finley (ed.), *Studies in Roman Property*, Cambridge: Cambridge University Press, 103–121.
——, 1985. *The Ancient Economy*, 2nd edition, Berkeley: University of California Press.
Fischer, S., R. Dornbusch, and R. Schmalensee, 1988. *Introduction to Macroeconomics*, 2nd edition, New York: McGraw-Hill.
Flynn, D. O., 1984. "Use and Misuse of the Quantity Theory of Money in Early Modern Historiography," in E. van Cauwenberghe and F. Irsigler (eds.), *Minting, Monetary Circulation and Exchange Rates: Akten des 8th International Economic History Congress*, Trier: Verlag Trierer Historische Forschungen, 383–417.
Foraboschi, Daniele, 2003. "'Free Coinage' e scarsezza di moneta," in Elio Lo Cascio (ed.), *Credito e moneta nel mondo romano: Atti degli Incontri capresi di storia dell'economia antica (Capri 12–14 ottobre 2000)*, Bari: Edipuglia, 231–244.
Forbes, H., 1989. "Of Grandfathers and Grand Theories: the Hierarchised Ordering of Responses to Hazard in a Greek Rural Community," in P. Halstead and J. O'Shea (eds.), *Bad Year Economics: Cultural Responses to Risk and Uncertainty*, Cambridge: Cambridge University Press, 87–97.
Forbes, H., and L. Foxhall, 1995. "Ethnoarchaeology and Storage in the Ancient Mediterranean: Beyond Risk and Survival," in J. Wilkins, D. Harvey and M. Dobson (eds.), *Food in Antiquity*, Exeter: University of Exeter Press, 69–86.
Foxhall, L., 1990. "The Dependent Tenant: Land Leasing and Labour in Italy and Greece," *Journal of Roman Studies* 80, 97–114.
Foxhall, L., and H. A. Forbes, 1982. "Sitometreia: The Role of Grain as a Staple Food in Classical Antiquity," *Chiron* 12, 41–90.
Frank, Tenney, 1920. *An Economic History of Rome to the End of the Republic*. Baltimore: The Johns Hopkins Press.
——, (ed.), 1935. *An Economic Survey of Ancient Rome*, Baltimore: The Johns Hopkins Press.
——, 1937. "Notes on Roman Commerce," *Journal of Roman Studies* 27, 72–79.
Frayn, J. M., 1979. *Subsistence Farming in Roman Italy*, Fontwell: Centaur Press.
——, 1984. *Sheep-Rearing and the Wool Trade in Italy during the Roman Period*, Liverpool: F. Cairns.
——, 1993. *Markets and Fairs in Roman Italy: Their Social and Economic Importance from the Second Century BC to the Third Century AD*, Oxford: Clarendon Press.
Frederiksen, M. W., 1975. "Theory, Evidence, and the Ancient Economy," *Journal of Roman Studies* 65, 164–171.
——, 1959. "Republican Capua: a Social and Economic Study," *Papers of the British School at Rome* 14, 80–130.
——, 1966. "Caesar, Cicero, and the Problem of Debt," *Journal of Roman Studies* 56, 128–141.
——, 1970–71. "The Contribution of Archaeology to the Agrarian Problem in the Gracchan Period," *Dialoghi di Archeologia* 4–5, 330–367.
Frézouls, E., 1986. "La fiscalité provinciale de la République au principat: Continuité et rupture," *Ktema* 11, 17–28.

Friedman, M. (ed.), 1956. *Studies in the Quantity Theory of Money*, Chicago: University of Chicago Press.

Frier, B. W., 1977. "The Rental Market in Early Imperial Rome," *Journal of Roman Studies* 67, 27–37.

——, 1978/79. "Cicero's Management of his Urban Properties," *Classical Journal* 74, 1–6.

——, 1981. "Roman Coinage and Army Pay: Techniques for Evaluating Statistics," *Numismatica e antichità classiche* 10, 285–295.

Früchtl, A., 1912. *Die Geldschäfte bei Cicero*, Erlangen: Junge and Sohn.

Fulford, M., 1987. "Economic Interdependence among Urban Communities of the Roman Mediterranean," *World Archaeology* 19.1, 58–75.

Gabba, E., 1980. "Riflessioni antiche e moderne sulle attività commerciali a Roma nei secoli II e I a.C.," *Memoirs of the American Academy in Rome* 36, 91–102.

——, 1988. *Del buon uso della ricchezza: Saggi di storia economica e sociale del mondo antico*, Milan: Guerini e Associati.

Gallant, T. W., 1991. *Risk and Survival in Ancient Greece: Reconstructing the Rural Domestic Economy*. Oxford and Stanford: Polity Press and Stanford University Press.

Garine, I. de, and G. Koppert, 1988. "Coping with Seasonal Fluctuations in Food Supply among Savanna Populations: the Massa and Mussey of Chad and Cameroon," in I. de Garine and G. A. Harrison (eds.), *Coping with Uncertainty in Food Supply*, Oxford: Clarendon Press, 210–259.

Garnsey, P. D. A., 1976. "Urban Property Investment," in M. I. Finley (ed.), *Studies in Roman Property*, 123–136.

——, 1979. "Where did Italian Peasants Live?" *Proceedings of the Cambridge Philological Society* 205, 1–25.

——, 1983. "Grain for Rome," in P. D. A. Garnsey, K. Hopkins and C. R. Whittaker (eds.), *Trade in the Ancient Economy*, London: Chatto and Windus, 118–130.

——, 1988. *Famine and Food Supply in the Graeco-Roman World. Responses to Risk and Crisis*, Cambridge: Cambridge University Press.

——, 1991. "Mass Diet and Nutrition in the City of Rome," in A. Giovannini and D. van Berchem (eds.), *Nourrir la plèbe: actes du colloque tenu à Genève les 28 et 29. IX. 1989 en hommage à Denis van Berchem*, Basel: F. Reinhardt, 67–99.

——, 1994. "L'approvisionement des armées et la ville de Rome," in *Le ravitaillement en blé de Rome et des centres urbains dès débuts de la République jusqu'au Haut Empire: Actes du colloque international organisé par le Centre Jean Bérard et l'URA 994 du CNRS; Naples, 14–1 février 1991*, Naples and Rome: Centre Jean Bérard and École Française de Rome, 31–34.

——, 1998. *Cities, Peasants, and Food in Classical Antiquity: Essays in Social and Economic History* (ed. W. Scheidel), Cambridge: Cambridge University Press.

Garnsey, P. D. A., T. W. Gallant, and D. Rathbone, 1984. "Thessaly and the Grain Supply of Rome during the Second Century," *Journal of Roman Studies* 74, 30–44.

Garnsey, P. D. A., K. Hopkins, and C. R. Whittaker (eds.), 1983. *Trade in the Ancient Economy*. London: Chatto and Windus.

Garnsey, P. D. A., and D. Rathbone, 1985. "The Background to the Grain Law of Gaius Gracchus," *Journal of Roman Studies* 75, 20–25.

Garnsey, P. D. A., and R. P. Saller, 1987. *The Roman Empire: Economy, Society and Culture*, Berkeley and Los Angeles: University of California Press.

Gazzetti, Gianfranco, 1995. "La villa romana in località Selvicciolo (Ischia di Castro–Vt.)," in Neil Christie (ed.), *Settlement and Economy in Italy, 1500 BC–AD 1500: Papers of the Fifth Conference of Italian Archaeology*, Oxford: Oxbow Books, 297–302.

Gianfrotta, P. A., 1980. "Ancore 'romane'. Nuovi materiali per lo studio dei traffici marittimi," *Memoirs of the American Academy in Rome* 36, 103–116.

Giardina, A., and A. Schiavone (eds.), 1981. *Società romana e produzione schiavistica*, Bari: Laterza.

Giovannini, A., 1995. "Catalina et le problème des dettes," in I. Malkin and Z. W.

Rubinsohn (eds.), *Leaders and Masses in the Roman World: Studies in Honor of Zvi Yavetz*, Leiden and New York: Brill, 15–32.
Glare, P. G. W., 1968. *Oxford Latin Dictionary*, Oxford and London: Clarendon Press.
Goldsmith, R. W., 1987. *Premodern Financial Systems: A Historical Comparative Study*, Cambridge: Cambridge University Press.
Gordon, W. M., and O. F. Robinson, 1988. *The Institutes of Gaius*, Ithaca: Cornell University Press.
Goudineau, C., 1983. "Marseilles, Rome and Gaul from the Third to the First Century BC," in P. D. A. Garnsey, K. Hopkins and C. R. Whittaker (eds.), *Trade in the Ancient Economy*, Berkeley and Los Angeles: University of California Press, 76–86.
Goujard, Raoul, 1975. *Caton: De l'agriculture*, Paris: Les Belles Lettres.
Greene, K., 1986. *The Archaeology of the Roman Economy*, London: B. T. Batsford.
Grierson, P., 1978. "The Origins of Money," *Research in Economic Anthropology* 1, 1–35.
Halstead, Paul, 1987. "Traditional and Ancient Rural Economies in Mediterranean Europe: Plus Ça Change?," *Journal of Hellenistic Studies* 107, 77–87.
Harl, K. W., 1996. *Coinage in the Roman Economy, 300 BC to AD 700*, Baltimore and London: The Johns Hopkins University Press.
Harris, W. V., 1971a. "On War and Greed in the Second Century BC," *American Historical Review* 76, 1371–1385.
——, 1971b. *Rome in Etruria and Umbria*, Oxford: Clarendon.
——, 1975. "Review of E. Badian, *Publicans and Sinners*," *American Journal of Philology* 96, 433–436.
——, 1976. "The Development of the Quaestorship, 267–81 BC," *Classical Quarterly* 26, 92–106.
——, 1979. *War and Imperialism in Republican Rome: 327–70 BC*, Oxford: Clarendon Press.
——, 1980. "Towards a Study of the Roman Slave Trade," *Memoirs of the American Academy in Rome* 36, 117–140.
—— (ed.), 1984. *The Imperialism of Mid-Republican Rome*, Rome: American Academy in Rome.
——, 1989. "Trade and the River Po: A Problem in the Economic History of the Roman Empire," in J.-F. Bergier (ed.), *Montagnes, fleuves, forêts dans l'histoire: Barrières ou lignes de convergence?*, St. Katharinen: Scripta Mercaturae Verlag, 123–134.
——, 1993. "Between Archaic and Modern: Problems in Roman Economic History," in W. V. Harris (ed.), *The Inscribed Economy: Production and Distribution in the Roman Empire in the Light of* Instrumentum Domesticum*: The Proceedings of a Conference Held at the American Academy in Rome on 10–11 January, 1992*, Ann Arbor: University of Michigan, 11–29.
——, 1999. "Demography, Geography and the Sources of Roman Slaves," *Journal of Roman Studies* 98, 62–75.
Hersh, C. A., 1977. "Notes on the Chronology and Interpretation of the Roman Republican Coinage: Some Comments on Crawford's *Roman Republican Coinage*," *Numismatic Chronicle* 137, 19–36.
Hersh, C. A., and A. Walker, 1984. "The Mesagne Hoard," *American Numismatic Society Museum Notes* 29, 103–134.
Herzog, Rudolf, 1919. *Aus der Geschichte des Bankwesens im Altertum. Tesserae Nummulariae.* Giessen: A. Topelmann.
Hollander, D. B., 1999. "The Management of the Mint in the Late Roman Republic," *Ancient History Bulletin* 13.1, 14–27.
——, 2005. "Veterans, Agriculture, and Monetization in the Late Roman Republic," in Z. Varhelyi, and Jean-Jacques Aubert (eds.), *A Tall Order: Writing the Social History of the Ancient World. Essays in Honor of William V. Harris*, Munich and Leipzig: K. G. Saur: 229–239.
Hollstein, W., 1993. *Die stadtrömische Münzpraegung der Jahre 78–50 v. Chr.*, Munich: Tuduv.

Hopkins, Keith, 1972. "Review of P. A. Brunt's *Italian Manpower 225 BC–AD 14*," *Journal of Roman Studies* 62, 192–193.
——, 1978. "Economic Growth and Towns in Classical Antiquity," in P. Abrams and E. A. Wrigley (eds.), *Towns in Societies*, Cambridge: Cambridge University Press, 35–77.
——, 1980. "Taxes and Trade in the Roman Empire (200 BC–AD 400)," *Journal of Roman Studies* 70, 101–125.
——, 1995/96. "Rome, Taxes, Rents and Trade," *Kodai* 6/7, 41–75.
Horden, P., and N. Purcell, 2000. *The Corrupting Sea: A Study of Mediterranean History*, Oxford: Blackwell.
Howgego, C., 1990. "Why Did Ancient States Strike Coins?" *Numismatic Chronicle* 150, 1–25.
——, 1992. "The Supply and Use of Money in the Roman World 200 BC to AD 300," *Journal of Roman Studies* 82, 1–31.
——, 1994. "Coin Circulation and the Integration of the Roman Economy," *Journal of Roman Archaeology* 7, 5–21.
——, 1995. *Ancient History from Coins*. London: Routledge.
Hutchinson, Sharon, 1992. "The Cattle of Money and the Cattle of Girls Among the Nuer, 1930-83," *American Ethnologist* 19, 294–316.
Johnson, A., and T. Earle, 2000. *The Evolution of Human Societies: From Foraging Group to Agrarian State*, 2nd edition, Stanford: Stanford University Press.
Johnson, L., 1998. "Review of Kenneth W. Harl's *Coinage in the Roman Economy, 300 BC to AD 700*," *American Journal of Philology* 119.1, 139–142.
Jones, A. H. M., 1966. *The Decline of the Ancient World*, London: Longman.
——, 1974. *The Roman Economy: Studies in Ancient Economic and Administrative History* (ed. P. A. Brunt), Oxford: Blackwell.
Jongman, W., 1988. *The Economy and Society of Pompeii*, Amsterdam: J. C. Gieben.
Jonkers, E. J., 1941. "'Wechsel' und 'Kreditbriefe' im römischen Altertum." *Mnemosyne: Bibliotheca Classica Batava* 10, 182–186.
Jonung, L., 1978. "The Long-Run Demand for Money—A Wicksellian Approach," *Scandinavian Journal of Economics* 80.2, 216.
Kehoe, D. P., 1988. *The Economics of Agriculture on Roman Imperial Estates in North Africa*, Göttingen: Vandenhoeck and Ruprecht.
——, 1993. "Economic Rationalism in Roman Agriculture," *Journal of Roman Archaeology* 6, 476–484.
——, 1997. *Investment, Profit and Tenancy: The Jurists and the Roman Agrarian Economy*, Ann Arbor: University of Michigan Press.
Keppie, L., 1983. *Colonisation and Veteran Settlement in Italy: 47–14 BC*, London: British School at Rome.
Keynes, J. M., 1936. *The General Theory of Employment, Interest and Money*, New York: Harcourt, Brace and World, Inc.
King, C. E., and D. G. Wigg (eds.), 1996. *Coin Finds and Coin Use in the Roman World: The Thirteenth Oxford Symposium on Coinage and Monetary History, 25.–27.3.1993*, Berlin: Gebr. Mann Verlag.
Kinns, P., 1987. "Asia Minor," in A. M. Burnett and M. H. Crawford (eds.), *The Coinage of the Roman World in the Late Republic: Proceedings of a Colloquium Held at the British Museum*, Oxford: B.A.R., 105–113.
Kirschenbaum, A., 1987. *Sons, Slaves and Freedmen in Roman Commerce*, Washington: The Catholic University of America Press.
Knapp, R. C., 1977. "The Date and Purpose of the Iberian *Denarii*," *Numismatic Chronicle* 137, 1–18.
——, 1982. "The Coinage of Corduba, Colonia Patricia," *Annali dell'istituto italiano di numismatica* 29, 183–202.
——, 1987. "Spain," in A. M. Burnett and M. H. Crawford (eds.), *The Coinage of the*

Roman World in the Late Republic: Proceedings of a Colloquium Held at the British Museum, Oxford: B.A.R., 19–42.

Kraay, C. M., 1964. "Hoards, Small Change and the Origin of Coinage," *Journal of Hellenic Studies* 84, 76–91.

Kurke, L., 1999. *Coins, Bodies, Games, and Gold: The Politics of Meaning in Archaic Greece*, Princeton: Princeton University Press.

Kuziscin, V. I., 1984. *La grande proprietà agraria nell'Italia romana II sec. a.C.–I sec. d.C.*, Rome: Editori Riuniti.

Laidler, D. E. W., 1985. *The Demand for Money: Theories, Evidence and Problems*, 3rd edition, New York: Harper and Row.

Lange, D., 1972. "Two Financial Maneuvers of Cicero," *Classical World* 65, 152–155.

Laurence, Ray, 1998. "Land Transport in Roman Italy: Costs, Practice and the Economy," in Helen Parkins, and Christopher Smith (eds.), *Trade, Traders and the Ancient City*, London: Routledge, 129–148.

Leclerc, H., 1998. "Recherches récentes sur les monétaires de la République," *Échos du Monde Classique/Classical Views* 42, 139–162.

Leiwo, M., 1989. "Philostratus of Ascalon, His Bank, His Connections and Naples in c. 130–90 BC," *Athenaeum: Studi periodici di letteratura e storia dell'antichità* 67, 575–584.

Leveau, P. (ed.), 1985. *L'origine des richesses dépensées dans la ville antique*. Aix-en-Provence: Université de Provence.

Lewis, Charlton T., and Charles Short, 1879. *A Latin Dictionary*, Oxford: Clarendon Press.

Lintott, A. W., 1990. "Electoral Bribery in the Roman Republic," *Journal of Roman Studies* 80, 1–16.

——, 1993. *Imperium Romanum: Politics and Administration*, London and New York: Routledge.

——, 1999. *Violence in Republican Rome*, Oxford: Clarendon Press.

Lirb, H. J., 1993. "Partners in Agriculture: The Pooling of Resources in Rural Societates in Roman Italy," in H. Sancisi-Weerdenburg, R. J. van der Spek, H. C. Teitler and H. T. Wallinga (eds.), *De agricultura: In memoriam Pieter Willem de Neeve*, Amsterdam: J. C. Gieben, 263–295.

Lo Cascio, E., 1979. "Carbone, Druso e Gratidiano: la gestione della *res nummaria* a Roma tra la *lex Papiria* e la *lex Cornelia*," *Athenaeum* 57, 215–238.

——, 1981. "State and Coinage in the Republic and Early Empire," *Journal of Roman Studies* 71, 76–86.

——, 1982a. "'Obaerarii' ('obaerati'): la nozione della dipendenza in Varrone," *Index* 11, 265–284.

——, 1982b. "Spesa militare, spesa dello stato e volume delle emissioni nella tarda Repubblica," *Annali dell'istituto italiano di numismatica* 29, 75–97.

——, 1996. "How did the Romans view their coinage and its function?" In C. E. King and D. G. Wigg (eds.), *Coin Finds and Coin Use in the Roman World: The Thirteenth Oxford Symposium on Coinage and Monetary History. 25.–27.3.1993*, Berlin: Gebr. Mann Verlag, 273–287.

Lo Cascio, E., and D. Rathbone (eds.), 2000. *Production and Public Powers in Classical Antiquity*, Cambridge: Cambridge Philological Society.

Lockyear, K., 1999. "Hoards and Ancient Coin Production," *The Numismatic Chronicle* 159, 215–245.

Lübtow, U. von, 1975. "Catos Seedarlehen," in H. Hübner, E. Klingmüller, and Andreas Wacke (eds.), *Festschrift für Erwin Seidl*, Köln: P. Hanstein, 103–117.

MacKinnon, Aran S., 1999. "The Persistence of the Cattle Economy in Zululand, South Africa, 1900-50," *Canadian Journal of African Studies* 33, 98–135.

MacMullen, R., 1970. "Roman Market Days," *Phoenix* 24, 333–341.

Macve, R., 1985. "Some Glosses on Ste. Croix's 'Greek and Roman Accounting'," in P. A. Cartledge and F. D. Harvey (eds.), *Crux: Essays in Greek History Presented to*

G. E. M. de Ste. Croix on His 75th Birthday, London: Duckworth and Imprint Academic, 233–261.

Maguire, R. A. J., 1928. "The Masai Penal Code," *Journal of the Royal African Society* 28, 12–18.

Malmendier, Ulrike, 2002. *Societas publicanorum: Staatliche Wirtschaftsaktivitäten in den Händen privater Unternehmer*, Köln: Böhlau Verlag.

——, 2005. "Roman Shares," in W. Goetzmann, and G. Rouwenhorst (eds.), *The Origins of Value. The Financial Innovations That Created Modern Capital Markets*, Oxford: Oxford University Press, 31–42, 361–365.

Manacorda, D., 1978. "The *Ager Cosanus* and the Amphorae of Sestius," *Journal of Roman Studies* 68, 122–131.

——, 1980. "L'*ager Cosanus* tra tarda Repubblica e impero: forme di produzione e assetto della proprietà," *Memoirs of the American Academy in Rome* 36, 173–184.

Mankiw, N. G., 1994. *Macroeconomics*, 2nd edition, New York: Worth Publishers.

Maróti, E., 1976. "The Vilicus and the Villa-System in Ancient Italy," *Oikumene* 1, 109–124.

Martin, R., 1971. *Recherches sur les agronomes latins et leurs conceptions économiques et sociales*, Paris: Les Belles Lettres.

Masselli, G., 1986. *Argentaria: banche e banchieri nella Roma repubblicana: organizzazione, prosopografia, terminologia*, Bari: Adriatica editrice.

Mattingly, D. J., 1996. "First Fruit? The Olive in the Roman World," in G. Shipley and J. Salmon (eds.), *Human Landscapes in Classical Antiquity: Environment and Culture*, London: Routledge, 213–253.

Mattingly, D. J., and S. Coccia, 1995. "Survey Methodology and the Site: A Roman Villa From the Rieti Survey," in Neil Christie (ed.), *Settlement and Economy in Italy, 1500 BC–AD 1500: Papers of the Fifth Conference of Italian Archaeology*, Oxford: Oxbow Books, 31–43.

Mattingly, D. J., and J. Salmon, 2001. "The Productive Past: Economies beyond Agriculture," in D. J. Mattingly and J. Salmon (eds.), *Economies beyond Agriculture in the Classical World*, London: Routledge, 3–14.

Mattingly, H. B., 1982. "The Management of the Roman Republican Mint," *Annali dell'istituto italiano di numismatica* 29, 9–46.

Mayerson, P., 1984. "Wheat in the Roman World: An Addendum," *Classical Quarterly* 34.1, 243–245.

McCann, A. M., J. Bourgeois, E. K. Gazda, J. P. Oleson, and E. L. Will (eds.), 1987. *The Roman Port and Fishery of Cosa: A Center of Ancient Trade*, Princeton: Princeton University Press.

McCusker, J. J. and J. C. Riley, 1984. "Money Supply, Economic Growth and the Quantity Theory of Money: France, 1650–1788," in E. van Cauwenberghe and F. Irsigler (eds.), *Minting, Monetary Circulation and Exchange Rates: Akten des 8th International Economic History Congress*, Trier: Verlag Trierer Historische Forschungen, 255–289.

Meiggs, R., 1980. "Sea-borne Timber Supplies to Rome," *Memoirs of the American Academy in Rome* 36, 185–196.

Meijer, F., 1990. "The Financial Aspects of the *Leges Frumentariae* of 123–58 BC," *Münstersche Beiträge zur antiken Handelsgeschichte* 9.2, 14–23.

——, 1993. "Cicero and the Costs of the Republican Grain Laws," in H. Sancisi-Weerdenburg, R. J. van der Spek, H. C. Teitler and H. T. Wallinga (eds.), *De agricultura: In memoriam Pieter Willem de Neeve*, Amsterdam: J. C. Gieben, 153–163.

Metcalf, W. E., 1974. "Roman Coins from the River Liri. II," *Numismatic Chronicle* 134, 42–52.

——, 1995. "Review of R. Duncan-Jones's *Money and Government in the Roman Empire*," *Swiss Numismatic Revue* 74, 145–159.

Millet, P., 2001. "Productive to Some Purpose? The Problem of Ancient Economic Growth," in D. J. Mattingly and J. Salmon (eds.), *Economies beyond Agriculture in the Classical World*, London: Routledge, 17–48.

Milne, J. G., 1940. "The 'Philippus' Coin at Rome," *Journal of Roman Studies* 30, 11–15.
Mishkin, F. S., 1992. *The Economics of Money, Banking, and Financial Markets*, 3rd edition, New York: HarperCollins.
Mitchell, S., 1976. "Requisitioned Transport in the Roman Empire," *Journal of Roman Studies* 66, 106–131.
Mommsen, T., 1865–1870. *Histoire de la monnaie romaine*, Paris: Rollin et Feuardent.
——, 1894. *Le droit public romain*, Paris: Thorin et Fils.
Morley, N., 1996. *Metropolis and Hinterland: The City of Rome and the Italian Economy, 200 BC–AD 200*, Cambridge: Cambridge University Press.
——, 1997. "Cities in Context: Urban Systems in Roman Italy," in H. Parkins (ed.), *Roman Urbanism: Beyond the Consumer City*, London: Routledge, 42–58.
Mors, P. O., 1954. "Cattle in Buhaya," *Anthropological Quarterly* 27, 23–29.
Mundell, R. A., 2001. "The Roman Monetary System: From Servius to Constantine," *Zagreb Journal of Economics* 7, 3–43.
Musti, D., 1980. "Il commercio degli schiavi e del grano: Il caso di Puteoli. Sui rapporti tra l'economia italiana della tarda Repubblica e le economie ellenisstiche," *Memoirs of the American Academy in Rome* 36, 197–216.
Nash, D. M., 1987. "Imperial Expansion under the Roman Republic," in M. Rowlands, M. Larsen and K. Kristiansen (eds.), *Centre and Periphery in the Ancient World*, Cambridge: Cambridge University Press, 87–103.
——, 1978. "Plus Ça Change: Currency in Central Gaul from Julius Caesar to Nero," in R. A. G. Carson and C. M. Kraay (eds.), *Scripta Nummaria Varia: Essays Presented to Humphrey Sutherland*, Oxford: Spink and Son, 12–31.
Netting, R. McC., 1993. *Smallholders, Householders: Farms Families and the Ecology of Intensive, Sustainable Agriculture*, Stanford: Stanford University Press.
Nicolet, C., 1971. "Les variations des prix et la 'théorie quantative de la monnaie' à Rome, de Cicéron à Pline l'Ancien," *Annales E.S.C.* 26, 1203–1227.
——, 1976. "Aperçus sur la fiscalité à Rome sous la République," *Ktema* 1, 187–194.
——, 1979. "Deux remarques sur l'organisation des sociétés de publicains à la fin de la République romaine," in H. van Effenterre (ed.), *Points de vue sur la fiscalité antique*, Paris: Le Centre, 69–95.
——, 1980. *The World of the Citizen in Republican Rome,* London: Batsford Academic and Educational.
——, 1988. *Rendre à César: Économie et société dans la Rome antique*, Paris: Gallimard.
——, 1991. *Space, Geography, and Politics in the Early Roman Empire*, Ann Arbor: University of Michigan Press.
——, 1994a. "Economy and Society, 133–43 BC," in J. A. Crook, A. W. Lintott and E. Rawson (eds.), *The Cambridge Ancient History* IX, 2nd edition, Cambridge, Cambridge University Press, 599–643.
——, 1994b. "Dîmes de Sicile, d'Asie et d'ailleurs," in *Le ravitaillement en blé de Rome et des centres urbains dès débuts de la République jusqu'au Haut Empire: Actes du colloque international organisé par le Centre Jean Bérard et l'URA 994 du CNRS; Naples, 14–1 février 1991*, Naples and Rome: Centre Jean Bérard and École Française de Rome, 215–229.
——, 1996. *Financial Documents and Geographical Knowledge in the Roman World*, Oxford: Leopard's Head Press.
Nightingale, D., 1989. "Review of J. Andreau's *La vie financière dans le monde romain: Les métiers de manieurs d'argent (IVe siècle av. J.-C.–IIIe siècle ap. J.-C.)*," *Journal of Roman Studies* 79, 176–177.
O'Donovan, John, 1940. *The Economic History of Live Stock in Ireland*, Dublin and Cork: Cork University Press.
Oliver, J. H., 1989. *Greek Constitutions of Early Roman Emperors from Inscriptions and Papyri*, Philadelphia: American Philosophical Society.
Parker, A. J., 1992. *Ancient Shipwrecks of the Mediterranean and the Roman Provinces*, Oxford: Tempus Reparatum.
Parkins, H. (ed.), 1997. *Roman Urbanism: Beyond the Consumer City*, London: Routledge.

——, 1998. "Time for Change? Shaping the Future of the Ancient Economy," in H. Parkins and C. Smith (eds.), *Trade, Traders and the Ancient City*, London: Routledge, 1–15.

Parkins, H., and C. Smith (eds.), 1998. *Trade, Traders and the Ancient City*, London and New York: Routledge.

Paterson, J., 1982. "'Salvation from the Sea:' Amphorae and Trade in the Roman World," *Journal of Roman Studies* 72, 146–157.

——, 1998. "Trade and Traders in the Roman World: Scale, Structure, and Organisation," in H. Parkins and C. Smith (eds.), *Trade, Traders and the Ancient City*, London and New York: Routledge, 149–167.

——, 2001. "Hellenistic Economies: The Case of Rome," in Z. H. Archibald, J. Davies, V. Gabrielsen and G. J. Oliver (eds.), *Hellenistic Economies*, London: Routledge, 367–378.

Patterson, C., 1972. "Silver Stocks and Losses in Ancient and Medieval Times," *Economic History Review* 2.25, 205–235.

Peacock, D. P. S., and D. F. Williams, 1986. *Amphorae and the Roman Economy: An Introductory Guide*, London: Longman.

Pekáry, T., 1980. "Les limites de l'économie monétaire à l'époque romaine," in *Les 'dévaluations' à Rome: Époque républicaine et impériale*, Rome: École Française de Rome, 103–120.

Percival, John, 1969. "Seigneurial Aspects of Late Roman Estate Management," *English Historical Review* 84, 449–473.

——, 1976. *The Roman Villa: An Historical Introduction*, London: B. T. Batsford Ltd.

Petrucci, A., 1991. *Mensam exercere. Studi sull'impresa finanziaria romana (II secolo a.C.–metà del III secolo d.C.)*, Naples: Jovene.

Picard, O., 1987. "Thrace," in A. M. Burnett and M. H. Crawford (eds.), *The Coinage of the Roman World in the Late Republic: Proceedings of a Colloquium Held at the British Museum*, Oxford: B.A.R., 79–94.

Pigou, A. C., 1917. "The Value of Money," *Quarterly Journal of Economics* 32, 38–65.

Pink, K., 1952. *The Triumviri Monetales and the Structure of the Coinage of the Roman Republic*, New York: American Numismatic Society.

——, 1956. "Special Coinages under the *Triumviri Monetales*," in R. A. G. Carson and C. H. V. Sutherland (eds.), *Essays in Roman Coinage Presented to Harold Mattingly*, London: Oxford University Press, 55–62.

Polanyi, K., 1957. "Aristotle Discovers the Economy," in K. Polanyi, C. Arensberg and H. Pearson (eds.), *Trade and Market in the Early Empires: Economies in History and Theory*, Glencoe, Ill.: Free Press, 64–94.

——, 1968. "The Semantics of Money-Uses," in G. Dalton (ed.), *Primitive, Archaic and Modern Economies*, Garden City: Anchor Books, 175–203.

Potter, T. W., 1979. *The Changing Landscape of South Etruria*, London: Paul Elek.

Preisigke, F., 1910. *Girowesen im griechischen Ägypten, enthaltend Korngiro, Geldgiro, Girobanknotariat mit Einschluss des Archivwesens*, Strasbourg: Druckerei Lokay.

Preston, H. S., 1983. "Roman Republican Coin Hoards: An Age Correction and Other Comments," *Annali dell'istituto italiano di numismatica* 30, 83–94.

Price, M. J., 1987. "Southern Greece," in A. M. Burnett and M. H. Crawford (eds.), *The Coinage of the Roman World in the Late Republic: Proceedings of a Colloquium Held at the British Museum*, Oxford: B.A.R., 95–104.

Pucci, G., 1983. "Pottery and Trade in the Roman Period," in P. D. A. Garnsey, K. Hopkins and C. R. Whittaker (eds.), *Trade in the Ancient Economy*, Berkeley and Los Angeles: University of California Press, 105–117.

——, 1985. "Città ed economia in età romana: Qualche riflessione," in P. Leveau (ed.), *L'origine des richesses dépensées dans la ville antique*, Aix-en-Provence: Université de Provence, 275–280.

Purcell, N., 1985. "Wine and Wealth in Ancient Italy," *Journal of Roman Studies* 75, 1–19.
——, 1994. "The City of Rome and the *Plebs Urbana* in the Late Republic," in J. A. Crook, A. W. Lintott and E. Rawson (eds.), *The Cambridge Ancient History* IX, 2nd edition, Cambridge: Cambridge University Press, 644–688.
——, 1995. "The Roman Villa and the Landscape of Production," in H. K. Lomas and T. J. Cornell (eds.), *Urban Society in Roman Italy*, New York: St. Martin's Press, 151–179.
Quiggin, A. H., 1949. *A Survey of Primitive Money: The Beginnings of Currency*, London: Methuen.
Raskolnikoff, M., 1977. "La richesse et les riches chez Cicéron," *Ktema* 2, 357–365.
Rathbone, D., 1981. "The Development of Agriculture in the *Ager Cosanus* during the Roman Republic: Problems of Evidence and Interpretation," *Journal of Roman Studies* 71, 10–23.
——, 1991. *Economic Rationalism and Rural Society in Third-Century AD Egypt: The Heroninos Archive and the Appianus Estate*, Cambridge: Cambridge University Press, 1991.
——, 1993. "The Census Qualifications of the *Assidui* and the *Prima Classis*," in H. Sancisi-Weerdenburg, R. J. van der Spek, H. C. Teitler and H. T. Wallinga (eds.), *De agricultura: In memoriam Pieter Willem de Neeve*, Amsterdam: J. C. Gieben, 121–152.
——, 1996. "Monetisation, not price-inflation, in third-century AD Egypt?" In C. E. King and D. G. Wigg (eds.), *Coin Finds and Coin Use in the Roman World: The Thirteenth Oxford Symposium on Coinage and Monetary History, 25–27.3.1993*, Berlin: Gebr. Mann Verlag, 321–339.
——, 1997. "Prices and Price Formation in Roman Egypt," in J. Andreau, P. Briant and R. Descat (eds.), *Économie antique: Prix et formation des prix dans les économies antiques*, Saint-Bertrand-de-Comminges: Musée Archéologique Départemental, 183–244.
Rauh, N. K., 1986. "Cicero's Business Friendships: Economics and Politics in the Late Roman Republic," *Aevum* 60, 3–30.
——, 1989a. "Auctioneers and the Roman Economy," *Historia* 38.4, 451–471.
——, 1989b. "Finance and Estate Sales in Republican Rome," *Aevum* 63, 45–76.
——, 1993. *The Sacred Bonds of Commerce: Religion, Economy, and Trade Society at Hellenistic Roman Delos, 166–87 BC*, Amersterdam: J. C. Gieben.
Rawson, E., 1976. "The Ciceronian Aristocracy and its Properties," in M. I. Finley (ed.), *Studies in Roman Property*, Cambridge: Cambridge University Press, 85–102.
Rea, J. R., 1997. "Private Account of Money and Wine," in E. W. Handley and U. Wartenberg (eds.), *Oxyrhynchus Papyri* LXIV, London: Egypt Exploration Society, 151–156.
Reger, G., 1997. "The Price Histories of Some Imported Goods on Independent Delos," in J. Andreau, P. Briant and R. Descat (eds.), *Économie antique: Prix et formation des prix dans les économies antiques*, Saint-Bertrand-de-Comminges: Musée Archéologique Départemental, 53–72.
Richardson, J. S., 1976. "The Spanish Mines and the Development of Provincial Taxation in the Second Century BC," *Journal of Roman Studies* 66, 139–152.
——, 1986. *Hispaniae: Spain and the Development of Roman Imperialism, 218–82 BC*, Cambridge: Cambridge University Press.
Rickman, G., 1971. *Roman Granaries and Store Buildings*, Cambridge: Cambridge University Press.
——, 1980a. "The Grain Trade under the Roman Empire," *Memoirs of the American Academy in Rome* 36, 261–276.
——, 1980b. *The Corn Supply of Ancient Rome*, Oxford: Clarendon Press.
Rosenstein, Nathan S., 2004. *Rome at War: Farms, Families, and Death in the Middle Republic*, Chapel Hill: University of North Caroline Press.
Roth, J., 1999. *The Logistics of the Roman Army at War (264 BC–AD 235)*, Leiden: Brill.

Rougé, J., 1980. "Prêt et societé maritimes dans le monde romain," *Memoirs of the American Academy in Rome* 36, 291–304.
Rowlandson, J., 1996. *Landowners and Tenants in Roman Egypt: The Social Relations of Agriculture in the Oxyrhynchite Nome*, Oxford: Clarendon Press.
——, 2001. "Money Use among the Peasantry of Ptolemaic and Roman Egypt," in A. Meadows and K. Shipton (eds.), *Money and its Uses in the Ancient Greek World*, Oxford: Oxford University Press, 145–155.
Saller, R. P., 2002. "Framing the Debate over Growth in the Ancient Economy," in W. Scheidel and S. von Reden (eds.), *The Ancient Economy*, New York: Routledge, 251–269.
Sancisi-Weerdenburg, H., R. J. van der Spek, H. C. Teitler, and H. T. Wallinga (eds.), 1993. *De Agricultura: In memoriam Pieter Willem de Neeve*, Amsterdam: J. C. Gieben.
Santalucia, Bernardo, 1982. "La legislazione sillana in materia di falso nummario," *Annali dell'istituto italiano di numismatica* 29, 47–74.
Savio, A., 1997. "La numismatica e i problemi quantitativi: Intorno al calcolo del volume delle emissioni," *Rivista italiana di numismatica e scienze affini* 98, 11–48.
Schapera, I., 1934. "Herding Rites of the Bechuanaland Bakxatla," *American Anthropologist* 36, 561–584.
Schaps, D. M., 2004. *The Invention of Coinage and the Monetization of Ancient Greece*, Ann Arbor: University of Michigan Press.
Scheidel, W., 1996. "Finances, Figures and Fiction," *Classical Quarterly* 46.1, 222–238.
——, 2005. "Human Mobility in Roman Italy, II: The Slave Population," *Journal of Roman Studies* 95, 64–79.
Scheidel, W. and S. von Reden (eds.), 2002. *The Ancient Economy*, New York: Routledge.
Schneider, H. K., 1974. "Economic Development and Economic Change: The Case of East African Cattle," *Current Anthropology* 15, 259–276.
Seaford, R., 2004. *Money and the Early Greek Mind: Homer, Philosophy, Tragedy*, Cambridge: Cambridge University Press.
Selden, R. T., 1956. "Monetary Velocity in the United States," in M. Friedman (ed.), *Studies in the Quantity Theory of Money*,. Chicago: University of Chicago Press, 179–257.
Serletis, A., 2001. *The Demand for Money: Theoretical and Empircal Approaches*, Boston: Kluwer Academic Publishers.
Shackleton-Bailey, D. R. (ed.), 1977. *Cicero, Epistulae Ad Familiares*. Cambridge: Cambridge University Press.
—— (ed.), 1980. *Cicero: Epistulae ad Quintum Fratrem et M. Brutum*. Cambridge: Cambridge University Press.
—— (ed.), 1965. *Cicero's Letters to Atticus*, Cambridge: Cambridge University Press.
—— (ed.), 1999. *Cicero, Letters to Atticus*. Cambridge: Harvard University Press.
Shatzman, I., 1972. "The Roman General's Authority over Booty," *Historia* 21, 177–205.
——, 1975. *Senatorial Wealth and Roman Politics*, Bruxelles: Latomus.
Shelford, Frederic, 1910. "Notes on the Masai," *Journal of the Royal African Society* 9, 267–269.
Siciliano, A., 1974–1975. "Ripostiglio di monete repubblicane da Policoro," *Annali dell'istituto italiano di numismatica* 21–22, 103–153.
——, 1976–1977. "Ripostiglio monetale tardo repubblicano da Policoro," *Annali dell'istituto italiano di numismatica* 23–34, 107–119.
Sippel, D. V., 1987. "Some Observations on the Means and Cost of the Transport of Bulk Commodities in the Late Republic and Early Empire," *The Ancient World* 16, 35–45.
Skydsgaard, J. E., 1980. "Non-Slave Labour in Rural Italy during the Late Republic," in P. D. A. Garnsey (ed.), *Non-Slave Labour in the Greco-Roman World*, Cambridge: Cambridge Philological Society, 65–72.

Small, Alastair M., 1974. "Excavations at Monte Irsi, Italy, 1971–1973," *Échos du Monde Classique/Classical Views* 18, 20–22.

Small, Alastair M., S. G. Moncton, Robert J. Buck, and C. J. Simpson, 1992. "Excavations at Gravina di Puglia, 1991: Interim Report," *Échos du Monde Classique/Classical Views* 36, 189–199.

Snell, D. C., 1995. "Methods of Exchange and Coinage in Ancient Western Asia," in J. M. Sasson (ed.), *Civilizations of the Ancient Near East*, New York: Charles Scribner's Sons, 1487–1497.

Spufford, P., 1988. *Money and its Uses in Medieval Europe*, Cambridge: Cambridge University Press.

Spurr, M. S., 1985. "Slavery and the Economy in Roman Italy," *Classical Review* 35, 123–131.

——, 1986. *Arable Cultivation in Roman Italy c. 200 BC–AD 100*, London: Society for the Promotion of Roman Studies.

Stannard, C., 1993. "The Adjustment *al Marco* of the Weight of Roman Republican *Denarii* Blanks by Gouging," in M. M. Archibald and M. R. Cowell (eds.), *Metallurgy in Numismatics*, London: Royal Numismatic Society, 45–53.

——, 1998. "Overstrikes and Imitative Coinages in Central Italy in the Late Republic," in A. M. Burnett, U. Wartenberg, and R. Witschonke (eds.), *Coins of Macedonia and Rome: Essays in Honour of Charles Hersh*, London: Spink, 209–229.

Stazio, A. 1973. "Poseidonia-Paestum: Problemi della circolazione monetale," in *La monetazione di bronzo di Poseidonia-Paestum: Atti del III convegno del Centro Internazionale di Studi Numismatici—Napoli 19-23 aprile 1971*, Rome: Istituto Italiano di Numismatica, 111–134.

Stephens, S. A., 1978. "Nine Orders to Pay from Oxyrhynchus," *Zeitschrift für Papyrologie und Epigraphik* 31, 145–160.

Stiglitz, J. E., 1997. *Economics*, 2nd edition, New York and London: W. W. Norton and Co.

Strong, D. E., 1968. "The Administration of Public Building in Rome during the Late Republic and Early Empire," *Bulletin of the Institute of Classical Studies* 15, 97–109.

Stuard, S. M., 1989. "Review of P. Spufford's *Money and its Uses in Medieval Europe*," *Journal of Economic History* 49, 206–208.

Sutherland, C. H. V., 1939. *The Romans in Spain*, New York: Barnes and Noble.

——, 1985. "*Monetae... Peculiares Servos Praeposuit*: Julius Caesar and the Mint of Rome," *Numismatic Chronicle* 145, 243–245.

Tchernia, A., 1983. "Italian Wine in Gaul at the End of the Republic," in P. D. A. Garnsey, K. Hopkins and C. R. Whittaker (eds.), *Trade in the Ancient Economy*, Berkeley and Los Angeles: University of California Press, 87–104.

——, 1986. *Le vin de l'Italie romaine: Essai d'histoire économique d'après les amphores*, Rome: École Française.

Temin, Peter, 2001. "A Market Economy in the Early Roman Empire," *Journal of Roman Studies* 91, 169–181.

Thompson, J., 1988. "Pastoralism and transhumance in Roman Italy," in C. R. Whittaker (ed.), *Pastoral Economies in Classical Antiquity*, Cambridge: Cambridge Philological Society, 213–215.

Thomsen, R., 1978. "From Libral 'Aes Grave' to Uncial 'Aes' Reduction: The Literary Tradition and the Numismatic Evidence," in *Les 'dévaluations' à Rome: Époque républicaine et impériale*, Rome: École Française de Rome, 9–30.

Tobin, J., 1958. "Liquidity Preference as Behavior towards Risk," *Review of Economic Studies* 25.2, 65–86.

Torrent, A., 1973. "Syngraphae cum Salaminiis," *Iura* 24, 90–111.

Touratsoglou, I., 1987. "Macedonia," in A. M. Burnett and M. H. Crawford (eds.), *The Coinage of the Roman World in the Late Republic: Proceedings of a Colloquium Held at the British Museum*, Oxford: B.A.R., 53–78.

Toynbee, A. J., 1965. *Hannibal's Legacy: The Hannibalic War's Effect on Roman Life*, London: Oxford University Press.

Travaglini, Adriana, 1988. "Presenza di moneta romana repubblicana in Puglia," in C. Marangio (ed.), *La Puglia in età repubblicana: Atti del I convengo di studi sulla Puglia romana, Mesagne, 20–22 marzo 1986*, Galatina: Congedo, 65–76.

Treggiari, Susan, 1969. *Roman Freedmen during the Late Republic*, Oxford: Oxford University Press.

——, 1999. "The Careful Paterfamilias' Views on Agrarian Investment," *Journal of Roman Archaeology* 12, 737–744.

Tucker, I. B., 1997. *Economics for Today*, Minneapolis/St. Paul: West.

Turyahikayo-Rugyema, B., 1976. "Markets in Precolonial East Africa: The Case of the Bakiga," *Current Anthropology* 17, 286–290.

van Minnen, P., 2000. "Agriculture and the 'Taxes-and-Trade' Model in Roman Egypt," *Zeitschrift für Papyrologie und Epigraphik* 133, 205–220.

Verboven, K., 1993. "Le système financier à la fin de la République romaine," *Ancient Society* 24, 69–98.

——, 1994. "The Monetary Enactments of M. Marius Gratidianus," *Studies in Latin Literature and Roman History* 7, 117–131.

——, 1997. "*Caritas Nummorum*. Deflation in the Late Roman Republic?" *Münstersche Beiträge zur antiken Handelsgeschichte* 16.2, 40–78.

——, 2002. *The Economy of Friends. Economic Aspects of Amicitia and Patronage in the Late Republic*. Brussels: Éditions Latomus.

——, 2003a. "54–44 BCE: Financial or Monetary Crisis?," in Elio Lo Cascio (ed.), *Credito e moneta nel mondo romano: Atti degli Incontri capresi di storia dell'economia antica (Capri 12–14 ottobre 2000)*, Bari: Edipuglia, 49–68.

——, 2003b. "The Sulpicii from Puteoli, Argentarii or Faeneratores?," in Pol Defosse (ed.), *Hommages à Carl Deroux III—Histoire et épigraphie, droit*, Brussels: Latomus, 429–445.

Veyne, P., 1979. "Mythe et réalité de l'autarcie à Rome," *Revue des études anciennes* 81, 261–280.

Virlouvet, C., 1985. *Famines et émeutes à Rome dès origines de la République à la mort de Néron*, Rome: École Française de Rome.

——, 1994. "Les lois frumentaires d'époque républicaine," in *Le ravitaillement en blé de Rome et des centres urbains dès débuts de la République jusqu'au Haut Empire: Actes du colloque international organisé par le Centre Jean Bérard et l'URA 994 du CNRS; Naples, 14–16 février 1991*, Naples and Rome: Centre Jean Bérard and École Française de Rome, 11–30.

Visonà, Paolo, and Frey-Kupper, Susanne, 1996. "The Romanization of the *Ager Bruttius* and the Evidence of Coin Finds. Part I," *Schweizerische numismatische Rundschau (Revue suisse de numismatique)* 75, 77–100.

Volk, T. R., 1987. "Mint Output and Coin Hoards," *Numismatica Lovaniensia* 7, 141–222.

Von Reden, S., 1995. *Exchange in Ancient Greece*, London: Duckworth.

——, 2001. "The Politics of Monetization in Third-Century BC Egypt," in A. Meadows and K. Shipton (eds.), *Money and its Uses in the Ancient Greek World*, New York: Oxford University Press, 65–76.

——, 2002. "Money in the Ancient Economy: A Survey of Recent Research," *Klio* 84, 141–174.

Walker, D. R., 1980. "The Silver Content of the Roman Republican Coinage," in D. M. Metcalf and W. M. Oddy (eds.), *Metallurgy in Numismatics*, London: Royal Numismatic Society, 55–72.

Wallace, S. L., 1938. *Taxation in Egypt from Augustus to Diocletian*, Princeton: Princeton University Press.

Watson, Alan, Theodor Mommsen, and Paul Krueger (eds.), 1985. *The Digest of Justinian*, Philadelphia: University of Pennsylvania Press.

Weber, M., 1927. *General Economic History*, New York: Greenberg.
——, 1988. *The Agrarian Sociology of Ancient Civilizations*, London and New York: Verso.
White, K. D., 1970. *Roman Farming*, Ithaca: Cornell University Press.
Whittaker, C. R., 1985. "Trade and Aristocracy in the Roman Empire," *Opus* 4, 49–75.
——, 1986. "La cliometria e lo storico," *Opus* 5, 127–132.
—— (ed.), 1988. *Pastoral Economies in Classical Antiquity*, Cambridge: Cambridge Philological Society.
——, 1989. "The Poor in the City of Rome," in A. Giardina (ed.), *L'uomo romano*, Rome: Laterza, 301–333.
Williams, J. H. C., 1998. "Coinage, Credit and the *Aerarium* in the 80s BC," in A. M. Burnett, U. Wartenberg, and R. Witschonke (eds.), *Coins of Macedonia and Rome: Essays in Honour of Charles Hersh*, London: Spink, 173–183.
Williams, W. G. (ed.), 1983. *Cicero. The Letters to His Friends*, Cambridge: Harvard University Press.
Wiseman, T. P., 1970. "Roman Republican Road Building," *Papers of the British School at Rome* 38, 122–151.
Woolf, G., 1992. "Imperialism, Empire and the Integration of the Roman Economy," *World Archaeology* 23, 283–293.
——, 2001. "Regional Productions in Early Roman Gaul," in D. J. Mattingly and J. Salmon (eds.), *Economies beyond Agriculture in the Classical World*, London: Routledge, 49–65.
Yavetz, Z., 1970. "Fluctuations monétaires et condition de la plèbe à la fin de la République," in C. Nicolet (ed.), *Recherches sur les structures socials dans l'antiquité classique, Caen 25–26 avril 1969*, Paris: Éditions du CNRS, 133–157.
Yntema, D., 1993. "Greeks, Natives and Farmsteads in South-Eastern Italy," in H. Sancisi-Weerdenburg, R. J. van der Spek, H. C. Teitler and H. T. Wallinga (eds.), *De agricultura: In memoriam Pieter Willem de Neeve*, Amsterdam: J. C. Gieben, 78–97.
Zehnacker, H., 1978. "L'évaluation des masses des émissions à l'époque républicaine," in *Les 'dévaluations' à Rome: Époque républicaine et impériale*, Rome: École Française de Rome, 31–52.
——, 1980. "Monnaies de compte et prix à Rome au IIe siècle avant notre ère," in *Les 'dévaluations' à Rome: Époque républicaine et impériale*, Rome: École Française de Rome, 31–48.

INDEX LOCORUM

I. *Literary Sources*

II. *Legal Sources*

III. *Epigraphical Sources*

IV. *Papyrological Sources*

GENERAL INDEX

www.ingramcontent.com/pod-product-compliance
Lightning Source LLC
Chambersburg PA
CBHW031325230926
51848CB00001B/88
9789004225497